SPIRITUAL PROGRESS

SPIRITUAL PROGRESS

Becoming the Christian You Want to Be

THOMAS D. WILLIAMS

New York Boston Nashville

Unless otherwise noted, Scripture quotations are taken from
THE JERUSALEM BIBLE. Copyright © 1966 by Darton, Longman & Todd Ltd.
and Doubleday & Company, Inc. Used by permission.
Scriptures noted NASB are taken from the New American Standard Bible®,
Copyright © 1960, 1962, 1963, 1968, 1972, 1975, 1977, 1995 by The Lockman
Foundation. Used by permission.
Scriptures noted RSV are taken from the REVISED STANDARD VERSION of
the Bible. Copyright © 1949, 1952, 1971, 1973 by the Division of Christian
Education of the National Council of the Churches of Christ in the U.S.A.
Used by permission.

FaithWords
Hachette Book Group USA
1271 Avenue of the Americas
New York, NY 10020

Visit our Web site at www.faithwords.com.

Printed in the United States of America

First Edition: February 2007
10 9 8 7 6 5 4 3 2 1

The FaithWords name and logo are trademarks of Hachette Book Group USA.

Library of Congress Cataloging-in-Publication Data
Williams, Thomas D., LC.
    Spiritual progress : becoming the Christian you want to be / Thomas D.
Williams.—1st ed.
        p. cm.
    Summary: "Thomas Williams draws on the knowledge that he's gained from
his own spiritual journey, exploring topics such as holiness, prayer, trust,
humility, and generosity."—Provided by the publisher
    ISBN-13: 978-0-446-58054-0
    ISBN-10: 0-446-58054-6
    1. Spiritual formation. I. Title.
    BV4520b.W52 2007
    248.4—dc22   2006026949

For My Mom and Dad
Whose Deep Faith Inspired My Own
and to Steve and Susie
Whose Growing Faith Inspired This Book

CONTENTS

Introduction

As life goes on, a certain maturing normally takes place. After years of schooling we pack away a reasonable stock of knowledge. Work experience brings practical know-how. Travels, readings, and conversations afford us a modest bit of culture. And we may even keep our physical health in check with diets, medical visits, and some regular exercise. Yet somehow in this forward wave of personal progress, one element—unfortunately, the most important—often gets left behind. Our spiritual lives often languish at the level where we left them back when Sunday school ended. Socially and professionally we are adults, but spiritually we may still be adolescents. I hope with this modest book to help bridge the gap between our practical, day-to-day lives and our spiritual lives.

Literature on Christian spirituality generally falls into three categories, which we could loosely term *self-help*, *devotional reading*, and *spiritual manuals*. Self-help books, even those with a Christian veneer, often smack of the spiritual narcissism where spirituality is pursued as a means of feeling better about oneself, rather than an earnest search for truth and transcendence. Our posttherapeutic generation is slowly realizing that the road to happiness does not pass through excessive self-absorption. Devotional reading, while very useful to some, can come across as sentimental and cloying, and somehow disconnected from the real problems and doubts of modern men and women. Spiritual manuals often contain hearty spiritual meat drawn from a long tradition of lived Christianity, but their rigorous structure and technical vocabulary can be off-putting to modern readers. Moreover, these manuals often presuppose much prior spiritual formation that today's Christians don't have.

This book aspires to offer something different. First, it takes the Christian proposal seriously, examining gospel teaching and its demands at face value. People who would follow Christ have a right to know what this entails, including both what Christ asks from us and what he promises. This must be done on his terms, not ours. Second, the book translates perennial spiritual concepts into familiar terms. Modern readers are starved for spiritual substance but would like it couched in accessible language that addresses modern problems and speaks to our generation rather than our forbears'. Finally, the book engages readers' critical intelligence, inviting rather than imposing a closer look at the Christian proposal. It seeks to explain not only the *whats* of the spiritual life, but just as important, the *whys* and the *hows*. Today's Christian seeks not only instruction, but also motivation and practical guidance. For example, it is one thing to present a general idea of what Christian prayer *is* and to reiterate the *necessity* of prayer, and quite another thing to show the real value and joy of prayer, to offer pointers for overcoming obstacles to prayer, and to give practical advice as to what to do during prayer time.

This book aspires to offer not only the whats *of the spiritual life, but just as important, the* whys *and* hows.

This work is meant to be a guidebook. A proper guide does not attempt to replace an experience but to accompany and enrich it. A trail guide does not supplant a hike over the mountain but prepares hikers to get the most out of the experience. A guide helps chart a course, explain the terrain, point out pitfalls, and accompany hikers as they confront the unknown. The spiritual life cannot be experienced vicariously but only lived personally, and thus a guide to the spiritual life can only offer hints and suggestions for living it well and recognizing the signs along the way. Reading this book cannot substitute prayer or the practice of virtue, but it can perhaps offer some helpful pointers and motivations to facilitate these activities.

This book is for beginners, but beginners in the broadest sense. It is for rank beginners, for whom the idea of spiritual progress presents a fresh, exciting quest into the unknown. It is for "experienced" beginners, for whom starting over and over again has become something of a profession. It is for humbled beginners, who realize that after much travel they need to retrace their steps and set out anew from square one. It is for curious beginners, who for the first time are considering the spiritual life as something worthy of pursuit. It is even for embarrassed beginners, who realize they should probably be far ahead of where they actually find themselves but simply aren't. In short, it is for anyone willing to take seriously Jesus' words: "Unless you turn and become like children, you will never enter the kingdom of heaven" (Matt. 18:3 RSV). Beginning, and a willingness to begin over and over again, is part and parcel of the Christian life.

For Christians, the spiritual life includes not only prayer, but also every dimension of friendship with God and the day-to-day experience of following Jesus Christ. This book deals with the aims and objectives of the spiritual life, as well as the natural and supernatural means we have at our disposal to reach our goal. It offers practical counsel, not lofty theory. In fact, I have made a concerted effort in these pages to render the spiritual life accessible and intelligible, rather than distant and esoteric.

As readers will quickly realize, this book tackles the spiritual life from a solidly Christian perspective. It unabashedly distances itself from New Age materials and self-help books by examining the Christian proposal at face value. Relying heavily on sacred Scripture, and especially the New Testament, the book lays out the basics of the spiritual life as gleaned from Jesus' life and teachings. I, the author, am a Catholic priest and naturally write from my own experience and tradition. Yet not only Catholics but other Christians as well will quickly discover that the perspective of the book is firmly based on the gospel.

The spiritual life presents an adventure unequaled by any other aspect of human existence. No other project or enterprise, no matter how absorbing or exciting, can match it. For spiritual explorers of every sort, this book aspires to be an introductory guidebook into the marvelous challenge of following Jesus Christ and living the riches of the Christian faith. It is Christ himself who assures us: Do not be afraid! I have conquered the world! (see John 16:33).

SPIRITUAL PROGRESS

Part I

WHERE WE ARE GOING

This book is more practical than theoretical, more a how-to book than a speculative essay. But how to what? "How-to" always begs another question: what do you want to do? Once you know the end you are pursuing, you can start looking for the best means. How to fix a leaky faucet, build a deck, rewire the family room, bake a pineapple upside-down cake, make curtains: all of these can be explained once you know what you are after. In the same way, if we are to embark on the spiritual life, we should have some idea of where it ought to lead.

This first part of the book deals precisely with this question. These first four chapters will look at the aim of the spiritual life and thereby set the stage for the following chapters, which will discuss the means to accomplish your objectives. The first chapter deals with *holiness*, debunking some typical misconceptions and showing how you can pursue and attain holiness in your ordinary life. The second chapter looks at *Christian charity*, or love, as a compendium of the commandments and the pinnacle of Christian perfection. The third chapter explores the elusive and sometimes mysterious notion of *God's will* as a sure source of orientation for our lives and choices. Finally, the fourth chapter shows how *imitating Christ*, following in his footsteps, is the quickest way to become holy—and happy.

CHAPTER 1

Redefining Success

Holiness and the Meaning of Life

Train yourself spiritually. "Physical exercises are useful enough, but the usefulness of spirituality is unlimited, since it holds out the reward of life here and now and of the future as well."

1 Timothy 4:7–8

Many years ago, as a junior in college, I unwittingly attended a recruiting session for Amway sales staff. The director of the session started out by speaking about success, and how to achieve our deepest aspirations. Yet every example he used referred to some material benefit. If we signed up for the program, he assured us, we could soon have everything we wanted: a huge house, a Mercedes in the driveway, luxury vacations in exotic places. In short, we would be *successful*.

Many expressed enthusiasm about what the director was proposing, but I couldn't help feeling empty inside, thinking, *Is that really all there is to life? Is that what it means to be successful? If so, why are so many "successful" people so unhappy?*

It struck me as a Christian that this materialistic vision seemed to be lacking the most essential element of true success. Christ's words came rushing back to me: "For what does it profit a man if he gains the whole world and loses or forfeits himself?" (Luke 9:25 RSV). Since life on earth is so short, any definition of success that confines itself to temporal goods that go with us to the grave cannot do justice to our deepest aspirations. Genuine success must be measured by eternity. Robert Bellarmine wrote,

> Prosperity and adversity, wealth and poverty, health and sickness, honors and humiliations, life and death, in the mind of the wise man, are not to be sought for their own sake. But if they contribute to the glory of God and your eternal happiness, then they are good and should be sought. If they detract from this, they are evil and must be avoided.

In Charles Dickens's classic novel, *A Christmas Carol,* Ebenezer Scrooge encounters the ghost of his former business associate, Jacob Marley, laden with yards of massive chains, which he must carry forever. Scrooge expresses astonishment at Marley's punishment and exclaims, "But you were always a good man of business, Jacob," to which Marley replies sharply: "*Mankind* was my business!" Our Christian faith declares to us in no uncertain terms: "Holiness is your business!" Holiness is not just one occupation among many, to be juggled along with our other affairs, but the central enterprise of our lives.

Our Christian faith declares to us in no uncertain terms: "Holiness is your business!"

In fact, holiness cannot really be classified as an "activity" at all, since it transcends and includes all our activities. The way we face life, the way we live our relations with our neighbors, the way we fulfill our responsibilities and spend our time—holiness embraces and synthesizes all of these elements. Holiness is, in short, the meaning of life.

God created us for holiness. Or as Paul succinctly put it, "What God wants is for you all to be holy" (1 Thess. 4:3). *Sanctification* (from the Latin *sanctus* for "holy") simply means growth in holiness. Holiness is our vocation, our calling—yours and mine. That is, "Even as he chose us in him before the foundation of the world, that we should be holy and blameless before him" (Eph. 1:4 RSV). Holiness not only defines the goal of the spiritual life, but the goal of human existence itself. Eventually all other tasks, occupations, projects, and ambitions fade in importance, and the only thing that matters in the final analysis is to be holy, to be saints. Since we were made for heaven, we were made for holiness.

What Holiness Is Not

All this talk about holiness, especially in a book for beginners in the spiritual life, may make some uneasy. The very word *holiness* may set off a whole series of red flags in our minds. We instinctively recoil at the proposal that we are called to holiness. The word itself may be off-putting and uncomfortable: "Holiness is not for me. Too hard, too weird, too radical."

Many of us, in fact, don't identify with holiness. Maybe it seems rare and unachievable, like Mother Teresa's work with lepers. Perhaps the word brings to mind even stranger images of past eras. After all, some officially recognized saints had pretty odd résumés. Saint Anthony of the Desert battled with demons in the form of wild beasts, Joseph of Cupertino experienced extraordinary levitations, and Vincent Ferrer led groups of flagellants through the streets doing public penance. At best these examples evoke admiration, but they hardly inspire imitation, like extreme stunts accompanied by the warning: Don't try this at home!

Not only do we feel incapable of many of these feats, but frankly many of us wouldn't *want* to imitate them even if we could, since they seem to border on the fanatical. And so we often think of holiness as a condition for eccentric people hatched from eggs, and not for normal folk with their feet on the ground, like us.

The good news is, these extraordinary spiritual phenomena and practices do not constitute holiness. In a few isolated cases they may accompany holiness, but they do not make up the *substance* of holiness. Nowhere in the gospel does Jesus command us to levitate, and unless recent modifications have been made to the book of Deuteronomy, none of the Ten Commandments deals with ecstasies, stigmata, or self-flagellation. The vast majority of holy men and women, in fact, clearly do not experience extraordinary spiritual phenomena like those I've mentioned, so these must not be essential to holiness.

> *We often think of holiness as a condition for eccentric people hatched from eggs, and not for normal folk with their feet on the ground, like us.*

Yet even if we leave aside these mistaken ideas, confusion regarding holiness abounds. Some nonbelievers admit the positive effects of religious belief (morals) while denying the objectivity of religious experience. Others see religion as inherently bad, the "opium of the people," as Marx said, nourishing false hopes and encouraging an unhealthy detachment from the world. Religious experience and devotion could even be a type of neurosis or an indicator of psychological immaturity.

To clear away some clutter of false ideas regarding holiness, let us briefly list and discard seven things that holiness *is not*. Then we can get down to the more important business of defining what holiness *is*, and how we are to go about attaining it.

1. Holiness Is Not Self-Improvement

Some approach spirituality in the generic sense, as a self-centered pursuit of psychological serenity and betterment. Holiness would then become the narcissistic quest of "magical me," standing before a spiritual mirror and gazing at myself, occasionally removing little stains that threaten to sully my immaculate ego. Yet this has nothing to do with the Christian understanding of holiness. Our own self-importance has to yield to other-centeredness and ultimately God-centeredness in order for us to grow in authentic holiness. In *Called to Communion*, Joseph Ratzinger wrote, "It is not the perfecting of one's self that makes one holy but the purification of the self through its fusion into the all-embracing love of Christ: it is the holiness of the triune God himself."

2. HOLINESS IS NOT JUST THE AVOIDANCE OF EVIL

Defining holiness as the avoidance of sin is like defining a good mother as one who does not beat her children. Of course a holy person will avoid evil, just as a good mother will refrain from beating her children, but holiness really isn't about avoidance at all. Jesus came

> *Holiness is about* doing *and* being, *not about avoiding.*

so that we might "have life and have it to the full" (John 10:10). Moreover, he sent us out to bear fruit that will last. Holiness is about *doing* and *being*, not about avoiding.

3. HOLINESS IS NOT MERE PHILANTHROPY

For the practical-minded, humanitarian aid may seem much more worthwhile than prayer and love of God. But just as holiness cannot be identified with prayers alone, nor can it be identified with philanthropy alone. The ultimate horizon of holiness is not some secular, earthly paradise, but heaven. "Storing up treasure for heaven" (see Matt. 6:20) includes but surpasses concern for our neighbor's temporal good. Almsgiving and works of mercy may be manifestations of true holiness, but they are not holiness itself.

4. HOLINESS IS NOT THE NUMBER OF DISCIPLINES YOU PERFORM

Many confuse devotion with *disciplines*, with excessive emphasis on external works such as fasting, abstinence, and lengthy prayers. While disciplines are a very good thing, they are not holiness itself but only a help to achieve it. Fasting alone hardly makes a saint. Whereas a certain puritanical spirit tempts us to identify virtue with stoic resistance, grim austerity, and duty for duty's sake, this doesn't square well with Jesus' express wish that our joy may "be complete" (John 15:11). Disciplines are a means to an end, but they are not holiness.

5. HOLINESS IS NOT ABOUT "FEELING" GOD'S PRESENCE
If the overemphasis on externals like disciplines misses the mark, so does an overemphasis on internals, like religious sentiment or sensible consolation. Some people have naturally cooler temperaments, while others wallow in sentimentality. Both are called to be saints, but their holiness doesn't stand or fall with sensible fervor. The waxing and waning of religious sentiment is a normal spiritual phenomenon and has little or nothing to do with growth in holiness. The greatest saints had moments or even long periods of aridity. Sentiment is not a reliable thermometer of holiness.

6. HOLINESS IS NOT A MEANS TO SOMETHING ELSE
Some try to manipulate their relationships with God as a means to curry his favor—like going to church on Sundays in exchange for financial success. Yet when we do this, we turn everything upside down, like getting married for the sake of a tax break. What God really wants is to transform our hierarchy of values, our way of gauging success—a real conversion or *metanoia* in the depths of our beings. Union with him can never be pursued as a means to something else, but only as our supreme end.

7. HOLINESS IS NOT AN UNREACHABLE UTOPIA
For some, holiness would be a pipe dream, an idealistic pie in the sky attainable at best only by a lucky few. If so, why strive for something unreachable, like Sisyphus forever pushing a huge stone uphill, only to

have it come rolling down again? Yet true holiness is within our grasp, a realistic possibility for each and every one of us. God calls each of us to holiness and provides all the means we need to attain it.

What Holiness Is

Having discarded inadequate notions of holiness, we can turn to the more interesting task of describing what holiness is. Far from a drab, fearful flight from something, holiness expresses the dynamic pursuit of what is most good and beautiful.

HOLINESS IS A GIFT

It gradually lifts us beyond the realm of the natural into the realm of the supernatural. It elevates us far beyond what we could achieve on our own. All the day-to-day striving and effort involved on our parts is nothing other than our constant "yes" to the Giver of this great gift; it expresses our desire and thanks for it. Holiness means tasting the infinite goodness and happiness of God despite the confines of our condition as creatures. It means appropriating, by his own free and generous gift, the very stuff of God.

> *Holiness means . . . appropriating, by his own free and generous gift, the very stuff of God.*

HOLINESS IS LOVE

And since the stuff of God is infinite supernatural love, in a word, holiness is *love*. To be holy is to be united with God, who is love itself. As John Paul II put it, "Holiness is intimacy with God." Holiness consists in a vibrant, living friendship with God in love, which overflows into true self-giving to our neighbor.

The book of Genesis tells us that God created man and woman in his own image and likeness. Further on in sacred Scripture, in John's first epistle, we read that "God is love" (1 John 4:8). In other words, we were created in the image and likeness of love. To live in love means to reach our full potential as a true reflection of God, who is love.

From a Christian perspective, man was made to love and be loved. And in this striving to live up to our nature we find holiness, since "he who abides in love abides in God, and God abides in him" (1 John 4:16 RSV). Just as there is no true holiness apart from love, so, too, there is no true love apart from holiness. We were not created to be alone, to seek some sort of abstract perfection in isolation from God and from our brothers and sisters, but rather to mirror God who is a community of persons: the Father, Son, and Holy Spirit. To love God above all things and our neighbor as ourselves means true human fulfillment.

Moreover, only love brings lasting joy. Generous self-giving to God and neighbor not only makes us good and holy, it also makes us happy. Is there anyone sadder and lonelier than the person who harbors hatred and distrust, who lives centered on himself? Is there anyone happier than a generous soul who lives for God and others? Happiness isn't found in a life of sin and selfishness, but in a life of love.

> *Generous self-giving to God and neighbor not only makes us good and holy, it also makes us happy.*

The Christian life, like all life, is progressive. Holiness does not refer to a state or condition to be reached, and much less does it resemble a certificate or diploma to hang on our walls. It is *life* and as such must grow and mature—growth is a law of life. A holding pattern is impossible—we either grow or diminish, advance or retreat, but we cannot stay still.

We can best monitor our progress in holiness by seeing whether or not we are growing in love. The more we forget about ourselves to serve God and others, the more we grow in genuine holiness. Self-giving—the core of love—makes us more like the Holy One, who is love. That is why authentic holiness does not parade about and often goes unnoticed. Think of all the men and women you know who serve others without pretensions, who, like Jesus, simply go about doing good. As long as we remember that sanctifica-tion is not about *our* perfection, but

We can best monitor our progress in holiness by seeing whether or not we are growing in love.

about loving God and others, our pursuit of holiness will stay on the right track.

Starting Out

Holiness is not an intellectual pursuit. One can understand much about holiness in theory without achieving it in practice. A doctor's knowledge of medicine does not guarantee his own health. In fact, the theory of holiness loses all value without the practice, since what is important is not understanding how holiness works, but being holy. How do we transfer speculative knowledge about holiness to the practical domain of life?

The rest of this book attempts to deal with this question by out-lining important means to achieve holiness, that is, means to grow in love of God and neighbor. Still, a couple of basic attitudes are necessary if we are to ever get out of the starting gate.

Since God wants you to be holy and will give you all the help you need, there are really only two re-quirements for becoming holy: desire and courage. Desire moves us to take the necessary steps to advance in holi-ness and courage helps us overcome the

God wants you to be holy and will give you all the help you need.

hurdles that are sure to appear. You *know* that God wants you to be holy, and that holiness is an ideal worthy of pursuit, but this knowl-edge is not enough. You need to really *want* to be holy and *decide* to be holy. You need to make holiness your number-one priority and be willing to take the necessary measures that will lead to holiness.

It's not enough to merely shrug our shoulders and say, "Yeah, I guess I probably should work more at that," somewhere around number thirty-nine on our list of New Year's resolutions, down among fixing the leaky roof of the garage, correcting our golf slice, and changing the living room upholstery. Holiness has to become our *passion*, our one overriding aspiration by which we judge our own success.

This means continually reevaluating our priorities so that holiness becomes a real ideal that moves us, rather than just a theory. We can ask ourselves: *How much time and effort do I devote to God and others, compared to the time I spend worrying about myself? How much am I willing to give up in order to be faithful to God? How many of my practical decisions are based on my desire to grow in holiness?* All other goals will find their proper place, prominent or otherwise, if measured in relation to this prime focus.

Jesus commands us to seek *first* his kingdom, and the rest will follow, and he also promises that whoever seeks, finds (Matt. 6:33, 7:7). We have to seek it more than anything else, like the Magi who left home and kin and set out to find the newborn king of the Jews, heedless of the many obstacles and hardships they would face. We need to become enthused with our spiritual lives, realizing that they are the most fruitful and fulfilling adventures we will ever embark on.

Our spiritual lives . . . are the most fruitful and fulfilling adventures we will ever embark on.

Nonetheless, desire alone does not suffice. Holiness comes at a price. Remember Jesus' parables of the treasure in the field and the precious pearl (Matt. 13:44–46)? When these treasures are unearthed, the lucky discoverer runs home and sells all he owns to buy the field or the pearl. You can afford to buy them only when you have sold everything else.

It's not enough to sell off a little excess stock or a few trinkets to "add" holiness to our little private portfolios. We have to want it so badly that we are willing to part with *everything else* in order to have it. Sell in order to buy, empty in order to fill, depose in order to enthrone. If we do not sell all, we cannot afford to buy. In our hearts nothing can be more important than God and we must be ready to make any necessary sacrifices, small or large, to possess him.

Thus the pursuit of holiness requires courage. We don't hear much about this ancient virtue in an age that places a premium on ease and comfort. Courage is the virtue of warriors, of those who know they have a battle on their hands and that they won't gain victory just by sitting around and waiting for it to happen.

Doing good requires more courage than doing evil. In wrongdoing you can often find someone to join you, to applaud your efforts, to justify your actions. In trying to maintain your personal integrity you will frequently find yourself all alone, making what appears to be a hopeless stand against a world that has chosen another path. Swimming upstream always demands more valor than going with the flow. On the cross Jesus felt so alone that he cried out in his anguish, "My God, my God, why have you forsaken me?" And yet in that very moment he was accomplishing our salvation and exhibiting the greatest love the world has ever known.

Courage goes hand in hand with hope. Holiness is possible. God wants it, and he is prepared to give us all the means we need to get there. The poet Francis Thompson has described God as "the hound of heaven," ceaselessly pursuing us simply because he loves us. What a beautiful source of courage to know that God loves us first, that he refuses to give up on us! After years of resisting God, Saint Augustine had to admit: "You made us for yourself, O Lord, and our heart is restless until it rests in you."

Courage can even mean heroism and a willingness to be different from the rest. Few obstacles hinder holiness more than the fear of standing out. No one wants to be labeled a "holy Joe" because he spends too much time in the chapel. We aspire to being "normal." Yet normality is overrated. Although we often associate normality

Normality is overrated.

with balance and levelheadedness, it frequently coincides with mediocrity and lukewarmness, a distinctly unevangelical quality. Sociologists coined the term "normal" to describe groups of subjects clustered around the "norm" or median, not standing out either for excellence or for deficiency. Here, "normal" means nothing more than average, mediocre, and run-of-the-mill.

Our urge to blend in with the crowd stands in direct opposition to a more noble yearning for greatness, an aspiration to lofty ideals, and a nostalgia for heroism. Jesus himself calls us to a certain radicalness. He taught that it is a narrow and hard road that leads to life and that few travel it, while the "gate is wide and the way is easy, that leads to destruction, and those who enter by it are many" (Matt. 7:13 RSV). If nothing else, these words should give us pause if we think that running with the crowd assures us of being on the right track. We wouldn't want to make like the lemmings that gleefully run off cliffs to their deaths in the subjective security that "everyone else is doing it."

Remember Christ's words as recorded in the book of Revelation: "So, because you are lukewarm [read: normal], and neither cold nor hot, I will spew you out of my mouth" (Rev. 3:16 RSV). Somehow, in this light, the idea of mingling in the masses of "normal" people begins to lose its appeal.

On the other hand, normality in another sense *does* have a place in our pursuit of holiness. It is precisely in ordinary, normal life that holiness comes about. We don't need special circumstances to grow in holiness; the ordinary will do just fine. Paul said, very simply: "Whether, then, you eat or drink or whatever you do, do all to the glory of God" (1 Cor. 10:31 NASB), and elsewhere adds, "And whatever you do, in word or deed, do everything in the name of the Lord Jesus, giving thanks to God the Father through him" (Col. 3:17 RSV). Every moment lived in union with God is an occasion to grow in holiness, since love for God must permeate all our activities, not only those specifically oriented to his praise. Our ordinary duties are not an obstacle, but a means for growing in holiness. They provide the setting, the backdrop for the drama of our holiness.

How many lament: "If it weren't for all the time I have to devote to my spouse and children, I would have more time to grow closer to God," or "If only I didn't have to work all day, I would be able to pray more." Yet God would be very strange indeed, and very unreasonable, if he were to command us to do two contradictory things. Why would he ask us to fulfill certain responsibilities if they served only to draw us farther from him?

We don't need special circumstances to grow in holiness; the ordinary will do just fine.

We must avoid creating an artificial dichotomy between activities that make us holy and merely human activities with no spiritual value. If we do our work wholeheartedly and well for God, everything serves to lead us to him. Paul again wrote, "Whatever you do, do your work heartily, as for the Lord rather than for men" (Col. 3:23 NASB).

Again, it all comes down to love, which gives value even to the smallest actions and ordinary activities. Love is, of course, one of the most hackneyed and least understood words in the world. For holiness to have real content, love needs to take flesh. This will be our task in the next chapter.

CHAPTER 2

True Love

The Heart of Christian Spirituality

God is love and anyone who lives in love lives in God, and God lives in him.

1 John 4:16

S ome words get so hammered over time that it is hard to remember what they originally meant. Just think of what has
happened to the word *charity*, for example. When you hear
charity, what comes to mind? You probably think of dropping a few
coins in a beggar's tin cup, sending a check to the Salvation Army,
or leaving some old clothes at your local shelter. This is fine and
good, but charity, in its original sense, goes far beyond holiday donations to the needy. If you ask a theologian what charity is, he will
tell you that charity is a theological virtue that disposes us to love
God above all things and our neighbor as ourselves, for the love of
God. True enough, but perhaps a bit academic for modern ears. In
its truest meaning, charity is simply *Christian love*.

Now we all know that love is important in the Christian life, but
we may not realize just how central it is. Earlier I made the auda-
cious claim that love is the essence of holiness. Two quick facts
from Jesus' life should suffice to drive home the point. First of all,
Jesus claimed that love would be the distinctive characteristic of his

followers (John 13:35). In other words, you might not be able to recognize a Christian by his hairstyle, the car he drives, the way he dresses, or some secret handshake, but you should be able to pick him out by his love.

Just take a moment to let that sink in. In the midst of the world, among so many people of different faiths and philosophies, folks should be able to spot a Christian by his love. Maybe not at first glance. Charity doesn't mean walking around wearing a goofy grin or greeting people with a smarmy, "I'm so neighborly" hypersincerity. But on closer observation, a Christian's self-giving and living for others should make him stand out.

Second, Jesus said that love (for God and one another) not only towers above the other commandments as the most important, it encapsulates in itself the entire moral law (Matt. 22:37–40). Paul likewise wrote, "Love . . . is the fulfilling of the law" (Rom. 13:10 RSV). Therefore, everything God expects from us, all the precepts and norms and commands, can be summed up in the commandment to love. This is how the great Saint Augustine could boldly claim: "Love and do as you please!" All the "shalt not's" and "remember to's" and "you must's" roll together in a single command: love!

Everything God expects from us, all the precepts and norms and commands, can be summed up in the commandment to love.

And if this weren't enough, along comes Paul to tell us that no matter what else we do, no matter how great or worthy, it all comes to naught if we do not love. Nothing else, he says—speaking in tongues, prophecy, mountain-moving faith—matters a whit if we do not love. In fact, Paul says we are just a "cymbal clashing" and a "gong booming" if we have these things without love (1 Cor. 13:1).

The value of the things we do comes more from the love we put into them than from their material worth. As Thomas à Kempis put it so well in *The Imitation of Christ*: "God regards more with how much affection and love a person performs a work, than how much he does. He does much who loves much." At the final reckoning, only one sort of work will survive the purifying fire: the work done in love and for love.

A Choice, Not a Feeling

The fact that we are commanded to love implies that love is within our grasp. It is something we can choose to do or not to do. This flies in the face of a typical notion of love as a wispy feeling that comes and goes as it pleases: now you feel it, now you don't. Feelings, as they say, have a mind of their own. But God does not command us to *feel* a certain way (which would be impossible) but rather to *act* a certain way and to adopt certain attitudes. His commandment to love our neighbor does not mean that we are obliged to experience warm, fuzzy feelings toward every specimen of the human race, but rather that we are to sincerely desire and work for their good. His commandment that we are to love him with all our hearts, minds, souls, and strength does not mean that our hearts have to go pitter-patter every time his name is pronounced, but that we are to strive to act in a way that pleases him.

To love our neighbor does not mean that we are obliged to experience warm, fuzzy feelings toward every specimen of the human race.

With disturbing frequency I hear husbands and wives tell me that they no longer love their spouses. My spontaneous response is always the same: "Then you had better start!" Romantic feelings come and go, but true love goes well beyond such feelings. Love is not something that happens *to you*, but something that you *choose to do*. Our society focuses so strongly on victimhood that we even conceive of ourselves as helpless victims of love's vicissitudes. We feel like pawns of the inexplicable movements of love, rather than the free decision-makers of whether we will love or not. Whether we *feel* love or not, we are called to love.

If love is a choice, then the first step in loving is to decide to love. In fact, the decision to love is already love, since love is a practical choice and not an irrational sentiment. Prayer is love, obedience is love, service is love, fulfilling our duties to God and others is love. Every time we prefer others to ourselves or choose to do something not because we feel like it, but because it is the right thing to do, we are loving.

Loving God

Jesus' "great commandment" is broken into two parts: love of God and love of neighbor. We usually jump over the first part and head right for the second, since love of neighbor seems more concrete and practical than love of God. In fact, if you ask someone whether he loves God, he is likely to look nervously at the ground and mutter something like, "I suppose so." If you were to press further and ask what it means to love God, his uneasiness would only increase. He would probably respond that loving God means going to church on Sundays and praying.

It isn't easy to define love for God, which means we have a hard time knowing whether we really love him or not. If love for God doesn't consist in warm, cozy feelings, in what does it consist? The answer is twofold: making him a part of our lives (the most important part), and doing his will.

We often think that the opposite of love is hate, but it isn't. The opposite of love is indifference. Love and hate are both passions and imply that another person is meaningful and important to us, albeit in radically different ways. Indifference means that the other doesn't matter to us at all, and as far as we are concerned the other could be dead. Now apply this to your relationship with God. How many people—starting with ourselves—conduct their lives as if God didn't exist? As if he weren't our greatest Benefactor who had given us life and all the qualities and gifts we possess?

We rarely deny him outright, but our lives betray a practical athe-

The first step in loving God is acknowledging him, making room for him, bringing him into our plans and decisions.

ism that leaves God out of our daily decisions and plans as if he didn't exist, or at least didn't matter. How often we are like the prodigal son, snatching up our inheritance without a thought or a word for our heavenly Father, source of our lives and every good! If we want to love God, we must acknowledge him, make room for him, bring him into our plans and decisions.

LOVING GOD MEANS COMMUNICATING WITH HIM

Practically speaking, making room for God means not only thinking *about* him but also talking *to* him. Recognizing God's presence shouldn't be like recognizing the existence of the Gobi Desert or Saturn—a purely speculative nod toward realities with little or no impact on our existence. We give God a place in our lives when we recognize him as a person, our Creator and Redeemer, and converse with him in friendship and gratitude.

Moreover, he deserves not just any place, but the *first* place, and this is what it means to call him *Lord*. For the saints, God's presence is a real and present reality, and he is the first one to be consulted before making a decision, the first to be thanked for blessings received, the first to be greeted in the morning before beginning the day. And the more we devote ourselves to loving God with our whole hearts, the more that love fills us with peace and joy.

Jean-Pierre de Caussade wrote in *Abandonment to Divine Providence,* "For those who abandon themselves to it, God's love contains every good thing, and if you long for it with all your heart and soul it will be yours. All God asks for is love, and if you search for this kingdom where God alone rules, you can be quite sure you will find it. . . . To love God is to want to love him in all sincerity."

LOVING GOD MEANS FREELY OBEYING HIM

The second dimension of loving God deals with obedience to his will. There has been much debate among theologians and people dedicated to the spiritual life concerning the role of obedience in the Christian life. Some have hazarded the hypothesis that obedience compromises love, and that true love releases us from the bonds of obedience. In one sense this is undoubtedly true, in that love frees us from slavish obedience to arbitrary norms, fulfilled out of fear. On the other hand, love clearly does not stand at odds with an active desire to please the one you love. In fact, it implies it: "Love consists, not in the extent of our happiness, but in the firmness of our determination to try to please God in everything, and to endeavor, in all possible ways, not to offend Him" (Teresa of Ávila, *Interior Castle*). Love would lose all meaning if it were to justify actions and attitudes that displeased the one loved.

For those who abandon themselves to it, God's love contains every good thing.

Jesus used rather forceful language when relating obedience to love. "If a man loves me, he will keep my word" (John 14:23 RSV). The first and most convincing sign of true love for God is obedience to his commands (1 John 2:4–5). Love indeed surpasses and completes the commandments, but it doesn't replace them. Love makes the commandments deeper, more demanding. We are no longer to obey out of strict obligation and fear, but out of filial love and a desire to respond to God's love for us by loving him in return. How could we possibly love God if we were to callously disregard or shun the demands he makes on us?

Much of our practical efforts to love God, therefore, consist in trying to find out what God wants from us and actively putting it into practice. For example, if at the beginning of your day, when planning your to-do list, you consciously ask yourself, *What does God want from me today?* you have already made great strides toward loving him better.

One final consideration on loving God relates to a practical means to grow in this love. Human love comes as a response to divine love. We love because we are loved (1 John 4:19). Though a firm resolution to love is important, the more we experience God's passionate love for us, the more we will be spontaneously moved to love Him. As one holy man put it: "Anyone who loves God in the depths of his heart has already been loved by God. In fact, the measure of a man's love for God depends upon how deeply aware he is of God's love for him" (Diadochus of Photice, *On Spiritual Perfection*).

And another great Christian, Ignatius of Loyola, ended his famous *Spiritual Exercises* with a "contemplation to obtain love." Very simply, this contemplation consists in recalling the many gifts we have received from God, beginning with the gift of existence itself. We are invited to slowly call to mind the countless material and spiritual gifts God has given us during our lives, and from this reflection on how much God loves us we are moved to want to love him better and better. A greater openness to God's love for us inevitably blossoms into an increased love for him.

> *A greater openness to God's love for us inevitably blossoms into an increased love for him.*

Loving Our Neighbor

Though love for God is the first of all the commandments, it cannot be separated from love for our neighbor. In fact, love for neighbor is often the best thermometer of our love for God. Teresa of Ávila wrote, "We cannot be sure if we are loving God, although we may have good reasons for believing that we are, but we can know quite well if we are loving our neighbor."

Jesus did say, after all, that whatever we do to the least of our brothers and sisters, we do to him (Matt. 25:40). And the apostle John forcefully added: "If any one says, 'I love God,' and hates his brother, he is a liar; for he who does not love his brother whom he has seen, cannot love God whom he has not seen. And this commandment we have from him, that he who loves God should love his brother also" (1 John 4:20–21 RSV).

Christian love involves seeing people with an eye to their own good rather than in terms of their usefulness. This virtue necessarily changes the way we deal with both people we like and people we don't like. Instead of treating them according to the pleasure or displeasure they cause us or the personal gain or loss they provide for us, we are called to love them for their *Acting for their genuine good . . . elevates our human relations to a truly supernatural level.* own sakes. Acting for their genuine good and not just for the profit we receive from our interaction with them elevates our human relations to a truly supernatural level.

Christian love cannot be reduced to a *quid pro quo*: I receive good, I give good back. I receive evil, I respond with evil. My treatment of others cannot simply be a conditioned response to their treatment of me and a strict meting out of what others "deserve." This would simply be an eye-for-an-eye, tooth-for-a-tooth, Old Testament–style justice. This is, as Jesus said, what comes naturally to tax collectors and pagans (Matt. 5:43–48). Jesus invites us to go beyond this and reminds us that the measure we use for others will be measured back to us (Mark 4:24–25; Luke 6:37–38). The model for Christians is the Father, who is good to all: the good, the bad, and the indifferent.

The Christian rule of thumb is as easy to understand as it is difficult to practice: Persons are not to be hated—period. They are to be loved—period. That means street cleaners and business moguls, drug dealers and shop clerks, bullies and babysitters—all men, women, and children without exception—are to be loved. Sometimes this is quite easy. Some people are lovable and kind, and we naturally love them in return. Things get sticky, however, when dealing with people who are unpleasant (or worse).

From personal experience I can say that on the Italian buses in summertime, it is very hard to love the smelly man next to me or the pushy woman who elbows me out of the way. It's harder still to love people who have intentionally wronged me or others I know. And here the essential Christian distinction between sin and the sinner becomes so important. Loving others does not mean condoning all their choices and actions. Some actions are clearly reprehensible and we do not fail to love when we acknowledge or even reprimand their evil. It is, in fact, true love that propels us to say something. Yet our driving attitude toward all people—our closest friends and those who have stabbed us in the back or dragged our names through the mud—can only be love, a true desire for their lasting good.

This beautiful, infinitely demanding virtue is not merely the fruit of willpower or superhuman effort, but of God's grace. At the same time, it will not come to fruition without our active cooperation. Sometimes it will cost us blood and the rending of our insides, but when we cease to love a single person we cease to be Christians and, in a real sense, we cease to live up to our humanity.

When we cease to love a single person we cease to be Christians and, in a real sense, we cease to live up to our humanity.

Charity means more than "putting up with others." It seeks communion, whence we speak of the "communion of saints" to be brought to perfection in heaven. And love is not just for me and my buddies, my clique, but for all of humanity. Christian love is universal in its scope. Charity gently prods our hearts open, enlarges and broadens them to include all persons, like the heart of Christ. When Christ looks on each of his brothers and sisters—sinners and saints alike—he looks on them with infinite love and a passionate desire to be united with them for all eternity. When we refuse to love, we risk creating an abyss between our hearts and Christ's. To willingly exclude a single brother or sister from the scope of our charity drives a wedge between us and Christ, since we are no longer united to him in his ardent, passionate love for that person.

An Open-Ended Challenge

Christ's new commandment of love encompasses the Ten Commandments and goes beyond. The minimalistic formulations "Thou shalt not steal. Thou shalt not kill . . ." are taken up and thrust forward to the immensely demanding, open-ended commandment to love God above all things and our neighbor as ourselves. Love certainly excludes all sorts of hurtful attitudes and actions toward others, but it also enjoins a positive, effective commitment to our neighbors' integral good. And being *effective*, this goodwill is always ready to manifest itself in practice whenever the opportunity presents itself.

Love impels us forward. It drives us farther and higher. It rejects minimalisms and refuses to be limited to what is strictly obligatory or necessary. Love doesn't ask: "How much am I obliged to do?" or "How far do I have to go?" but rather "What more *can* I do?" Traditional expressions of Christian love include the corporal and spiritual works of mercy: feeding the poor, clothing the naked, instructing the ignorant, comforting the afflicted. But there are myriad forms of exercising charity throughout the day.

One particularly fruitful form of charity is patience—or the bearing with the faults, defects, and limitations of others. Paul, in his splendid description of love, enumerated the qualities of this virtue and patience tops the list (1 Cor. 13:4). Patience, from the Latin *patior* ("to suffer"!), means a willingness to bear with others—with all their quirks—as we hope that they will bear with ours. Sometimes the smallest things—the guy who loudly chews gum in the office cubicle next to mine, the woman who holds up the checkout line at the grocery store—demand nearly heroic patience.

Since charity means an active desire for the good of others, it cannot neglect their highest good. If we are truly convinced that it profits a person nothing to win the whole world and lose his soul, our love would be severely lacking if we do all sorts of nice things for others but do nothing to bring them nearer to Christ.

By the same token, the worst faults against charity involve leading others into sin, because in this way we damage them in what is most precious: their friendship with God. Remember Jesus' severe admonition: "It is inevitable that stumbling blocks come, but woe to him through whom they come! It would be better for him if a millstone were hung around his neck and he were thrown into the sea, than that he would cause one of these little ones to stumble" (Luke 17:1–2 NASB). Obviously the opposite also holds true: charity reaches its apex when we lead others by our example, words, and encouragement to a deeper faith in and love for Jesus Christ. Faith is the true "gift that keeps on giving," both now and in eternity.

They'll Know We Are Christians

Of course *charity* isn't just any sort of love. It is specifically *Christian love*. That means to love as Christ loves and on Christ's terms. At the Last Supper, when Jesus laid down his "new commandment," he didn't just enjoin his disciples to "love" in a generic sort of way but rather told them: "Love one another; just *as I have loved you*" (John 13:34, emphasis mine). This gives us a clue to the importance of imitating Christ, since he himself is the model of what it means to love. If we really want to know how to love in a Christian way, we must look more closely at his life (which we will do in chapter 4). For the moment, it will suffice to sketch a few characteristics of Christ's love in broad strokes.

GRATUITY

A first trait of Christ's love for us is its gratuity. In other words, his love is thoroughly unearned and undeserved. When Jesus came to earth to save us from our sins, he didn't do so in response to mankind's record of good behavior. The human race hadn't stacked up so many brownie points that God felt compelled to reward us. In fact, quite the opposite. He loved us when we were sinners, rebels, enemies of God (Rom. 5:8). He took the initiative, the first step. He didn't wait for us to apologize, to humble ourselves and beg for his indulgence, or even to ask him for help. Like the good Samaritan, he saw us lying by the roadside, unable to save ourselves, and came to our assistance.

The gratuity of Christ's love can be seen over and over throughout his life. He continually reached out, offered himself, came to the aid of those in need. And what about our own lives? What did I do to deserve the gift of faith, my baptism as a child, so many experiences of God's love just when I needed it most—and deserved it least?

We can practice this same gratuity in our own lives. Instead of only giving people what they *deserve*, we can deliberately go further. If we are attentive, we can discover numerous occasions where people need our assistance and we can love them as Jesus loves us. Helping an elderly woman to put her purchases in the trunk of her car, holding the door for the person behind you, making an overture of peace to your estranged sister that you haven't spoken to in months—how many opportunities to love as Christ loves!

COMPASSION

A second characteristic is Christ's compassion. When Jesus looked out over the crowds, what did he see? Somehow he was able to overlook all the malice, the pettiness, and the self-seeking that was surely present. Remember, these were just ordinary people, like any human gathering today. Yet Jesus saw them as sheep without a shepherd and was moved to compassion. Sometimes love is a question of focus, a predisposition to concentrate on the good rather than the bad.

This compassion is another quality that we can practice in our own lives. Instead of feeling disgust for the many unfortunate people we run into every day, we can try to see them as Christ sees them. Poor people, uneducated people, morally weak people, petty people, people that just seem to be in the way—in all these cases we need to exchange a natural reaction of contempt or avoidance for a truly Christian response of compassion.

PERSONAL

Third, Christ's love bears a personal stamp and focuses on the individual. His was not a generic love of humanity or a comfortable philanthropy, but a personal, singular love for each one. The Good Shepherd is disposed to leave the ninety-nine in the wilderness and go in search of the stray, because each one is of infinite value for him. With God, everyone counts. The individual does not escape his attention because he loves each one as if he were the only one.

In our own lives it is much easier to love "humanity" than to love individual persons. We can become more like Jesus when we make an effort to love the person we have before us: the clerk at the cash register, the coworker who shares office space with us, our spouses who are in a particularly foul mood. How many chances we have every day to love personally, concretely, individually!

MERCY

A fourth characteristic of Christ's love is mercy. He insisted over and over again on the need to forgive, up to "seventy times seven" (Matt. 18:22 NASB), and he practiced what he preached. Jesus' disciples were painfully slow learners, yet he did not give up on them. He spent time with them, teaching by word and example, and led them gently forward. When they fell, he did not abandon them. Even when Peter betrayed him three times, denying that he even *knew* him, Jesus forgave him and immediately Peter was back by his side.

Jesus foresaw all their sins and failings yet continued to hope in them, to confide in them, to bring out the best in them by his persevering love. Who among us has not experienced the same steadfast, merciful love in our relationship with Christ? How many times should he have given up on us, left us to our own devices, and yet he didn't!

How many times should he have given up on us, left us to our own devices, and yet he didn't!

Here once again, we are called to practice this same virtue in our own lives. A merciful heart bears with the failings of a wayward son or daughter, makes room for the foibles of coworkers, and reaches out to heal rifts in relationships even when "it's not my fault." There is, perhaps, no harder aspect of Christian morality than the command to forgive those who trespass against us and to love even our enemies, yet it is in the practice of these eminently Christian virtues that we most resemble the Master. We cannot, in fact, forgive as we are called to without the assistance of divine grace. Fortunately, God offers this grace to those who ask for it.

SELF-GIVING

And finally, and most distinctively, Christ's love involves self-giving: "My life for yours." Jesus himself declared that the greatest love a person can have for others is to lay down his life for them, and this is precisely what Jesus did. This is why if we really want to understand Jesus' love for us, we need to look at his Passion and death, freely embraced for love of us. On seeing our need, Jesus didn't sit back at a comfortable distance in heaven and "send a check" to remedy the situation. He came in person to give his life. Whenever we prefer others to ourselves, we imitate Christ in his love. When we give them our time (that we could have used for ourselves), when we listen to their concerns (instead of expressing our own), when we oblige their suggestions and preferences (instead of forcing our own), our love resembles Christ's. And resembling Christ is what it's all about, as we will see in the next chapter.

CHAPTER 3

WWJD?

What It Really Means to Follow Christ

We can be sure that we are in God only when the one who claims to be living in him is living the same kind of life as Christ lived.

1 John 2:5–6

You have no doubt seen kids walking around with those 1970s-looking nylon bracelets with the letters WWJD embroidered on them. These letters cut across denominational lines and pierce the heart of Christian ethics: *What would Jesus do?* That is, here and now, if Jesus were in my place, what would he do? What sort of decisions would he make? What sort of person would he be if he were living now, in my shoes?

When I was in high school I toyed with the idea of taking up acting as a career. In my junior year the theater group at my school announced it would be putting on the Frank Loesser musical *Guys and Dolls*. I auditioned and received the role of Sky Masterson. Soon I began diligently memorizing my lines, rehearsing my stage movements, and doing my best to identify with my character.

In the midst of our rehearsals we learned that a professional troupe was putting on *Guys and Dolls* at a small theater in downtown Detroit. A group of us attended the opening night performance and I was mesmerized. Sky Masterson came alive for me. He was no longer a two-dimensional set of lines and stage movements loosely held together by the personality I imposed on him. That actor had *become* Sky Masterson, and I felt that somehow I could too.

Have you ever watched a really good tennis match or soccer game and wanted to run out right afterward and play? I used to love to watch Bjorn Borg play tennis, with his incredible top-spin forehand and devastating net game. It's that thrilling "Aha!" experience that makes us exclaim, "So that's how it's done! Now I understand!" and makes us want to run out and try it ourselves. Not only do we better understand what is required, but we actually feel capable of carrying it out. Seeing our ideal in action, lived out, can be more motivating and instructive than reams of theory.

WWJD doesn't propose a set of rules to obey but points to a person to follow. Jesus Christ wasn't just a good interpreter of the human condition, a worthy representative of one of the best ways to go about the business of living. He was humanity itself, "the Son of Man"—man the way he was meant to be, the way God dreamed of when he first said, "Let us make man in our own image" and breathed life into Adam's nostrils. Christ, the perfect man, truly does reveal what it means to be a human being. He came to earth not only to be our Savior, but also our model of holiness and humanity.

WWJD doesn't propose a set of rules to obey but points to a person to follow.

We may well balk at this proposal. Isn't that putting the bar a little high? After all, Jesus was God. Shouldn't we look for a model a little closer to our own level? Jesus' divinity shone so brightly that it threatened to overshadow and negate his humanity. Yet just because Jesus was God didn't make him less a man. The fatigue, fear, sadness, anguish, joy, and loneliness that are part and parcel of human existence marked Jesus' life as well, and the expressions of these realities in the gospel are not some sort of theatrical performance "as if" Jesus were just like us. He really was. He really experienced these human conditions, just as we do.

Some days he woke up with a headache, other times his nerves were on edge, other times he was so drowsy that he just wanted to roll over and sleep—and still he was faithful to his Father. The author of the Letter to the Hebrews takes pains to assure us that "we have not a high priest who is unable to sympathize with our weaknesses, but one who in every respect has been tempted as we are, yet without sin" (Heb. 4:15 RSV).

A Christian is not first and foremost a virtuous person, a law-abiding citizen, or a righteous fellow who lives up to certain standards of conduct. A Christian is a follower of Christ. A Christian is, in the first place, a believer and a disciple. The Christian life does not comprise a set of prescriptions and counsels, which, when properly applied, give rise to a Christian. The Bible is not a playbook or a Christian owner's manual. The Christian life means following Christ himself, since God the Father "intended [us] to become true images of his Son" (Rom. 8:29). Jesus is not a theory, an idea, a cause, or a program. He is a living person. *He*, and not merely his *doctrine*, constitutes the center and goal of the Christian life.

Christ didn't shy away from this dramatic truth, and if he weren't God himself, his boldness would be obnoxious: "I am the way, and the truth, and the life; no one comes to the Father, but by me" (John 14:6 RSV). Jesus did not claim to be *a* way—along with Buddha, Mohammed, and psychological self-help books—but *the* Way. He didn't claim to be *a* truth or *your* truth, but *the* Truth, with all the unfashionable absolutism that that implies. And he didn't claim to be *a* life, and

> *If he weren't God himself, his boldness would be obnoxious.*

still less one "alternative lifestyle" among many, but rather *the* Life, the only true life for which we all were created. As Peter reminds us, "There is no other name under heaven that has been given among men by which we must be saved" (Acts 4:12 NASB).

Christian life, we are told, is a call to discipleship. Perhaps this idea of discipleship is lost on our modern ears. An illustration may help. Renaissance Italy produced some of the finest artists the world has ever known. When in the Renaissance a youngster aspired to become a painter or sculptor, he attached himself to a master. Rather than read books on artistic technique or set off immediately on his own, he lived with a great artist and spent his days studying him, afterward to practice and imitate what he had learned.

An apprentice sculptor or painter could spend hours contemplating the master and would try to imitate his style so closely that often an apprentice's works could be recognized as coming from the "school" of Perugino or Ghirlandaio or Botticelli. Some apprentices got so good that their works could even be confused with works of the masters themselves. Perusing museums, one occasionally comes upon works attributed to a well-known artist "or one of his disciples," so closely did their styles resemble one another.

As a disciple, a Christian is a learner, an apprentice, enrolled in the school of the Master to observe and learn. Gregory the Great wrote, "Our Lord and Savior sometimes gives us instruction by words and sometimes by actions. His very deeds are our commands, and whenever he acts silently he is teaching us what we should do." Jesus spoke of just such an identification between him and his disciples: "A disciple is not above his teacher, nor a servant above his master; it is enough for the disciple to be like his teacher, and the servant like his master" (Matt. 10:24–25 RSV). What a beautiful goal for a Christian: to be recognizable for our resemblance to Christ!

What It Means to Imitate Christ

Flipping through the pages of the Gospels could dishearten a would-be disciple. We see Jesus healing lepers, calming unruly seas, multiplying loaves and fishes, and walking on water. How are we to imitate that? Jesus himself provides the answer to this question. He never asks us to imitate him in his miracle-working or in those specific actions that we attribute to his divinity. He asks us, rather, to imitate him in his fundamental attitudes of humility, self-sacrificing love, and dedication to the Father's will.

"Learn from me," Jesus invited his followers, "for I am gentle and humble in heart" (Matt. 11:29). He focused our attention on his interior dispositions, which are then translated into concrete actions. He invited us to humility, to peacefully take our rightful places before God as his creatures and children, and to take our places alongside our brothers and sisters as fellow travelers on the road to eternity.

He invites us to humility, to peacefully take our rightful places before God as his creatures and children.

As we saw in the previous chapter, Jesus also commands us to imitate him in his love. "Love one another *as I have loved you*" means to take Jesus as our model in living out the commandment to love God and neighbor. This love does not remain at the level of good feelings and noble intentions but takes shape in service. After washing his disciples' feet at the Last Supper, Jesus once again says to his disciples: "If I then, your Lord and Teacher, have washed your feet, you also ought to wash one another's feet. For I have given you an example, that you also should do as I have done to you" (John 13:14–15 RSV). Jesus' love expressed itself in real service, and ours should too.

Following Christ's example means adopting his moral framework. The structure or dynamic of Christ's moral life provides a model for his disciples. How did Jesus go about making choices? What was his scale of values? When he woke up in the morning, how did he decide what to do that day? What seems to stand out most is Christ's awareness that the Father had a plan for him, that he had received a mission that he was called to carry out. The Father's will furnished a stable point of reference for his decisions, and his overriding desire was to please the Father in all things. Often in the Gospels Jesus made reference to his mission, what he was sent to do, and why he was on earth. Rather than ask himself what he *felt* like doing, Jesus asked what the Father wanted from him.

Imitating Christ, then, means more than imitating his actions and extends to his way of thinking, his words, his reactions, his feelings, his perspectives on persons and events, all summed up in Paul's packed expression: "Put on the Lord Jesus Christ" (Rom. 13:14 NASB). Thus WWJD becomes WWJT (*What would Jesus think?*), WWJS (*What would Jesus say?*), and so on. His attitudes, his criteria, his way of accepting humiliation, of dealing with his Father, of forgiving offenses become a pattern of life for us. The imitation of Christ encompasses all the dimensions of our personalities and all the elements of our lives. A heart like his, a mind like his, standards like his, feelings like his, thoughts like his: these are the path to holiness—and to true humanity.

Enroll in My School

Imitation involves assiduous study. Think of how sports aficionados study the moves of their idols in order to better replicate their style. The better we know Christ, the truer our imitation will be. How can we know what Jesus would do if we haven't taken the time to get to know him inside and out? If we don't know Christ deeply, our so-called imitation will be nothing more than an expression of our own idiosyncrasies in the name of Christianity.

Knowing *persons* differs from knowing *facts*. We may know a lot about Billy Graham, but that isn't the same as having met him and spent time with him. Our knowledge of Christ cannot be merely an academic, antiseptic knowledge as if Jesus were nothing more than a great historical figure of the distant past. It must be a vital, personal knowledge of the One who is the same yesterday, today, and forever, the Alpha and the Omega. We imitate him not only as the perfect model, but through intimate friendship with him, love for him, and union with him. He is not only the perfect man, but my Savior, the One who gave his life for me on the cross. He took my place and accepted the punishment due to my sins, so that in him I could find mercy and be united with him forever in heaven. Thus knowledge leads to love, and love to imitation.

We imitate him not only as the perfect model, but through intimate friendship with him, love for him, and union with him.

Jesus tells us: "Learn from me." The French version of that phrase offers a beautiful nuance: "*Mettez-vous à mon école*"—"Enroll in my school." But how can we go about learning from Jesus? We can't just pack up and move to Sienna or Florence (or the Holy Land, for that matter) to become apprentices of the Master. Where are the "workshops" where we can find him so as to learn from him? The practical answer to that question is threefold: in the Gospels, in the Eucharist, and in the Cross.

The Gospels

The Gospels recount the life of Jesus and offer us a special window into his heart. We learn about his birth, his home life, his relationships with his disciples, his dealings with the poor and suffering, his Passion, death, and resurrection. Reading a passage or two from the Gospels every day grants us a familiarity with Jesus' life, his teaching, and the way he thinks. But unlike other historical documents, the Gospels are God's living Word. We find Jesus present in them in a way that other historical figures are not present in texts about their lives or even in their written correspondence. God continues to speak to us personally through his Word, and in it we not only find out *about* Jesus, we actually *meet* him.

The unexpected bonus of this contact takes the form of an increased love for Christ. The hackneyed phrase "To know you is to love you" takes on a whole new meaning in the case of Jesus. The richness of his personality, the strength of his character, and the attractiveness of his whole being make us want to be like him, to be his friends. Thus greater knowledge of Christ provides not only the content of our imitation, but also an ever-growing *desire* to resemble him. Knowledge of Christ and the experience of his love for each of us fill us with a longing to love him in return, and this love in turn leads to imitation.

> *The experience of his love for each of us fills us with a longing to love him in return, and this love in turn leads to imitation.*

THE EUCHARIST

The Eucharist is the second "workshop" where Jesus meets his apprentices. On the night before he died, Jesus left us a perpetual memorial of his Passion: the sacrament of his body and blood. He promised his disciples that he would not leave them orphans (John 14:18), that he would be with them all days, till the end of time (Matt. 28:20). Catholics believe that whenever we enter a church or chapel where the Eucharist is present, we are with Jesus not only spiritually, but even physically. How much we can learn from him in the Eucharist! He awaits in silence, ready to console, enlighten, and strengthen those who approach him. The humility that characterized him when he walked the earth continues to shine as he makes himself available to us in great simplicity, under the form of a piece of bread. How many Christians of times past overcame their defects, grew strong in faith, and found consolation through their daily contact with Jesus in the Eucharist!

THE CROSS

The third "workshop" where we learn from him is the *Cross*. Jesus' love for us, his obedience to the Father, his total self-giving are all summed up in his sacrifice on the cross. When we look at Jesus' suffering for us, freely accepting the punishment due to our sins (not his!), our own little crosses seem very small in comparison, and we find strength to love better. Can't I accept this little hardship if Jesus was willing to suffer so much for me? Can't I be a little more forgiving when Jesus forgave his executioners even in the midst of so much agony? Can't I be a little more faithful to what God is asking of me when I see Jesus obedient up to death, death on the cross?

From *Imitatio Christi* to *Imitatio Patris*

Some preachers speak of Jesus as a radical innovator. He is painted as some sort of revolutionary—the Che Guevara of the ancient Jewish world, upsetting the status quo and rebelling against the institutional leaders of his time. While Jesus did forcefully upbraid the Pharisees for their hypocrisy, he was anything but a headstrong maverick obstinately out to "do things his way." The closer we look at the Gospels' accounts, the better we realize that Jesus was no megalomaniac, but a humble imitator of the Father, carrying out the mission for which he was sent.

"My teaching is not mine, but his who sent me," Jesus said to the Jews (John 7:16 RSV). Further along he added, "I do nothing on my own authority but speak thus as the Father taught me" (John 8:28 RSV). Jesus not only looked to his Father as his origin and guide, but also as a model. "The Son can do nothing of his own accord, but only what he sees the Father doing; for whatever he does, that the Son does likewise" (John 5:19 RSV). His model and ideal is the Father, the One who sent him. In this way, the *imitatio Christi* (imitation of Christ) leads us to the *imitatio Patris* (imitation of the Father).

Jesus passed this ideal of imitation along to his disciples, summing up his Sermon on the Mount with the words, "You must therefore be perfect just as your heavenly Father is perfect" (Matt. 5:48). Not only does Jesus offer himself as an example to follow, but he also points beyond himself to the Father. In his preaching, Jesus invited his disciples to look to the Father and take his example as a pattern for their own lives. Thus could Paul write to the Ephesians: "Be imitators of God" (Eph. 5:1 NASB).

This is especially the case in universal charity. Jesus enjoins his followers to love their enemies and pray for their persecutors: "So that you may be sons of your Father who is in heaven; for he makes his sun rise on the evil and on the good, and sends rain on the just and on the unjust" (Matt. 5:45 RSV). Christ holds up the Father's example for imitation, promising that through their imitation of his indiscriminating love for all, his disciples will be children of the heavenly Father.

This love also entails mercy. "Be merciful," Jesus teaches, "just as your Father is merciful" (Luke 6:36 NASB). Such imitation sets us squarely on the road to heaven. "Your reward will be great," Jesus promises, "and you will be sons of the Most High; for he is kind to the ungrateful and the selfish" (Luke 6:35 RSV).

In all things Jesus looked to the Father. He took his cues from heaven and consulted his Father in prayer before making big decisions or facing difficult moments. Before he chose his twelve apostles from among his many disciples, he spent an entire night in prayer to make his choices according to the Father's will (see Luke 6:12–16). Before his Passion and death, he prayed for hours in the Garden of Gethsemane, asking for his Father's will to be done, not his own (Luke 22:39–44). Rather than do things his own way, Jesus sought to do things the Father's way.

In this light, WWJD becomes *What Was Jesus Doing?* and the answer is clear: he was doing his Father's will. Always. What is this will of God? How are we to follow it in our own lives? To this topic we now turn.

CHAPTER 4

The Road to Happiness
Reevaluating God's Will

I want to do what you ask of me,
In the way you ask,
For as long as you ask,
Because you ask it.

"Universal Prayer" attributed to Pope Clement XI

O bedience is no fun. One of the chief reasons many adolescents want so desperately to grow up is that they imagine that they won't have to answer to anyone but themselves. Isn't this the dream of our age, to be one's own boss? To no longer have to "report in" to someone else? No one enjoys submitting his will to another's, especially in our day where individual freedom has become the supreme value.

That's why Jesus' example impresses us so much. He submitted to the Father's will in Gethsemane, embracing the cross despite the revulsion he experienced. Yet on describing his own relationship with the Father's will, Jesus didn't talk about long-suffering resignation to the divine plan. He could have chosen many analogies to illustrate his compliance with the Father's will. He could have spoken of the prompt obedience of a soldier, or the way an arrow springs from the bow and faithfully follows the path marked by the archer's keen eye. Jesus opted for the peculiar image of *food*. "My food is to do the will of him who sent me" (John 4:34 RSV). Jesus isn't like the obedient little boy who stoically accepts the decision of his parents ("I would love to, but my parents won't let me"). Rather he presents submission to God's will as refreshing, liberating, nourishing. It is his *food*.

Imitating Christ in carrying out God's will for your life entails, in the first place, a recognition that God has a plan for you. He created you out of love and entrusted you with a mission. If you conceive of your life as the result of happenstance and not the fruit of God's loving designs, the notion of God's will simply makes no sense. If you acknowledge that God *intended* for you to exist, then the idea of his will starts to take shape. God wants certain things *for* you, expects certain things *from* you, and moreover since he is God, he has a right to make demands *on you*. Why he does so, and in what these demands consist, will be the topic of this chapter.

Misconceptions of God's Will

God's will is not an easy concept to understand. Some conceive of the divine will as impersonal fate or "destiny," an irresistible, cosmic force to which we must succumb or be swept along regardless. Written in the stars, or etched into the universe, this "will" would simply represent the way things must be, the immutable reality of past, present, and future. People consult fortune-tellers and horoscopes to get some clue as to what this fate entails. All in all, irrepressible destiny provides neither guidance nor comfort.

Much of our attitude toward God's will stems from our understanding of God himself. For those who conceive of God as something more than impersonal fate, another option is the cosmic chess player. We are the pieces, the "pawns" in God's hands, and he moves us whether we like it or not. Man's life on earth would simply be a bit of afternoon entertainment for a whimsical god with too much time on his hands. According to this scenario, God's "will" simply represents his moves, where he wants us to go. Such was the conception of the ancient Greeks, who viewed the gods as capricious deities, with their own ambitions and infighting, and their own arbitrary designs over the lives of mortals.

Others see God as a sort of celestial factory foreman. He has work to do, some tasks to accomplish, and we—the witless instruments—provide the manpower for his projects. In this case, a utilitarian taskmaster god would be using us for his goals, trying to squeeze all the work—or entertainment—out of us he can. Something like Tennessee Williams's Gipsy, who quipped that we're all of us "guinea pigs in the laboratory of God." Indifferent to *our* needs and happiness, he would be concerned only with the accomplishment of his master plan, in which we would be mere cogs in a machine. Such a slavish conception of God, far from the filial perspective shown by Christ, leaves us squirming for independence, anxious to get out from under the divine yoke.

Such a slavish conception of God . . . leaves us squirming for independence, anxious to get out from under the divine yoke.

The pendulum can also swing the other way. Where some see God as indifferent to our needs, others see him as overly concerned for our well-being, like a benevolent but controlling father who decides our future for us regardless of our own preferences and plans. His will—the way *he* thinks our lives should go—may or may not coincide with our own aspirations and goals. As with a father who desperately wants his son or daughter to be a doctor or a lawyer, we feel his will to be an imposition. Perhaps deep down he wants the best for us, but we perceive his interventions into our lives as invasive meddling, rather than genuine help toward our happiness and fulfillment.

In moments of frustration and anger, haven't we sometimes wondered why God won't leave us in peace? According to this mind-set, the best we can do is keep a low profile and hope God doesn't notice us. Maybe that way he will let us go about our business.

Yet do these conceptions of God and his will match up with what Jesus Christ revealed to us? In other words, are they Christian? Not at all. Jesus presents God's will as something liberating, a plan that gives sense to our lives, rather than an oppressive, arbitrary set of rules designed to make life difficult or unpleasant. Let us take a closer look.

What Is God's Will?

If God is love, then everything he does must be born of love and express love. God doesn't ordain some things out of love, others out of anger, others out of justice, and others out of amusement. All he does, no matter how we may view it, is an act of love. The more deeply and perfectly we realize that God is love, the more beautiful life becomes. We start experiencing how he really does know how to work all things to good for those who love him (Rom. 8:28).

He created us, in fact, out of love, to be with him forever in heaven and share his life and his joy. That is the essence of his will for us. He created us to know him and love him in this life, and he marked out a plan for each of us, the best possible course to reach him. To conceive of our lives apart from him, independent of his design, means unmooring ourselves from our origins and destinies. Because we are free we can disregard God's plan or even reject him, but that path will surely not lead to happiness but to misery and emptiness.

He created us to know him and love him in this life, and he marked out a plan for each of us, the best possible course to reach him.

So many times we don't know what to do and we yearn for guidance, for someone to show us the way. And often we cannot just figure it out on our own, since the right thing to do does not always coincide with a moral calculation of what is *absolutely* best. Otherwise we would never leave the chapel, since prayer and commerce with God undoubtedly are "better" than, say, playing basketball, studying, or going to the market. Yet recreation, study, and shopping all make up part of God's will for us. Likewise, we cannot deduce God's plan for our lives simply by inquiring into which state of life is "higher" or "better" than the others, since what is better depends on what we are specifically called to do.

God's will for me expresses his personal love for me in a concrete way. By it, he manifests his desire for my happiness and shows me where this happiness is to be found. As Jesus said, "I have come so that they may have life and have it to the full" (John 10:10). Those are hardly the words of a taskmaster.

How can I be happy and holy? Where is the right path for me? God knows better than I, and incredible as it may seem, he wants my happiness even more than I do. Many high schools and colleges provide their students with "guidance counselors" who help students match their inclinations and talents to specific career paths. God is the guidance counselor par excellence, since he made us and only he knows exactly what for. He shows his love for us by making known his will.

God's will resembles a treasure map, indicating where great riches are buried. In a well-known parable Jesus said: "The kingdom of heaven is like treasure hidden in a field, which a man found and covered up; then in his joy he goes and sells all he has and buys that field. Again,

We can spend our lives trading in pearls, but the one precious pearl of God's will makes all the others appear deformed and worthless in comparison.

the kingdom of heaven is like a merchant in search of fine pearls, who, on finding one pearl of great value, went and sold all that he had and bought it" (Matt. 13:44–46 RSV). Conforming ourselves to

God's will means sacrificing many other things, "selling all," but it is worth it. We can spend our lives trading in pearls, but the one precious pearl of God's will makes all the others appear deformed and worthless in comparison.

Though God does have a specific plan for each of us, that plan requires the responsible use of our freedom and creativity. We work in unison with God, but he does not micromanage our every decision or send signs for every little move we make. God's will is not like a GPS (Global Positioning System) cuing us to "turn right" here, "turn left" there, requiring only the mechanical execution of his orders. He gives us indications of what sort of people he wants us to be and accompanies us on our journeys as a loving Friend and Father, gently guiding us in the exercise of the freedom and intelligence he gave us.

Rigorously interpreting every single thing that happens as a "sign" from God can lead to serious psychological imbalances and a very unpleasant existence. God is not a Ouija board to be consulted before we choose what to wear for a party or select a first course at a restaurant, but our dearest Friend who lives in, with, and through us.

God's will has two dimensions: (1) a *moral* dimension, whereby he indicates to us—through his commandments and counsels, his example, the natural law, the Church he founded, or the inspirations of the Holy Spirit—what he wants us to do, how he wants us to act, what sort of people he wants us to be, and (2) a *providential* dimension, whereby he governs all of human existence, directing events according to his wisdom and love. This providential will is manifested in what occurs inside us and around us. As the great French Christian, Jean-Pierre de Caussade, wrote: "The realization that God is active in all that happens at every moment is the deepest knowledge we can have in this life of the things of God. It is a continuous revelation, an endlessly renewed traffic with God" (*Abandonment to Divine Providence*).

Let us look at the moral and providential dimensions of God's will in greater depth.

GOD'S MORAL WILL

Conformity with God's *moral* will means wanting everything that God wants us to do and be and putting our full effort into living it out. "What God wants" includes the truths he wants us to believe, the good things he wants us to hope for, the punishment he wants us to fear, the commands he wants us to obey, the attitudes he wants us to cultivate, the counsels he wants us to follow. As a consequence, we are to desire the *means* necessary to achieve these things: the duties of our state in life, the practice of the virtues that help us live charity, the avoidance of the occasions of sin, and so forth.

As sovereign Lord and Creator, God has the right and authority to command us, his creatures. And being infinitely wise and good, he commands us only what is truly good for us and what will lead us to eternal happiness (John 15:9–11). God's will and his love are the same thing. His will is not arbitrary but based entirely on his love for us and his wisdom, and by it he leads us sure-footedly to our true fulfillment and happiness.

His will is not whimsical or arbitrary but based entirely on his love for us.

Some have fallen for the destructive lie that God's commands are given not to aid us in our pursuit of happiness, but as hurdles strewn along our path to test us and make life more difficult. We often hear about original *sin*—the sin of Adam and Eve—but we easily forget that this was the fruit of the original *lie*. In the garden Satan told Eve that God's commands proceeded from selfish motives rather than pure love. He coaxed her and her husband, Adam, into doubting God. And where distrust of God's goodness was accepted, sin entered the world.

Sometimes the goodness of God's precepts isn't readily evident. He asks many things that are costly to our nature, and others that frankly seem unreasonable or illogical. Moreover, he often asks us to take his goodness on faith, to act out of loving obedience rather than the pure logic of what appears good or attractive to us. Yet often the reasons become clearer with the passage of time, or when we put them in the larger context of those around us.

An analogy may help illustrate this. Think of a carefully choreographed dance, synchronized swimming, or a football game. On a football team, individual players receive instructions as to their specific roles in a given play. An offensive lineman may be told to knock the defensive tackle to the right, to the left, or straight back, depending on the play. This may be tough to do, and it doesn't have any logic in itself but only in the context of the whole play. If the guard has seen how the play is laid out, he will understand why he must do this, but otherwise he simply has to trust the coach. Often only the coach sees the broader picture and coordinates how the different tasks fit together to create a harmonious play.

If the players trust the coach, they will do their jobs with the assurance that they fit into the larger scheme of things. Life is like this. God often conceals the whole play from us and simply asks us to fulfill our parts with the knowledge—in faith—that he knows exactly what he is doing, and how our part fits into the whole. Only he sees the big picture, and he asks us to trust him.

John Henry Newman summed up this trusting attitude in one of his most beautiful meditations:

> I am created to do something or to be something for which no one else is created; I have a place in God's counsels, in God's world, which no one else has; whether I be rich or poor, despised or esteemed by man, God knows me and calls me by my name.
>
> God has created me to do Him some definite service; He has committed some work to me which He has not commit-

ted to another. I have my mission—I never may know it in this life, but I shall be told it in the next. . . . I am a link in a chain, a bond of connection between persons.

He has not created me for naught. I shall do good, I shall do His work; I shall be an angel of peace, a preacher of truth in my own place, while not intending it, if I do but keep His commandments and serve Him in my calling.

Therefore I will trust Him. Whatever, wherever I am, I can never be thrown away.

If I am in sickness, my sickness may serve Him; in perplexity, my perplexity may serve Him; if I am in sorrow, my sorrow may serve Him. My sickness, or perplexity, or sorrow may be necessary causes of some great end, which is quite beyond us.

He does nothing in vain; He may prolong my life, He may shorten it; He knows what He is about. He may take away my friends, He may throw me among strangers, He may make me feel desolate, make my spirits sink, hide the future from me—still He knows what He is about.

(Meditations on Christian Doctrine)

Jesus came to renew our trust in God by revealing his extraordinary love for us. As he said to the Pharisee Nicodemus: "For God so loved the world, that He gave His only begotten Son, that whoever believes in Him shall not perish, but have eternal life. For God did not send the Son into the world to judge the world, but that the world might be saved through Him" (John 3:16–17 NASB). A God who is willing to die for me surely deserves my absolute trust.

A God who is willing to die for me surely deserves my absolute trust.

Christ also showed us how to love the Father in return. The deepest, most real union takes place at the level of the will: to want what the other wants, to strive to please the other in all things. This was the most convincing manifestation of Christ's love for his Father: "I always do what pleases him" (John 8:29). "The Father and I are one" (John 10:30). Embracing the Father's will unites us to Christ more deeply than blood unites brothers and sisters: "For whoever does the will of my Father in heaven is my brother, and sister, and mother" (Matt. 12:50 RSV).

In the Lord's Prayer Jesus taught us to pray: "Your will be done, on earth as in heaven" (Matt. 6:10). Though stated in a general way, this petition commits us personally and can be translated as "Help me to do your will here and now, as perfectly as the saints do it in heaven." Here, too, the imitation of Christ is essential. On the night before he suffered, knowing full well what was in store for him, Christ prayed in the Garden of Gethsemane: "My Father, if this cannot pass unless I drink it, thy will be done" (Matt. 26:42 RSV). This short prayer summed up Jesus' attitude toward his Father. In similar fashion, each of us plays his or her part in the work of salvation by our own loving obedience to the Father.

The petition "Thy will be done" can be seen as a more detailed explanation of the prior petition of the Lord's Prayer: "Thy kingdom come." Christ's kingdom exists in souls where he reigns as King, where his will is the rule of life. Thus "Thy kingdom come" expresses itself in "Thy will be done." Likewise, union with God consists first and foremost as a union of wills. Conformity with the divine will is the surest sign of true holiness, where God reigns as King, just as opposition to God's will is the surest sign of the absence of holiness.

Conformity with the divine will is the surest sign of true holiness, where God reigns as king.

Unlike pagan conceptions of God's will as impersonal and irresistible fate, the Christian sees God's will as an invitation to love freely. God does not impose his will but appeals to our freedom to follow him. It would be tragic to love someone and have no way of expressing that love. Lovers are always anxious to get to know the other's tastes and desires, in order to be able to please. When God manifests his will to us, he not only points out the way to our happiness but indicates the way for us to love him. His will is not a cold *rule* but a personal *request*; it's what *Jesus* is asking of me. Many hard things become easy when we do them in order to please Jesus, rather than to "be good" in the abstract, or just to "follow the rules."

> *His will is not a cold rule but a personal request; it's what Jesus is asking of me.*

GOD'S PROVIDENTIAL WILL

Conformity with God's *providential* will means accepting and actively cooperating with his sanctifying activity through the circumstances and events he permits in our lives. It means embracing all the providential events willed or permitted by God for our benefit. Nothing happens to us or in us without God's willing or permitting it, and God, being infinitely good and wise, wills and permits only what can be directed to our eternal good. God can even bring good out of evil. What an immense consolation to know that there is nothing in life, no matter how terrible, that God cannot turn to good!

Often this good is not readily apparent, and faith is necessary to trust that God will bring good out of even the most trying ordeals. Even death, sickness and heartbreak can become an occasion for great good. Our faith reminds us over and over: God is love, therefore everything that proceeds from him can have only love as its source and motivation. We must then ask ourselves: *What good is God trying to produce in me through this occasion? What response does he expect from me?*

This trust in God's power to bring good even out of tragedy proves especially necessary when considering our own faults and sins. The ancient Easter hymn "Exultet," sung by Christians for many centu-

Our faith reminds us over and over: God is love, therefore everything that proceeds from him can have only love as its source and motivation.

ries, speaks of the "happy fault" of Adam that won for us such a Savior. In a sense, when we turn to God with repentance, all our sins can become "happy faults," since God is able to bring good even out of our own greatest misfortune: personal sin. This means that even when we have strayed far from the path of God's plan for our lives, we haven't irremediably de-

stroyed God's project. He is able to turn even the most disastrous existence into a spiritual masterpiece.

Only the light of faith—and the perspective of eternity—gives us the assurance that God brings good out of all things. If we limit our vision to this life only, such an assertion makes little sense. Or, as Paul would put it, "If our hope in Christ has been for this life only, we are the most unfortunate of all people" (1 Cor. 15:19). Our firm conviction in any circumstance—joyful or painful—must be one of confidence and submission to God's will: not stoic resignation or apathy, biting the bullet with grim resolve, but deep Christian hope and confidence in a God who is love, a God who did not hesitate to die on the cross for us.

Thus God's providential will requires our active acceptance and cooperation with his plans so that they will bear all the fruit that he intends. This trusting acceptance of God's will furnishes us with an excellent way to show our true love for him. If we love him only when his gift pleases, we may well wonder whether we really love God, or just his gifts. If we view them rightly, even God's less-pleasant gifts call for thanksgiving, since behind everything that happens to us—even what seems to be misfortune—we discover the love of God. The saints recommend that we endeavor to be just as grateful for those things that are immediately pleasing as for those that run contrary to our nature.

Adversities and trials can be spiritually beneficial if a person uses them well. Sorrows and troubles remind us that we are exiles in this life; we have here no lasting home. The joys we experience in this life make the journey more pleasant, but their fleetingness and inability to satisfy our spirits leads us to place our hope for lasting joy not here but in heaven.

Contradictions and failures keep us humble, make us distrust ourselves and trust in God, and provide an effective antidote to vanity. When the world treats us badly, we better understand how much we need God and find in him a true and faithful Friend. The experience of life's trials benefits the soul, since we learn that no genuine security or lasting peace can be found in this life, which will one day come to an end. Our sorrows and miseries here teach us to fix our gaze on heaven, where "God will wipe away every tear from [our] eyes" and where "no eye has seen, nor ear heard, nor the heart of man conceived, what God has prepared for those who love him" (Rev. 7:17 RSV; 1 Cor. 2:9 RSV).

A disposition to bear even the sufferings that God allows doesn't mean we shouldn't seek to avoid or mitigate them. A headache permitted by God may indeed be a source of sanctification, but we mustn't infer from that that we may not take a couple of Extra-Strength Tylenol to make it go away. Whereas some suffering is unavoidable, other times we can and should take the necessary measures to avoid it with no qualms of conscience.

The key to living these occasions well is to unite ourselves to Christ and offer our sufferings—small or great—for the salvation of souls and out of love for God. All we need to do is place these sufferings in God's hands and ask him to unite them to his own. He can use them for great good and bring spiritual fruit out of what would have otherwise been sterile irritation.

A particular case of God's providential will deals with temptations. As James reminds us, God never tempts us to sin, since that would go against his very nature: "God cannot be tempted by evil,

The very same stone in our path can trip us up or allow us to climb to greater heights—it all depends on how it is used.

and He Himself does not tempt anyone" (James 1:13 NASB). Yet if God permits temptations in our lives, it can be only for our good, not so we will fall but so we will triumph. The very same stone in our path can trip us up or allow us to climb to greater heights—it all depends on how it is used.

Even though they are bothersome to our nature, temptations may be very beneficial to our souls. They urge us to have recourse to God's grace, the way a child runs to his mother or father when danger appears. They also purify us and teach us much about ourselves as well as give us the chance to show God how much we love him and prefer him to all things. Temptations are not sins, unless we give in to them. There is an essential difference between *feeling* an evil inclination and *consenting* to it. Thus what the devil would throw in our path to make us stumble God intends for us to use as a means to greater union with him.

The normal means God employs to help us grow in virtue are the struggles and temptations he permits in our lives. It is in the battle to be true and faithful that virtue is forged. We should always assume when we experience temptation—provided we haven't deliberately stumbled into it—that God intends us to grow through it, especially in those virtues directly opposed to the temptation. Temptations to pride give us the chance to grow in humility, and temptations to laziness give us the chance to grow in diligence. In all this we need to cling to the assurance that Christ will always give us the sufficient grace to overcome any and all temptations, as he promised Paul (2 Cor. 12:9; 1 Cor. 10:13).

Knowing God's Will

Let us suppose for a moment that we are well disposed to do God's will and are anxious to know what it is. How can we be sure what God is asking of us? We have at our disposition a precious little tool, called *moral conscience,* "the most secret core and sanctuary of a man," where "he is alone with God, whose voice echoes in his depths."[1] Through conscience we apply the objective principles of right and wrong to particular situations and the Holy Spirit enlightens our minds to know how best to act. Conscience not only evaluates possible courses of action, but it also urges us to pursue the right course and to avoid whatever displeases God.

> *Conscience not only evaluates possible courses of action, but it also urges us to pursue the right course and to avoid whatever displeases God.*

"Do not be conformed to this world, but be transformed by the renewing of your mind, so that you may prove what the will of God is, that which is good and acceptable and perfect" (Rom. 12:2 NASB). This renewal of our minds comes about when we open ourselves to God's grace and the working of the Holy Spirit in our lives, and when we sincerely look for the will of God and not our own will.

Fortunately God gave us objective criteria to know his will for us in the big things, and these provide the raw material for conscience to act. The Gospels, the Ten Commandments, the natural law that urges us to do good and avoid evil, the teachings of the apostles and their successors, and "lights" of the Holy Spirit all provide guidance in knowing what God expects from us. Let's take a quick look at each of these elements.

THE GOSPELS

We have already examined the importance of God's Word, and especially the Gospels, for gaining firsthand knowledge of Jesus, his life, and his teachings. If he provides the example of how we are to live and pleased the Father in all he did, we can learn much from studying his life. By reading and meditating on the Gospels we learn to live with Jesus and to see all things through his eyes, which provides a whole new optic for viewing our lives and choices. Jesus' commands to love God and neighbor, to forgive those who hurt us, to bless even our enemies, to keep our hearts pure, and to actively serve rather than lord power over others all teach us what God wills for us in our day-to-day lives.

THE TEN COMMANDMENTS

The Ten Commandments (or Decalogue) are a series of moral injunctions that God gave to Israel, which many of us memorized as children in Sunday school. They provide a basic framework or moral minimum for our lives, letting us know what pleases or displeases God in our conduct with him or other people. These precepts that enjoin us to worship God, honor our parents, and treat others and their property with respect, haven't lost any of their relevance. In fact, when Jesus was asked what was needed in order to enter eternal life, the first reply he gave was: "Keep the commandments" (Matt. 19:17). As we saw earlier, all of these commandments are summed up in love of God and love of neighbor, but these ten help to make the demands of this love more explicit.

NATURAL LAW

Third, we have the capacity to know what God wants from us in many situations through "natural law," a law "written on our hearts" (see Rom. 2:15) by which we recognize good and evil. Thomas Aquinas describes this law as "the light of understanding infused in us by God, whereby we understand what must be done and what must be avoided. God gave this light and this law to man at creation." The ability even of little children to recognize fair and unfair treatment bears witness to this moral sense that God has given to us. It enjoins us to do good and shun evil, to treat others as we would have them treat us, seeking for them all the good things that we want for ourselves.

THE CHURCH'S TEACHING

The fourth tool for knowing what God expects from us comes in the form of the Church's teaching. Remember that Paul called the Church "the pillar and support of the truth" (1 Tim. 3:15 NASB) and Jesus himself promised that the gates of hell "will not overpower it" (Matt. 16:18 NASB). What a consoling and reassuring promise, especially in our day and age when she is battered from within and from without!

Moreover, with the many difficult moral questions arising from biomedical discoveries, shifting geopolitical structures, and social unrest, we need divine assistance to sort out what we *should* do from what we *are able* to do. Jesus never taught about cloning, stem cell research, or manipulating the human genome, and Christians need guidance to know what God expects from them in these areas as in many others.

Despite the evident flaws and sinfulness of her members, the Church is a means of sanctification and sure guidance for Jesus' followers, because Jesus himself, head of the Church, stands at her helm. Jesus sent his apostles and their successors to teach in his name and assured them that "if they kept my word, they will keep yours also" (John 15:20 RSV). Like the early Christian community, we are called to be united in faith, devoted "to the apostles' teaching and to fellowship, to the breaking of bread and to prayer" (Acts 2:42 NASB).

Moreover, Jesus promised he would send his Holy Spirit who would lead us to the fullness of truth and remind us of all he had taught. This promise was made not to individuals—who can and do often disagree—but to the whole body of believers, the Church, under the guidance of her pastors.

LIGHTS OF THE HOLY SPIRIT

Finally, "lights" of the Holy Spirit refer to particular inspirations that he gives us to guide us and spur us on to a greater charity and perfec-tion in living out our duty. The Holy Spirit plays a more active role in our lives than we would imagine, and he enlightens us to know what God wants from us, especially when we desire this above all things. On our part these lights require a prompt, generous response. The Holy Spirit may suggest, but he will never twist our arms. It is up to us to follow his lead. How many times do we experience simple inspirations to telephone a friend who is suffering, help a struggling sibling, or swallow our hurt pride! It is up to us to act on these inspirations or not.

The Church is a means of sanctification and sure guidance for Jesus' followers, because Jesus himself, head of the Church, stands at her helm.

How can we distinguish true lights from the Holy Spirit from our own overexcited imaginations? All of us experience doubt at some point regarding whether a given "inspiration" really comes from God. For the best assurance, we should check out such ideas with our spiritual mentor or director, an objective third party who can help us sift through our spiritual experiences and separate the real from the imaginary.

Nonetheless, a simple rule of thumb can also save us many head-aches in this area. Generally, we walk with assurance when we trust the ordinary and distrust the extraordinary. Inspirations that en-courage us to do our duty with greater vigor and enthusiasm, that help us live the requirements of our state in life with greater fidel-ity and joy—such inspirations can be followed without hesitation. When our "inspirations" induce us to undertake strange practices or to do things at odds with what we already know to be God's will for us, such ideas should be filed away for consultation before we take any action.

For example, when we see a person evidently in need and feel the urge of conscience to assist him, we can be reasonably sure such an inspiration comes from the Holy Spirit. When we start getting ideas that we are to do out-of-the-ordinary things (move to another country, go talk to that person we don't know, perform weird penances) with no apparent reason to do so, a healthy dose of skepticism is in order.

Having looked at where we are going in the spiritual life, we now turn to the specifics of how we are to get there. We have seen that we are on earth to become holy, to learn to love, which consists especially in embracing the Father's will in imitation of Jesus Christ. How are we to do this in practice, and what supports can we rely on to accomplish it? In the Christian conception of life, we are not simply told what to do and sent to do it. The Christian works together with God's grace, which is an indispensable aid to spiritual and moral growth. The Good Shepherd doesn't just hand his sheep a map and send them on their merry way; he accompanies them all along the route, fighting off wolves, encouraging, strengthening, and even carrying them when necessary. Let us now look at some of the practical helps Jesus offers in this undertaking.

Part II

WHAT GOD DOES FOR US

A t the Last Supper, in that final, long, intimate conversation with his apostles before his Passion, Jesus said and did some wonderful things. He gave them his body and blood in the Eucharist, gave them the authority to celebrate it in his name, and entrusted them with his new commandment of love. He also taught them a very important truth that was to guide Christians forever: he compared his relationship with them to a vine and branches, pointing out how a branch can bear fruit only when firmly attached to the vine, since the vine provides the branches with their life-sustaining sap and nourishment. And he concluded with a categorical statement: "Cut off from me you can do nothing" (John 15:5).

Now Jesus was not given to hyperbole, and if we take him at his word, that is a strong declaration. He doesn't merely say that without him we won't be able to get nearly as much done, or without him things won't go quite so well, or without him our yield will be pitifully small. Having Jesus on our side (better: being on *his* side) isn't like adding Miracle-Gro to our strawberry patch and reaping baseball-sized strawberries instead of normal ones. It is rather like the difference between trying to grow strawberries in rich soil or trying to grow them in concrete. When he says "nothing," he means *nothing*. In our spiritual work, union with Jesus is the prerequisite, the indispensable condition, of fruitfulness.

Fortunately, the acknowledgment of our spiritual impotence without Jesus also has a flip side. If it is true that without him we can do nothing, it is equally true that with him we can do *anything*. "With God, all things are possible," were Jesus' encouraging words to his disciples (see Matt. 19:26; Mark 10:27, 14:36). There is literally nothing we cannot do without God's help, since God is all-powerful. Nothing is beyond him. Tasks and projects that seem gargantuan and thoroughly beyond us, desperate situations that seem to have no possible solution: these are small potatoes to the Lord of the universe.

He asks for our cooperation, of course. Whereas without him we *can* do nothing, without our cooperation he often *will* do nothing, because he wants us to freely choose him instead of passively watching him act without us. I have divided these two sections of the book into What God Does for Us and What We Are to Do. This division, while hopefully helpful to readers, is nonetheless somewhat forced and artificial. After all, a clear-cut separation between God's part and ours simply doesn't exist. God's gifts demand our acceptance and response, and our works presuppose God's grace and ongoing assistance. The beauty of cooperating with God's action in our lives is that we simply can't tell where his activity leaves off and ours begins, since both become thoroughly intermingled. Still, at least on a conceptual level, this section will focus especially on God's gifts and the need for his aid.

How, then, do we gain access to this divine assistance? What specific help does Jesus provide to usher us along our spiritual journey? The next five chapters will deal with these questions. First we will explore the world of Christian prayer. Even though prayer most certainly involves human creativity and effort, it is essentially a gift. God makes himself available for communication with his children:

he hears us, understands us, and answers us. We will first examine the nature of this gift, along with the obstacles that most hinder us from taking advantage of it and then proceed to look at its inner dynamics and offer some practical pointers for getting started in prayer.

Next we will look at the sources of Christian grace, especially those means that Christ himself offered to the Christian Church as channels of his mercy and assistance. Here we will ponder the gift of baptism, which Jesus referred to as a rebirth in the Spirit, as well as other sacraments instituted by Christ and celebrated by the Church since the very first centuries of the Christian era.

We will also reflect on Christ's great gift to his Church: the Holy Spirit, the Promised One who would lead us to the fullness of life and truth. Jesus called him the Consoler, the Advocate, who would provide guidance and comfort to all Christians. He is moreover the Sanctifier, the one who fashions the image of Christ in our souls and strengthens us to do things we never would have thought possible.

Finally we will explore the gift of Christ's own mother, Mary, as a model for the Church and a special heavenly intercessor for Christians. Few Christian teachings are less understood than devotion to Mary, a poor creature like ourselves, but dedicated for a special mission, that of being Christ's mother. I hope that this chapter helps both Catholics and other Christians to better appreciate the role of Mary in salvation history and in our own personal journeys.

Clearly these five chapters don't exhaust "God's part" in our Christian lives, but they do hopefully open us to a deeper awareness of just how active God is in our lives, and how committed he is to our eternal happiness and success. Let's begin by looking at the gift of prayer.

CHAPTER 5

Talking with God

Prayer and Why It Matters

Pray constantly.

1 Thessalonians 5:17

I magine you got a phone call from your favorite movie star inviting you to breakfast. "Hey, Sally, this is Brad Pitt. I know we've never met, but I was wondering if you were free for breakfast this Wednesday. . . ." You'd probably jump at the opportunity. The honor of the invitation combined with the excitement would be overwhelming. While we probably won't be receiving any phone calls of this sort in the near future, all of us have an open invitation for an even more important encounter whenever we want. The King of Heaven himself awaits our company in his presence.

Prayer is a Christian duty, to be sure, but even more it is a privilege. Moses remarked in admiration to the Israelites, "For what great nation is there that has a god so near to it as the Lord our God is to us, whenever we call upon him?" (Deut. 4:7 RSV). Our God is not an unapproachable legislator or a distant, indifferent cosmic architect, but a *Father* personally interested in his children. Christ revealed to us a God who listens, a God who has counted every hair on our heads (Matt. 10:30; Luke 12:7), a God who hastens to give good things to those who ask him (Matt. 7:11; Luke 11:13). The same almighty Lord who spoke a single word and all things came to be, now bends his ear to listen to every word that you utter.

Holiness, we have said, is friendship with God, a dynamic relationship of love. Friendships thrive on communication, and friendship with God is no different. Good friends speak often and prefer to do things together rather than apart. Frequent contact cements friendships by building up a history of common lived experiences and a continuous exchange of gifts. The converse also holds true. A lack of contact through indifference or neglect can over time create chasms between friends, and a loss of intimacy and mutual trust.

What is prayer, after all, if not a heartfelt conversation with God? Teresa of Ávila described prayer as "nothing else than an intimate sharing between friends; it means taking the time frequently to be alone with Him who we know loves us." In prayer we lift our hearts and minds to God: we think of him, we speak with him, we listen.

> *In prayer we lift our hearts and minds to God: we think of him, we speak with him, we listen.*

Prayer gives us the chance to grow daily in our personal knowledge of Christ and opens us to the immensely edifying experience of living with him and for him. Our Christian faith means more than assent to a series of principles and doctrines. It means throwing in our lot with Jesus of Nazareth and accepting him into our lives as our best Friend and constant Companion. He is, indeed, the best and most faithful of friends, the true Friend who never fails us. Remember the illuminating words of Thomas à Kempis: "He who finds Jesus finds a rare treasure, indeed, a good above every good, whereas he who loses Him loses more than the whole world. The man who lives without Jesus is the poorest of the poor, whereas no one is so rich as the man who lives in His grace."

In prayer we talk with him, listen to him, tell him of our needs, ask his forgiveness for our failures, praise him, and thank him for his gifts. The practice of prayer reminds us that we are never alone, never abandoned, never left to our own devices.

Fruits of Prayer

The benefits of prayer are so manifold and stupendous, in fact, that a more thorough examination is in order. Our modern, pragmatic outlook risks seeing prayer as a luxury. Instead of being an essential element of our daily existence—like breathing, sleeping, or eating—we may be tempted to conceive of prayer as a leisure activity to be engaged in only when our work is done. Worse still, some see prayer simply as useless endeavor that pulls us away from needed activity. In this regard, Pope Benedict's words are especially illuminating: "Prayer, as a means of drawing ever new strength from Christ, is concretely and urgently needed. People who pray are not wasting their time, even though the situation appears desperate and seems to call for action alone."[1] In reality, prayer is the key by which our work yields the results we seek.

At the Last Supper Jesus compared our relationship to him with a vine and its branches. Jesus told us we can bear no fruit unless we are united to him. "Abide in me, and I in you," Jesus said. "As the branch cannot bear fruit by itself, unless it abides in the vine, neither can you, unless you abide in me" (John 15:4 RSV).

This relationship of total dependence on Christ for the fruitfulness of our lives is exemplified for us by Christ's own relationship with his heavenly Father. Jesus maintained continual contact with God in prayer, whether the short, spontaneous prayers he often uttered or the long hours he spent in conversation with his Father. Jesus kept plugged in with his Father's plan, and prayer was the plug.

Jesus kept plugged in with his Father's plan, and prayer was the plug.

Of the many fruits of prayer, I propose five for your consideration.

Prayer strengthens, orients, and consoles; it also unites us to God's will and works great good for those we love and for the whole world.

1. PRAYER STRENGTHENS US

In the book of Exodus, Israel engaged Amalek in battle (Exod. 17:8–13). While the armies clashed, Moses stood on the top of a hill overlooking the battleground with his hands raised in prayer. As long as Moses kept his hands raised, the battle went well for Israel, but when Moses grew tired and lowered his hands, the battle shifted in favor of Amalek. Eventually Moses' companions Aaron and Hur supported his arms on either side, and Israel won the day. While common sense would dictate that superior military strength and tactics determine the outcome of a battle, the biblical account drives home a different message: the deciding factor in our enterprises is often prayer.

God frequently asks us to do things that exceed our capabilities. He does so not to watch us squirm but to increase our reliance on him and on his grace. We are not a race of supermen; if anything, we are even weaker than we think. The night before his death Jesus cautioned his disciples to watch and pray because "the spirit is willing, but the flesh is weak" (Matt. 26:41). Sure enough, a few hours later Peter denied Jesus three times and the other disciples fled into the protection of the night. As a man, Jesus felt this human weakness and in his prayer God sent an angel to strengthen him (Luke 22:43). The lesson? We simply can't do it alone.

At the same time, with God by our side as Friend and Guardian, our weakness itself becomes our strength. Christianity is full of paradoxes and this is one of them. Paul says that in a moment of anxiousness he prayed to the Lord to take away the "thorn in his flesh," and Christ answered him, "My grace is enough for you: my power is best in weakness" (2 Cor. 12:9). From this Paul derived the conclusion that "when I am weak, then I am strong" (v. 10). What seems to be a liability becomes an asset to the Christian.

Recall how often in the history of Israel God made use not of

Israel's strength, but of its weaknesses. None of those God chose to do his work seemed particularly well suited to the task. David and Jeremiah were young and inexperienced, Abraham too old, Zacchaeus too small; Moses stuttered and Jonah and Peter were cowards. The list goes on.

Recall how often in the history of Israel God made use not of Israel's strength, but of its weaknesses.

Acknowledgment of our neediness, instead of being an impediment, opens us to a greater reliance on God.

Reliance on God in prayer does not, however, supplant the need for personal effort. The old adage "God helps those who help themselves" carries an important message for those who would replace needed activity with prayer. Prayer and activity complement each other. God rarely wants us to pray and then cross our arms waiting for him to act. Rather we must pray *and* work, knowing that God will bring forth good fruit from our actions.

2. PRAYER REORDERS OUR PRIORITIES

We discover and continually rediscover what is really important in life through prayer. Prayer reminds us that God is the Source and the End of all things: the One for whom we act, the One we aim to please in all things, the One to whom we tend as our greatest good and final happiness. Prayer lifts our gaze beyond our daily concerns to look toward eternity.

Medieval writers proposed a simple formula for judging the worth of our pursuits. They would ask: "*Quid hoc ad aeternitatem?*"— "What does this have to do with eternity?" This refers not just what we stand to gain or lose in the short run, but to the bearing of events on life after death. Prayer offers a continual reminder of eternity, of a world beyond this world, a world that is more important, lasting, and beautiful. In prayer we learn the value and true importance of all things, not assessing them according to their appearance but according to their objective worth—seeing them as God sees them, from the perspective of eternity (1 Sam. 16:7).

This eternity-based perspective does not discount the importance of the world in which we live—quite the contrary. This present world itself gains importance when considered in relation to eternity, since our daily actions transcend this short life and have eternal consequences. Our belief in eternal life increases our engagement with this world in which we live. Though we need not cling to the many things of this world that will pass away, this is the stage where we act out our faith and the school where we learn to love.

The reorientation provided by prayer acts like a compass. We pray not only to make headway, but to make headway in the right direction. Nothing is more frustrating than to be tooling along the freeway making great time, only to find out we are going the wrong way and need to turn around. Constant contact with God in prayer helps us gain a heavenly perspective of earthly realities, which keeps us heading in the right direction.

> *We pray not only to make headway, but to make headway in the right direction.*

3. PRAYER OFFERS CONSOLATION

No one is a spiritual superhero all the time. We try to keep upbeat, but sadness and frustration inevitably make an appearance now and again. Difficulties accompany human existence and we all need consolation sometimes. Prayer is balm for the heart and salve for the soul. Then again, it isn't *prayer* per se that consoles us, but *God* who consoles us *in* prayer.

> *It isn't prayer per se that consoles us, but God who consoles us in prayer.*

Unlike yoga or other relaxation techniques, Christian prayer doesn't seek simply to calm our nerves but to put us in personal contact with the living God, who knows us through and through and never stops thinking of us. It isn't the method or the exercise that matters most, but the God to whom we turn. In prayer God provides a shoulder to cry on, a word of encouragement to the downtrodden, and above all the assurance that we are known and unconditionally loved. As a mother or father comforts a little child, God comforts us and reassures us that everything is all right—which it truly is. He is in control.

The psalmist offered these deeply comforting words:

For as high as the heavens are above the earth,
So great is His lovingkindness toward those who fear Him.
As far as the east is from the west,
So far has He removed our transgressions from us.
Just as a father has compassion on his children,
So the LORD has compassion on those who fear Him.

(Psalm 103:11–13 NASB)

Even in moments of distress and suffering, God stands by our sides to comfort us. We find him in prayer.

4. PRAYER TRANSFORMS US

Perhaps the most beautiful and characteristic fruit of prayer is not what it provides for us, but the fact that it *transforms us*. Prayer makes us better. Spending time with God makes us more like him. If prayer doesn't make us better, something is wrong with our prayer, as Thomas Dubay wrote in *Fire Within*: "Advancing in communion with God does not happen in isolation from the rest of life. One's whole behavior pattern is being transformed as the prayer deepens. So true is this that if humility, patience, temperance, chastity and love for neighbor are not growing, neither is prayer growing."

Our Lord's yardstick for measuring the authenticity of discipleship—"You will know them by their fruits" (Matt. 7:20 NASB)—can be similarly applied to the quality of our prayer. Real Christian prayer goes hand in hand with an increase in virtue. Contact with God produces likeness to God. When asking whether we are "praying well," the key question is not *How do I feel?* nor even *How much light and consolation, or how many good ideas, come to me in prayer?* but rather *How is prayer helping me become a better, more Christlike person?*

True prayer is not divorced from life. Prayer affects our mode of living, just as our mode of living necessarily affects our prayer. If we live in a way that we know is displeasing to God, it is very difficult to approach him in prayer with simplicity and forthrightness. Sometimes what most disturb our prayer are our own consciences that reproach us for having been unfaithful to our best Friend and Father. The door is always open, however, and God's forgiving hand is always outstretched. He is always ready to bring about the transformation we need.

This transformation consists principally in a deeper union with God's will. Prayer helps us conform our wills to God's. It should come as no surprise that the real goal of prayer is union with God's will. "The whole aim of any person who is beginning prayer," Teresa of Ávila wrote, "should be that he work and prepare himself with determination and every effort to bring his will into conformity with God's will." In our intimate contact with God we learn to hate sin and anything that displeases him. Similarly, we learn to avidly seek all that pleases him.

The real goal of prayer is union with God's will.

All Christian prayer converges on Gethsemane. Christ's prayer— "Not my will, but your will be done" becomes the prototype of all Christian prayer. No matter what we ask for and how desperately we want it, we should always end our prayer as Christ did—asking that above all, God's will be done.

Prayer does not seek to make God conform to our plans but to conform ourselves to his. In prayer, we don't look for our own interests but plug into God's interests. The more we trust in God's love and wisdom, the easier it is to embrace his will. Our assurance that he loves us better than we love ourselves and would give us nothing but the best things grants serenity even in life's toughest moments.

The fruits of prayer don't end here, however.

5. PRAYER HELPS OTHERS

Prayer for others—often called *intercessory prayer*—forms a pillar of the Christian prayer tradition. During Christ's public life, numerous people approached him not with their own needs but someone else's. Recall, for instance, how four men carried a paralytic and lowered him through the roof to place him before Jesus, resulting both in the man's cure and in the forgiveness of his sins (Mark 2:1–12). They simply placed the man at the feet of Jesus, knowing that he would do what needed to be done.

Similarly, how many people do you know who have intense need of God's assistance but lack the will or inclination to ask for it themselves? Prayer gives us the chance to take their necessities before a Father who loves them, even if they may not know it. Those who suffer, those who doubt, those who are discouraged need us to "lay them at the feet of Christ" so that he can give them the healing they need.

We often wonder how to channel our desire to help others. How many times do we find ourselves earnestly wanting to come to the assistance of a friend in need and feel there is nothing we can do? We would like to change the world for better and feel incapable of doing so! Yet the most powerful aid possible is right at our fingertips. We can pray. We must pray. Our love for one another is transformed into prayer. What we cannot do, God *can* do. God can melt hearts, change minds, rectify situations, and soften even rock-hard opposition.

We may sometimes mistakenly think of prayer as a last resort, to which we have recourse when all other efforts have failed. Such an attitude doesn't do justice to the power of prayer. Even when we must take practical measures to resolve problems, we should accompany them with prayer, asking for God's assistance and protection. He works with us. He works through us. And he wants us to pray.

Finally, though prayer unquestionably brings great benefits to those who pursue it, we should guard against a utilitarian attitude to prayer. It is not merely a "useful" exercise. No one would ask friends or lovers what they "get out of" time spent together, as if their activity were always ordered to some other good. In like manner prayer is good *in itself*, independent of its consequences. It serves not only as a means to other good things, but as an end in itself. Spending time with God, basking in his presence, can be a foretaste of heaven. And even when prayer seems more like arduous labor than a pleasant pastime, it is a great good to be in God's presence.

Prayer is good in itself, independent of its consequences.

Typical Excuses for Not Praying (and Their Rebuttals)

If prayer is so wonderful—you may wonder—why do so few people practice it with any regularity? Prayer is the sort of thing we all know is necessary but never seem to find enough time for. Despite our good intentions, other affairs always seem to take precedence over prayer time and effectively crowd our prayer. Many wax eloquent on the beauty and fruitfulness of prayer, but scratch beneath the surface and even prayer's most ardent apologists often fail to live up to their own spiritual ideals.

This nearly pandemic neglect of prayer undoubtedly has multiple causes. The following list presents some of the more common rationalizations I have heard (and used!) over the years. Like most good excuses, each of these bears an element of truth, but also an element of falsehood. Unmasking them may help us overcome them.

1. "I Don't Have Time to Pray"

No one has time to pray, really. The idyllic notion of "free time" simply doesn't exist. We all have twenty-four hours in a day, and we all fill those hours with something. Yet in these twenty-four hours some people pray; others don't. Why is that? Here a glance at Christ's life can prove instructive.

The first striking feature of Christ's prayer life is not the *way* he prayed, or *what he said*, but the *fact* that he prayed. Simply put, Christ was a man of prayer. Since Jesus was God, we may think that he wouldn't have needed to pray. And yet in the Gospels we find him praying all the time: in the morning, at night, alone, and with others.

We don't have much disposable time in our hectic lives, but the same was true in the case of our Lord. His days were packed with activities (just as ours often are): foot travel from town to town, long hours of preaching and teaching, visiting people, listening to their questions and problems, curing the sick, and so forth. And still, he always had time to pray. Or, to be more exact, he always *made* time to pray.

This seems to be the key to Christ's prayer life. He made it a priority. He preferred prayer to other activities. He specifically set aside blocks of time to speak with his Father in prayer. And if he did this, it was because he was convinced of his need for prayer. It's not that he had "nothing better to do," but rather that for Him prayer was not a filler activity but a priority.

Prayer doesn't just happen. It doesn't automatically occur like breathing or a heartbeat. It doesn't impose itself on our organisms like eating and drinking. If we don't make time to pray, it simply won't happen. Sure, on occasion we can spontaneously be moved to direct a word or two to our Lord, but a vigorous, constant life of prayer and union with God is more the result of hard work and willpower than chance occurrence.

We often allow other "urgent" activities to crowd prayer out of our lives. The more work we have to do, the less time we leave for prayer, under the pretext that we simply have no time to pray. Our Lord teaches us by his example that the contrary is true. The more we have to do, the more we *need* prayer. The bigger our business decisions, the more transcendent our choices for our family and future, the more we need prayer. Meetings, strategic planning, and careful consideration are important, but they don't match the impact of prayer. Otherwise, what value does all our work have? "Unless the LORD builds the house," the psalmist reminds us, "they labor in vain who build it" (Ps. 127:1 NASB). Prayer gives meaning and direction to our many activities.

2. "I Don't Know How to Pray"

Some approach prayer the way they would approach windsurfing or glassblowing. It can seem so daunting that we approach it with exaggerated reserve. We think that prayer requires extensive training to master complicated techniques. And since we "don't know how" to pray, we don't do it.

Even if we do attempt prayer, we may quickly abandon it out of discouragement. Knowing that we possess no special spiritual credentials, we may feel that our prayer is second-rate, that we aren't doing it right, and that God surely has more interesting people to listen to. If we compare our ramblings, say, to the soaring spiritual poetry of John Donne or John of the Cross, we can't help but feel more than a little inadequate.

These considerations would be valid if God were a professional prayer critic whose primary concern was the technical perfection of our performance. But God isn't a critic, or an Olympic prayer judge, but a father. Think, instead, of a small child who brings home a crayon drawing from school for Mother's or Father's Day. A child's drawing will lack the technical expertise of the practiced artist, but it will charm a mother or father's heart more than a work by Raphael or Rembrandt. Its value to a parent does not depend on its artistic merits, but on the effort and love invested in the work, and the fact that it is done by a son or daughter. In a similar fashion, God is predisposed to be delighted with whatever we offer him, by the mere fact that we are the ones offering it. Sincere manifestations of our desire to please him, however imperfect, do indeed please him.

> *God is predisposed to be delighted with whatever we offer him, by the mere fact that we are the ones offering it.*

Others simply don't know what to *do* during prayer time. Like an adolescent boy calling a girl for the first time, many would-be pray-ers quickly run out of topics of conversation and end with a clumsy and premature good-bye. Such failed attempts sometimes lead to the abandonment of prayer with a shrug of the shoulders and resignation to the sad fact that "I guess I wasn't made for prayer." In these cases, some revert to the rote recitation of standard formulae, which, in spite of their real value, often leave one with the vague, interior nagging that prayer should somehow be more than that.

We mustn't be afraid to dive into prayer and to stick with it. We learn to pray by praying. We learn to love by loving. We make progress when we get out of the theoretical stage and move on to the active. We will make more progress in prayer by praying than by reading a hundred good books on prayer techniques, just as we will learn more about swimming by jumping in the water than by sitting on dry land consulting swimming manuals. But we must persevere despite setbacks. Prayer is an act of love, a lifting up of the heart to God. The more we do it, the more natural it becomes.

3. "Nothing Happens When I Pray"

Our prayer can often feel ineffectual. We experience no interior heat, hear no angelic choirs, see no flashes of light, and often get no quick answers to our problems and queries. Yet we would be wrong to think that nothing happens when we pray. True, we may not get the result we expect, but something happens nonetheless.

Even without its many consequences, prayer is good. Spending time with God is never time wasted, but time well spent. We should find it very strange if a young man valued time spent with his girlfriend according to the gain it brought him. And a girlfriend treated in such a way could rightly feel used. Surely God must often feel used if we see him only as a sugar daddy whose sole purpose is to grant us favors. God is worth loving for his own sake, regardless of the favors he bestows.

But prayer does bring favors as well. Things do indeed happen every time we pray. They may not coincide exactly with our expectations, but that doesn't mean our words fall on deaf ears. Remember that prayer is not meant to "bring God around" to our way of seeing things. We do not present ourselves before our Maker armed with convincing arguments like attorneys pleading cases. Nor do we say a magic word and expect an automatic result.

In prayer we praise God, place our needs before him, thank him, and enjoy his company. And he in turn transforms us. We may not feel it right away, but all experienced pray-ers know that God answers every prayer we utter. True, he does so in his own time and in his own way, but that is part of the adventure of living a personal relationship with your Creator. By persevering in prayer, we experience the special delight of discovering, little by little, how wonderful and unexpected God's responses are.

> *By persevering in prayer, we experience the special delight of discovering, little by little, how wonderful and unexpected God's responses are.*

4. "I Get Along Fine Without Prayer"

Though most of us would assert the necessity of prayer for the Christian life, in practice it often seems that we can get by all right without it. Some writers compare the spiritual life to our corporal existence, saying that what eating, breathing, and sleeping are to the body, prayer is to the spirit. Yet like all analogies, the comparison only goes so far. If we fail to sleep at night, the effects make themselves felt on our next day's performance, whereas a day without prayer often produces no such immediate consequences. Parallels to eating and breathing seem even more forced. Neglect of prayer often produces no evident harm, especially in the short run.

Yet the absence of prayer does produce negative effects in our lives, just as its presence produces positive ones. They are often gradual effects, but real ones nonetheless. Removing prayer from the Christian life is like watching a black-and-white TV, which is acceptable unless you have seen television in color. Life without prayer slowly becomes a drudgery. It dries up, grows dull and sad, and saps our energy and enthusiasm. Prayer doesn't only affect prayer time; it affects all the moments of our lives and colors them with excitement, depth, and meaning.

Prayer means going through life in the company of the One who loves us, instead of trying to wing it on our own. Though it seems we can get along without it, how much richer and more colorful life is when we travel it in God's company through an active prayer life!

> *Prayer means going through life in the company of the One who loves us, instead of trying to wing it on our own.*

5. "I'm a Spiritual Person, but I Don't Pray"

Often these days people make the pseudosophisticated claim of being interested in "spirituality" but not particularly big on "religion." Personal prayer is out; yoga is in. Given the many flaws of organized religion, this position is understandable but still mistaken. For many it may even be a cop-out. Like live-in lovers who want all the benefits of marriage with none of the commitment, chasing "spirituality" in lieu of "religion" substitutes a sham for the reality.

What does it mean to be a "spiritual" person? For many, it seems to be nothing more than a justification to feel somehow engaged with the transcendent without those bothersome demands of a personal God. Instead of having to adore one's Creator and live up to his expectations, we would rather lower the bar, creating a comfortable little spiritual world under our own control. That way we feel "spiritual" but are accountable to no one but ourselves.

Those advocating a religion-free spirituality remind me of what Holocaust victim Dietrich Bonhoeffer called "cheap grace." Bonhoeffer, a Lutheran theologian, described cheap grace as "preaching forgiveness without requiring repentance. Cheap grace is baptism without church discipleship. . . . It is grace without discipleship, grace without the cross. Cheap grace is grace without Jesus Christ, living and incarnate" (*The Cost of Discipleship*).

This is why people who pursue religion-free spirituality often become victims of fashion. They end up following the most popular guru-du-jour for a little while, until the novelty wears off. Then they have to find another one, and another. They are trying to get into shape by eating potato chips when what they really need is some hearty meat and fresh vegetables—spiritual nourishment, not a sideshow.

Christian revelation can be uncomfortable, since we must give up the reins of our lives and allow someone else to be God. The last word is his, not ours. Yet letting God be God is also immensely liberating. The weight of the world sits on his shoulders, not ours. He is the Savior, we are not. And in our personal lives as well, he has the solutions even to our most difficult problems. Christian prayer recognizes God for who he is and accepts him on his own terms. It doesn't try to downsize him to our own measure or to replace authentic discipleship with a vague, feel-good spirituality.

6. "I Am an Active Sort, Not a Contemplative"

Many people find prayer difficult and naturally prefer action to contemplation. Isn't doing good to others, after all, the essence of true religion? And all that precious time wasted in idleness—couldn't it be better invested in fruitful activity? Well, no. Both prayer and action are essential to the Christian life, but prayer takes precedence. Prayer is not idleness, and as odd as it may seem, prayer provides more good for the world than all sorts of human activity.

There was a saint who once tried this excuse on Jesus, but it backfired. You probably remember the Gospel story of two sisters named Martha and Mary who invited Jesus over to their house. While Martha bustled about preparing supper and waiting on her guest, Mary sat "idly" by at Jesus' feet, listening to him. Martha finally reached the end of her rope and came over to Jesus

> *Both prayer and action are essential to the Christian life, but prayer takes precedence.*

in a huff. "Lord, do you not care that my sister is leaving me to do the serving all by myself? Please tell her to help me." Yet rather than acknowledge Martha's complaint, Jesus defended her sister. "Martha, Martha," he said, "you worry and fret about so many things, and yet few are needed, indeed only one. It is Mary who has chosen the better part; it is not to be taken from her" (Luke 10:40–42).

As good and worthwhile activity is, prayer is more needful still. It is prayer, indeed, that gives meaning and worth to action. Prayer is, as Jean-Baptiste Chautard puts it, "the soul of the apostolate"; it breathes life into our evangelism. Our activity would be an empty shell without personal contact with our Lord. No number of good works, no matter how useful, can compensate for our lack of prayer.

Some have gone so far as to accuse contemplatives of escapism. Instead of getting their hands dirty with hard work, contemplatives would hide away in their safe, inner retreats. I think that those who allow themselves such criticisms must never have tried praying. Once we strip away its romantic trappings, prayer is really hard work. Beautiful moments of inner peace and consolation do indeed sweeten the task, but ongoing struggles against distractions and listlessness are just as common. Of the three types of work—physical, intellectual, and spiritual—spiritual is the hardest. Far from being a dreamer's escape, prayer requires a good deal of mettle.

Wasn't it that great woman of prayer Teresa of Ávila herself who said that for a long period of her religious life she would have preferred to do *anything* rather than pray? Her words can console those of us who often find prayer difficult:

> And very often, for some years, I was more anxious that the hour I had determined to spend in prayer be over than I was to remain there, and more anxious to listen for the striking of the clock than to attend to other good things. And I don't know what heavy penance could have come to mind that frequently I would not have gladly undertaken rather than recollect myself in the practice of prayer.
>
> (*The Autobiography of Saint Teresa of Ávila*)

Improving our prayer lives begins with honestly looking at the excuses *we* have been using not to pray or not to pray as we should. A sincere examination of conscience will help us to overcome the rationalizations we often hide behind to avoid spending more time alone with God. But improvement in prayer cannot be achieved by willpower alone. Here, too, we need the assistance of God's grace, which he is all too happy to give. "Lord, give me the strength to pray and to pray well!"

Once we have cleared the obstacles out of the way and have truly made up our minds to pray, we come down to the nitty-gritty of prayer itself. How do we begin this conversation with God? What shall we talk about? Where do we go? This will be the matter for our next chapter.

CHAPTER 6

How to Pray

The Inner Dynamics of Christian Prayer

But when you pray, go into your private room and, when you have shut your door, pray to your Father who is in that secret place, and your Father who sees all that is done in secret will reward you.

Matthew 6:6

Many of us learned to pray as little children. I remember kneeling by my bed every night as a boy, often with my mom and dad by my side, repeating memorized prayers and asking God to take care of the people I loved before crawling into bed to go to sleep. My parents let me pray spontaneously but also gently reminded me of things or people I needed to pray for, and thus they guided my petitions and taught me to pray. Examples of prayer help immensely. The example of my parents as persons of prayer made *me* want to pray.

The best example of prayer comes from Jesus himself. The Twelve had observed Jesus at prayer. They had seen him steal away at the close of day to spend hours in conversation with his Father, while they had dinner and prepared for bed. They had rubbed the sleep from their eyes at the first glint of dawn only to find that Jesus had long since arisen from his sleeping place to spend a good while in commerce with God before beginning the day's grueling agenda of foot travel, preaching, and healing. So one day the disciples finally made the request that had been on their minds for some time: "Lord, teach us to pray" (Luke 11:1).

Jesus' reply tells us much about Christian prayer. It took the form not of a treatise, but a concrete, "formal" prayer, which has come down to us as The Lord's Prayer or the "Our Father." Jesus offered content rather than technique. He didn't recommend that the disciples attend an intensive weekend prayer seminar. Nor did he bid them assume the lotus position and, while carefully regulating their breathing, to repeat a special mantra known to them alone. In fact, he didn't mention a single word about technique, posture, or method. He gave them words to say, a content for their prayer, which in turn enfolded fundamental dispositions for prayer.

The Forms of Prayer

Prayer is an act of love, a dialogue between friends. It surpasses simple thought exercises or interior discourse. Again, Teresa's words are helpful: "If you would

Prayer is an act of love, a dialogue between friends.

progress a long way on this road and ascend to the mansions of your desire, the important thing is not to think much, but to love much" (*Interior Castle*). Prayer involves communication and being with another: sometimes passionate, sometimes quiet, sometimes warm, and sometimes serious and deliberate. Prayer is not just something I do, as if it consisted in a well-constructed monologue. Prayer is interpersonal communion with God, under the impulse of the Holy Spirit.

Christian prayer takes many forms, as many forms as love itself can devise. It can be private or public, mental or vocal, spontaneous or formal. All of these forms are good and add to the richness of one's prayer life. It isn't so much about choosing one form of prayer to the exclusion of others, but rather integrating many expressions of prayer into our spiritual lives and drawing the beauty and bounty out of each one.

Public or Private?

Which is better, private prayer or public? Both are good, really. Jesus denounced one sort of "public" prayer, which he likened to a kind of spiritual exhibitionism. He recommended discretion in prayer, not praying to be seen but for God alone. Unlike hypocrites who love to flaunt their prayers, he enjoined his followers to "go into your room and shut the door and pray to your Father who is in secret; and your Father who sees in secret will reward you" (Matt. 6:6 rsv). Prayer shouldn't be a show, but a living expression of friendship with God.

Importantly, private prayer doesn't exclude prayer in common, especially liturgical prayer, since Jesus also reminded us that praying together, as a community, we will be heard. "Again I say to you, if two of you agree on earth about anything they ask, it will be done for them by my Father in heaven. For where two or three are gathered in my name, there am I in the midst of them" (Matt. 18:19–20 rsv).

Jesus himself prayed both in the synagogue and alone in the mountains or the desert. At the Last Supper, Jesus offered his priestly prayer in the presence of his apostles, renewing the Passover feast by offering his own body and blood for the forgiveness of sins, and he enjoined his disciples to "do this as a memorial of me" (Luke 22:19). All prayer has an ecclesial *dimension*, which means that we address God not merely as individuals, but as members of a family, a community united in faith and love. That is why we speak to God as "Our Father," and not merely "My Father." I've mentioned that the early Christian community was united in common prayer (Acts. 2:42). Even so, prayer requires interior quiet and an awareness that we are addressing our Lord, and not merely socializing with friends.

MENTAL OR VOCAL?

Prayer can be mental or vocal. The prayer that Jesus taught his disciples was vocal, and the prayers he uttered in the Gospels were also of this sort. But Jesus also taught that his disciples must worship God "in spirit and truth" (John 4:23), not merely with their lips. He warned against prayer becoming a mere repetition of words (Matt. 6:7–8). Prayer always involves the heart. Vocal prayer means uniting your heart to the meaning of words already composed (like the Psalms, or your favorite prayers handed on from generation to generation), whether recited out loud or silently. Mental prayer is the dialogue with God that takes place in our hearts, not using ready-made compositions. Both are useful and necessary. Sometimes they dovetail. The greatest saints didn't leave vocal prayer behind, and even children can engage in mental prayer.

Mental prayer can be meditation on a passage from Scripture or a simple gaze of our hearts on the face of Christ. Saint John Vianney saw a poor peasant come to the parish church daily and sit in silence at the back of the church for a half hour or so, then leave. Curious, Father Vianney asked the peasant what he did during that time. The man simply replied, "I look at him, and he looks at me." In prayer as in all friendships, there is a time for speaking and a time for silence.

In prayer as in all friendships, there is a time for speaking and a time for silence.

So which is better, vocal, prepared prayers or a simple dialogue of the heart? Again, each has its place. On the one hand we want the best quality prayer for the Lord, on the other we want it to be extremely personal and from the heart. At first glance, the lofty thoughts and eloquent phrases of certain formal prayers may not appear to be appropriate material for sincere, spontaneous prayer. Yet often they are the very words we want to say but never formulized, and as a result we were unsatisfied by the inadequacy of our expression. It is a relief and a joy to find words that resonate with one's own emotions, desires, and ideals. We appropriate them because they say what we would like to say, and we make them our own. In the gospel we often find Jesus reciting the Psalms, making their words his own, and they never lessened the intense personal nature of his prayer.

Formal prayers also teach us what to ask for and how to ask. They express beautifully what we already longed to say and also put new and wonderful ideas and sentiments into our minds and hearts. Jesus taught his disciples *content* when they requested a lesson in prayer. He taught them to praise God, to ask for his kingdom to come and his will to be done, as well as begging forgiveness for their sins and promising to forgive others. When we pray as Jesus taught us, we learn to desire what he desires for us. We look above and beyond immediate concerns—my math test, my headache, my not being invited to that party—and care more and more about things that really matter.

Yet mental prayer is essential for our faith and love to grow. Being alone with Christ, meditating on his life, talking over our concerns in a heart-to-heart dialogue, all help our friendship with God to grow deeper and stronger. Sometimes books help, in that they provide us with ideas and reflections, but prayer is more than just reading and thinking. Above all, prayer is love and requires our active participation and attentive listening to God.

Being alone with Christ, talking over our concerns in a heart-to-heart dialogue . . . help our friendship with God to grow deeper and stronger.

Try this simple exercise. Pull out your Bible and turn to any passage from the Gospels: maybe one of Jesus' parables, maybe some of his teachings or cures, or his Passion and crucifixion. Read the passage slowly, aware that you are in God's presence, that he is really with you. Close your Bible and talk with him. Reflect on what he did for you, what teachings he offers you now, in your real-life situation.

Ask him for wisdom to know what he wants from you and strength to carry it out. Ask him what you can do to please him more, and how you can live more faithful to his word and to his love for you. Thank him for revealing himself to you, for being such a good and true Friend. Ask him to accompany you throughout your day as you try to live it as best you can. You'll be surprised how prayer can become natural to you, like talking with your best friend.

SPONTANEOUS OR STRUCTURED?

There is a time for spontaneity and a time for structure in prayer. The awareness that we are never alone, that God is always with us, gives rise to many spontaneous prayers throughout the day. A simple word here or there, a request for assistance or strength, an expression of thanks, a heartfelt act of love all add to the richness of our relationship with Christ in prayer. We shouldn't, however, fall into the trap of thinking that prayer must *always* be spontaneous. At certain times of our lives we may not feel like praying at all, but even in these moments, or perhaps *especially* in these moments, we should continue to pray. Prayer is not primarily an overflow of sentiment but rather an act of love, a work of the heart. Many times love requires sacrifice and it certainly demands constancy.

If we look at Jesus' constancy in prayer, we see that it was grounded on more than the ebb and flow of his feelings. As a human like us, he undoubtedly woke occasionally with discomforts or distractions that could have lessened his resolve to pray. And yet, Jesus kept on praying. Structure in our prayer lives leads to similar constancy and fruitfulness. Jesus himself reminds us that a vigorous prayer life requires perseverance and not only a good initial intention (Luke 11:5–8, 18:1–8).

Realistically, we have only so many hours in a day, despite the need for daily prayer. Practical exercises in prayer for a busy, modern Christian could be the following: a short offering of our whole day to God in the morning, asking for his grace to live the day well; five or ten minutes of Scripture reading and prayer, giving pride of place to the four Gospels; ten or fifteen minutes of mental prayer, maybe before leaving for work in the morning or ending your lunch break a little early; a short prayer of thanksgiving and examination of conscience before going to bed at night, putting your day in Christ's hands and entrusting your loved ones to his care. Again, this won't be the exact formula for everyone, but some regularity and structure are sure to strengthen your prayer life.

Distinctions between forms of prayer—private or public, mental or vocal, spontaneous or structured—tell us something of the richness of Christian prayer. But they don't tell the whole story. When should we pray? We have so little time for such an important enterprise. The answer can seem far from hopeful . . . until we dig a little deeper.

Praying "Always"

We may imagine that Paul was exaggerating when he recommended that we "pray without ceasing" (1 Thess. 5:17 NASB). After all, how would that leave any time for work, study, eating, sleeping, sports, or television? A little realism would help. Yet, when we look at Jesus' life, we find that he, too, admonished his disciples to "to pray continually" and led by example (Luke 18:1). He didn't just pray once or twice, a token word addressed to his Father now and again. Jesus prayed when he was joyful and he prayed when in distress; he prayed when he was satisfied and he prayed when he felt weak and in need of strength; he prayed alone and in the presence of his disciples; he prayed in the morning and he prayed in the evening. He prayed on the mountain, in the desert, in the temple, in the garden and on the cross. Jesus prayed . . . always.

The gospel writers make clear that Jesus prayed at length before the decisive moments of his mission. He prayed after his baptism, at the Transfiguration, for an entire night before the election and call of the twelve apostles, before Peter's confession of faith in Jesus as the Christ, before his Passion, in the garden of Gethsemane, and from the cross. The apostles learned their lesson well. In Acts we see the disciples gathered together, dedicated to prayer. Time and time again, in the temple, in jail, next to a river, or even on the beach we find the apostles praying, individually or together.

"Praying always" is not as impossible as it seems. We already hinted at how to pray always when speaking about the need for some structure and regularity in our prayer lives. We need times earmarked just for prayer during the day, such as the early morning upon waking or before we go to bed at night. The beautiful practice of offering our entire day to God in the morning in a sense converts our entire day into a prayer, as all our actions become a part of our offering and worship.

Offering our entire day to God in the morning in a sense converts our entire day into a prayer, as all our actions become a part of our offering and worship.

Those who strive for a regular prayer life inevitably run up against obstacles, such as distractions and dryness. As much as we would like to think only of God during prayer and give him our full attention, our thoughts easily slip away and we find ourselves thinking about other things. One minute we can be thanking Christ for giving his life for us on the cross, the next we could be thinking about whose turn it is to pick up the kids at school. This can be frustrating, but it also provides an opportunity for loving God more. Our perseverance, even in the midst of trials, reminds us how important God is and that prayer is worth the struggle. In these cases, the best thing we can do is simply turn our minds back to God without getting upset or anxious. Our efforts to focus on him, even when we often fail, pleases him immensely.

Another way to "pray always" comes through ordering our whole lives to God. If we seek God's glory in everything we do, conforming our intentions and activities to his plan, our whole lives—work, study, rest, meals, play—become a continuous prayer of praise to God. Our workbench or office desk becomes an altar, and our work a pleasing sacrifice in God's eyes. A Christian who lives in God's grace and seeks to please him in all things truly prays "always."

Yet praying always requires some content as well. Should all our prayer be praise of God, or thanksgiving? Is it right to ask God for things, or is that just selfishness cloaked in a spiritual guise?

The Content of Prayer

Christian tradition has long classified prayer along the lines of its content—its *orientation*. Four typical forms of prayer can be found throughout sacred Scripture and Christian liturgical tradition, namely: thanksgiving, praise, petition, and contrition. When we refer to the content of prayer, we mean the underlying attitudes or dispositions that determine the orientation of the prayer.

Some claim that content is not the most important aspect of prayer, and that higher levels of prayer and union with God are without content, images, or words. There is indeed a type of prayer that could be called in a certain sense "contentless"—the habitual awareness of the presence of God or the intense union with him experienced by some in infused prayer and contemplation. Yet we should recall once again that Christ's answer regarding prayer emphasized the *content* that should fill our conversation with God, expressed in the Lord's Prayer.

That doesn't mean that prayer necessarily involves words or images. Often prayer from the heart is a true dialogue of love without ever reaching verbal expression. An attentive gaze directed toward Christ, permeated with love and adoration, is an eloquent prayer of praise. The deep thirst for union with God and a longing for Christ

Often prayer from the heart is a true dialogue of love without ever reaching verbal expression.

to reign in our hearts and in the lives of all men and women is the nonverbal petition of a soul in love with God. Tears that flow from sorrow for having offended our Lord, or the pain in our hearts for not having loved as he deserves, is the most perfect prayer of contrition.

And finally, the spontaneous recognition of God's hand in the many gifts we receive each day and a smile of acknowledgment and gratitude speeds to the Lord's heart as a stirring prayer of thanksgiving. Let us look briefly at each of these orientations separately.

1. Prayer of Thanksgiving

One of the first signs of a well-mannered child is the use of polite expressions such as "please" and "thank you." Even in adults these expressions reveal a noble soul capable of recognizing favors received. People who always remember to *ask* but always forget to *thank* reveal an adolescent self-centeredness. Yet as unpleasant as ingratitude is in other people, an honest examination of our relationship with God often shows that we ask much and thank little.

Jesus had a great appreciation for thankfulness. In one of the more moving episodes of his public life, Jesus cured ten lepers, allowing them to reenter society healed of their malady. One day, as Jesus was making his way toward Jerusalem, he met ten men afflicted with leprosy, a virulent skin disease. From a distance they shouted out to him, begging for mercy. He sent them off to show themselves to the priests and while they were on their way, they found themselves miraculously cured. Yet on finding themselves healed, only one of the ten came back to give thanks to God. The tone of our Lord's response to the situation reflects a certain sadness: "Were not ten cleansed? Where are the nine? Was no one found to return and give praise to God except this foreigner?" (Luke 17:17–18 RSV).

All ten begged and pleaded; all ten were cured. Yet only one thought to come back and give thanks. Simple math reveals a grim statistic: 10 percent. It clearly shows the rarity of thanksgiving. Gratitude is truly a virtue of noble souls. It is the 10-percent virtue. Where were the other nine? Christ expressed disappointment not because he felt slighted, but because he hadn't finished yet. The physical healing was only the lead-up to the really big gift he wanted to give: the gift of faith. Because of ingratitude, nine out of ten missed out on what was most valuable.

We are all lepers. Let no one think that he hasn't been healed, that he doesn't have reason to come back and thank God. Yet, our pride can lead us to believe that the gifts we receive are in reality only our just desserts. How hard for the proud to be genuinely thankful! How hard to give thanks if we believe that everything is due to us! Humility, on the other hand, reminds us that in truth we deserve nothing, and that everything is a gift. Even our personal talents are not the result of our merit but are a free gift of God.

Jesus himself showed the same thankful attitude in his own prayer to his Father. Instead of taking his blessings for granted, he acknowledged the Father's love behind each one. Time and time again in the gospel we find him thanking God for benefits received: lifting his eyes to heaven to give thanks at the multiplication of the loaves and the fishes, before raising Lazarus from the dead, at the Last Supper. He often expressed his love for the Father in terms of gratitude and he invites us to follow his example.

How much richer and more beautiful our prayer lives would be if we filled them with thanksgiving! Who of us has not received immense benefits from our Lord? True, it is often difficult to recognize God's hand in some day-to-day occurrences. Why do some people naturally thank God for a sunny day or a pay raise and others do not? Simply because some are more attuned to God's action in their lives and thus quickly discern his hand at work. Often we don't thank simply because we fail to see.

Prayer of thanksgiving not only flows from our awareness of God's action in our lives, it also teaches us to see. It teaches us to focus on the good received, the half-full glass, rather than life's pains and crosses. Paul recommended: "Give thanks in all circumstances; for this is the will of God in Christ Jesus for you" (1 Thess. 5:18 RSV). That is the formula for a prayer that truly pleases God and for a more joyful life. More attention to thankfulness means more attention to God's gifts, and the more aware we are of God's gifts, the more we realize how much he loves us.

2. PRAYER OF PRAISE AND ADORATION

Of the four forms of prayer, perhaps the prayer of praise is the hardest for our generation to understand. It seems to accomplish little. Telling God how great and wonderful he is, well, it obviously adds nothing to God, and it seems to have little benefit for us either. Such obsequiousness just gets in the way of heart-to-heart dialogue, doesn't it?

Moreover, we are very horizontalistic and egalitarian. We are proud to have eliminated the concept of nobility and we tend to eliminate titles as well. No one bows before anyone else. Everyone is the same. We call our presidents "Abe," "Ike," "Jimmy," "Slick Willy," and "W." No one is above anyone else. This is good. It means a recognition of each person's fundamental human dignity as a child of God, and the equality of all human beings. But it has negative effects as well. A loss of praise and adoration can mean a loss of respect, a loss of a sense of the sacred. Though we may like to treat God as an equal, he isn't an equal—he is our Lord and Creator.

Prayer of adoration sets us on our proper footing before God. It calls to mind certain important truths: that God made me, and I

wouldn't have existed without him; that
he is more important than I am, and that
his wishes weigh more than mine; that I
am unworthy to be in his presence, and
I am here only because his immense love
surpasses my unworthiness.

Prayer of adoration sets us on our proper footing before God.

A salutary trend toward a renewal of adoration has begun in the last few years. People crave the chance to treat God as God, to acknowledge a power infinitely superior to the powers of this world. It is "natural" for man to worship his Creator. Adoration brings hope, since it reminds us of the existence of one who can do all things, and even save us from ourselves. When man sets himself up as God, he realizes how wretched he really is. When he adores the one, true God, he discovers his own dignity and greatness. Far from belittling man, the worship of God elevates him.

The Christian tradition abounds in such prayer. The book of Psalms, prayed by Jesus himself, sings of God's goodness and mercy. Take, for example, the first few lines of Psalm 145:

I will extol thee, my God and King,
and bless thy name for ever and ever.
Every day I will bless thee,
and praise thy name for ever and ever.
Great is the LORD, and greatly to be praised,
and his greatness is unsearchable.

One generation shall laud thy works to another,
and shall declare thy mighty acts.
On the glorious splendor of thy majesty,
and on thy wondrous works, I will meditate.
Men shall proclaim the might of thy terrible acts,
and I will declare thy greatness. (vv. 1–6 RSV)

In praising and adoring God, we honestly proclaim that without Him we can do nothing, but that with him we can do all things. We put ourselves before Christ with great humility and say, "You are my God. You made me. I need you. I praise you. I adore you."

It is true—we're not doing God any favors. But we are wrong if we think we do not benefit from adoration. By adoring God we live in the truth and grow as persons. Though we may often take it for granted, to stand in the presence of God is an unspeakable blessing, an honor beyond our imagining. Here we could apply Christ's words to his disciples, "Blessed are the eyes which see the things you see, for I say to you, that many prophets and kings wished to see the things which you see, and did not see them, and to hear the things which you hear, and did not hear them" (Luke 10:23–24 NASB). To recognize this blessing is to praise the One who is the Source of every good thing.

3. PRAYER OF PETITION

With the nobility of gratitude and praise before our eyes, perhaps the prayer of petition seems a little petty. We may think twice before approaching him for favors. We shouldn't. Jesus commands us to ask. He doesn't merely permit it. Jesus tells us to pray for "laborers for the harvest" (see Luke 10:2), for "strength to survive all that is going to happen" (Luke 21:36). He tells us to ask that we may receive, to seek that we may find, and to knock in order to have the door opened to us. And Jesus himself didn't hesitate to ask his Father for everything he needed. In his prayer to the Father, Jesus said, "I know you always hear me," which implies that Jesus constantly made such petitions (see John 11:42). Asking is an essential part of Christian prayer.

If God is truly a father, this makes good sense. What father

What father doesn't love to be asked, to be able to meet the needs and desires of his children?

doesn't love to be asked, to be able to meet the needs and desires of his children? Of course God already knows what we need, but he likes to see us turn to him with confidence and faith to ask for all we desire. Jesus' words are very consoling, and very instructive:

> Ask, and it will be given you; seek, and you will find; knock, and it will be opened to you. For every one who asks receives, and he who seeks finds, and to him who knocks it will be opened. Or what man of you, if his son asks him for bread, will give him a stone? Or if he asks for a fish, will give him a serpent? If you then, who are evil, know how to give good gifts to your children, how much more will your Father who is in heaven give good things to those who ask him!
>
> (Matthew 7:7–11 RSV)

The one who asks "always receives." God always hears and always answers. True, he asks us to request "good things," not bad. "If you then, who are evil, know how to give your children what is good, how much more will the heavenly Father give the Holy Spirit to those who ask him!" (Luke 11:13). God wouldn't be very good if he were to grant our foolish requests. A loving mother or father doesn't cede before a child's pleading to watch more television or eat more chocolate than is good for him. This is another reason to preface our petitions with a request that above all, his will be done, not ours. If we truly believe that God knows and loves us better than we love ourselves, we can trust him to give us only good things.

Though in the Lord's Prayer Jesus taught us to ask for big and important things—the coming of the kingdom and the accomplishment of his will—we shouldn't be shy to ask for little things as well. The great saints combined an immense respect for God with an endearing, childlike simplicity and confidence in dealing with him. Thus, though Teresa of Ávila would refer to God as "His Majesty," she didn't hesitate to take all her needs to him, even the smallest and most mundane—like the famous petitions she wrote asking God to rid her convent of a louse infestation.

The more we see God as a Friend (rather than a genie in a bottle), the more spontaneous and simple our requests will become. At the same time, a quick look at our typical requests tells us a lot about the focus of our hearts. It's not the same to always ask God for help on our tests or for a raise at work as it is to ask for the spiritual well-being of our children, comfort for the lonely, and wisdom for our world leaders.

In the little things and the great, it is imperative to trust and to seek God's will above all else. In the house I grew up in hung a simple plaque with the words: "God gives the best to those who leave the choice to Him." God may give us better things than we ask, but never worse. The more we want what he wants, the easier it is to spot his answers to our prayers.

We ask. God answers. Sometimes he responds in the way we expect, often he surprises us, but he always answers.

Prayer is not a magic power over the supernatural, but a personal relationship. Even when it is petition, it is an interpersonal request and not a formula to control or convince God. We ask. God answers. Sometimes he responds in the way we expect, often he surprises us, but he always answers. And he always answers with love, even when he says no.

4. PRAYER OF SORROW

The 1970s were a time of crazy slogans and catchphrases and none was so crazy and utterly false as the famous line from the movie *Love Story*: "Love means never having to say you're sorry." As poetic as this made-for-Hollywood wisdom sounds, nothing could be farther from the truth. Indeed, it is love's opposite—indifference—that never says "I'm sorry." Love means saying you're sorry as often as it takes, as often as you have offended your loved one. In fact, asking for forgiveness is an essential part of true love. Offenses, thoughtlessness, sin—these create walls in our relationships with other people and with God. And love can't bear walls.

This isn't easy. The prouder we are, the more (as Elton John wrote) "sorry seems to be the hardest word." No one likes admitting mistakes. No one likes to say: "It was my fault. Forgive me." And yet penitence and pardon are integral parts of Christian life, and of Christian prayer. The Lord's Prayer states: "Forgive us our trespasses." We all sin, and we all need forgiveness.

Some say that this is the "negative" part of Christianity, and that we would be better off focusing on the "positive" part, such as God's love for us and the happiness he promises. Out with sin, in with joy. These people have a point, or at least half a point. Christianity is essentially good news, not bad news. But this good news means that God's love has triumphed over my selfishness, that his obedience and love have triumphed over my disobedience and egoism. The more I recognize my sickness, the more I appreciate the remedy. The more I acknowledge my slavery, the more Christian liberation will mean to me. The more I recognize my sinfulness, the more I will experience the singular joy of God's mercy and forgiveness.

Jesus did not come to call the virtuous, but sinners (Luke 5:32). Our membership cards in Jesus' band of followers do not consist in our lists of good deeds, but in our misery and need for forgiveness. Asking forgiveness for our sins highlights our misery instead of hiding it away. "God, be merciful to me, a sinner" is that prayer that always wins God's favor (Luke 18:13). It shows both humility and trust: humility to recognize our faults and the trust that God loves us anyway, and that his mercy is more powerful than our wretchedness.

Some of the most beautiful spiritual poetry ever written expresses contrition. One example is Psalm 51, the poem attributed to the repentant King David after his adultery with Bathsheba and murder of her husband, Uriah.

Have mercy on me, O God, according to thy steadfast love,
according to thy abundant mercy blot out my transgressions.
Wash me thoroughly from my iniquity,
and cleanse me from my sin!

For I know my transgressions, and my sin is ever before me.
Against thee, thee only, have I sinned,
and done that which is evil in thy sight,
so that thou art justified in thy sentence
and blameless in thy judgment.

. . . Create in me a clean heart, O God,
And put a new and right spirit within me.

(Psalm 51:1–4, 10 RSV)

Christian contrition is more than regret. Regret means feeling bad that things are the way they are and wishing they were different, but with no implication of personal responsibility or guilt. For example, to express our condolences at a funeral, we often use the words "I'm sorry" to express our sadness and sympathy toward the person who is suffering the loss of a loved one. Contrition, on the contrary, means the sorrow we feel for having freely done wrong, and our remorse for having hurt others through our own fault. Prayer of contrition—telling God we're truly sorry—is not less beautiful than praise, petition, or thanksgiving. It is a necessary component of our prayer lives and one that draws us closer to God.

Finally, when we speak of these four basic prayer orientations, a question must surely arise: Where in this four-part scheme is the most fundamental prayer attitude of all? Where is love? What has happened to the most important prayer, and the end to which all prayer tends: love of God?

Love is not one orientation among others. It does not form a separate category but rather shapes all the categories of prayer. The four orientations of prayer are really four different ways of expressing love of God. To truly love God embraces sorrow for our offenses, gratitude for his benefits, praise of his admirable attributes, and confidence in his unfailing providence.

As expressions of love, these four modes of prayer also tend toward and bring about union with God. Praise, as the contemplation and recognition of God's goodness, draws us toward Him who attracts us by his goodness. Petition goes beyond the mere request for something and leads us to trust the provident Father who cares for us in our needs. Contrition looks to remove the barrier of sin and to restore the union that was wounded through offending the beloved. Thanksgiving transcends the gift of the lover to focus on the love of the Giver and reciprocates love for love. Just as in the Christian life love is the axle around which everything else revolves, so, too, it is in our life of prayer.

Prayer puts us in direct contact with God who is love. In it he grants us grace and strength to be what we are called to be. But prayer doesn't exhaust all the means God has of communicating his grace to us. Christ himself instituted ingenious ways of remaining with his Church and feeding his people. To these means we now turn.

CHAPTER 7

Where to Draw Water

The Sources of Christian Grace

A sacrament is a concrete something, that when you bump into it, it puts you in contact with a divine reality.

Jeremy Driscoll, *What Happens at Mass*

As important as the spiritual life is, it always runs the risk of becoming overspiritualized. That may sound like a contradiction, but it isn't. An exaggerated emphasis on the spiritual can lead to a disdain for the created world. "Spirit is good, matter bad," said the Manicheans, a religion dating back to third-century Babylon. This contempt for matter doesn't seem to reflect God's perspective on things. He created the material world, after all, so it must be good.

In fact, on becoming man and taking human flesh, God reaffirmed his love for the whole human person: soul *and* body. Similarly, the *tools* God employs for our sanctification unite the spiritual world with the physical world.

In his public ministry, Jesus continually offered *signs*—outward manifestations of the kingdom he came to establish. Take, for example, Jesus' healing ministry. When Jesus encountered a man born blind, he spat on the ground, made a mud-paste with the spittle, and anointed the man's eyes so he could see again. Did his spittle or the mud have some special thaumaturgic powers? Of course not. Jesus accompanied his cure with an outward sign for the sake of the people's faith.

When Jesus gave his apostles the gift of the Holy Spirit, he simultaneously "breathed on them" so they could physically perceive the gift they were receiving. Was his breath magical? Hardly. And when he healed the deaf and dumb man in the region of the Decapolis, he touched the man's tongue and ears with saliva and uttered aloud the command "*Ephphatha!*" which means "Be opened" (Mark 7:34). At once his ears were opened and he could speak clearly.

Why all these words and gestures? Why didn't Jesus just confer his grace silently, in a purely spiritual way? He could have communicated his grace directly into people's hearts and souls, but he chose to accompany them by visible actions that everyone could witness. He could have healed the man born blind just by willing it. Why rely on physical signs to work these miracles?

One thing is clear: he does so not because he needs to, but because he *chooses* to. The outward signs, which Catholics call *sacraments*, help our faith. We are able to witness *physically* what is happening *spiritually*. Because they are signs they also instruct. They not only presuppose faith, but by words and objects they also nourish, strengthen, and express it. Jesus opens our minds to the spiritual reality of what is occurring by signifying it in a physical way.

Jesus opens our minds to the spiritual reality of what is occurring by signifying it in a physical way.

In the sacraments that he entrusted to the community of believers, Jesus uses the same material-spiritual duality. Anointing with oil, bathing in water, eating a small piece of bread—these and other external signs help us experience outwardly a much deeper reality that is taking place on the spiritual level. Again, the water and oil have no special powers of their own—it is Jesus who acts through them. But the external signs are necessary elements of the sacraments Jesus established. Then and now, Jesus doesn't fall into the trap of overspiritualizing the spiritual life.

At the same time, the sacraments aren't merely symbols either, in the sense that they really do *confer* what they signify, just as the mud-paste on Jesus' fingers truly healed the man's eyes. The sacraments don't just dispose us to receive God's grace, they are the vehicles though which his grace is communicated. Baptism, for instance, doesn't just symbolize cleansing and rebirth; it brings it about. For Catholics, the Eucharist does not merely recall Jesus' body and blood, in his own words it *is* his body and blood. This beautiful intermingling of the physical and the spiritual can be found throughout salvation history, and in each of our own lives.

In the history of salvation we find sacred times, sacred places, and sacred actions. Sacred *times*—times set apart especially for God—include, first and foremost, the Sabbath, but also other liturgical feasts, seasons, and moments of special grace. Sacred *places* immediately call to mind the temple in Old Testament times, and churches, sanctuaries, and shrines in our own. Sacred *actions* comprise blessings, common prayer, and especially the sacraments. Now these sacred times, places, and actions don't mean that God doesn't act outside of them, but only that they have been the vehicle he instituted, and that he uses them in a particularly effective way.

The sacraments are channels of God's grace that allow all generations of believers to participate in the benefits and blessings of the redemption Christ won for us. The sacraments touch all the stages and all the important moments of Christian life. There is a certain parallel between the stages of natural life and the stages of the spiritual life. The sacraments imitate and perfect in the spiritual realm what we see in man's earthly existence.

Baptism is to the spirit what birth is to the flesh. The rich symbolism of water representing both death and cleansing brings about spiritual rebirth, what Jesus called being "born through water and the Spirit" (John 3:5). The Holy Eucharist, the gift of Jesus' body and blood as real food and real drink (John 6:55), parallels in our spiritual lives the physical nourishment our bodies receive from food and drink. For Catholics, the sacrament of penance, or reconciliation,

The sacraments are channels of God's grace that allow all generations of believers to participate in the benefits and blessings of the redemption Christ won for us.

heals our souls from sin just as surely as medicine cures our physical bodies from their maladies. In the same way, holy matrimony accompanies and seals the exclusive, life-giving love between a man and woman, and the anointing of the sick accompanies our infirmity and, when necessary, prepares us for a good death. In each of these cases outward gestures and words convey interior, invisible grace.

I've mentioned that Jesus promised his disciples that he would not leave them orphans, that despite his ascension into heaven he would stay with them "always, to the close of the age" (Matt. 28:20 RSV). One of the ingenious, practical ways he chose to carry out his promise was the institution of the sacraments, by which he would truly remain with them—with all of us. They were gifts to his Church through which every Christian could encounter him.

So did God need the sacraments in order to work? Of course not. Can't God communicate his grace directly, without them? Sure he can and often does. The sacraments don't limit God's action, they extend it. Jesus offers us these precious gifts and he wishes us to make use of them. They are for us, not for him. They are especially efficacious channels of God's grace for us, gifts that he prepared for us with infinite love. When we approach the sacraments, we are assured of the graces they offer.

Do we need them, then? Yes, we do. Jesus promised Paul that his grace was sufficient for him, but we need to take advantage of the sources of that grace—sources that he offered. It would be strange if a miner, on being outfitted with boots, helmet, pickaxe, dynamite, and a lantern, were to ask, "Do I really need these?" That question would seem strangely out of place and irrelevant. Sure, the miner could probably scrape away at the mountain with a teaspoon or his bare hands, but his progress would be unbearably slow and at day's end he wouldn't have much to show for his work. In other words, why would anyone *want* to go without these means when he has them at his disposal? For Catholic Christians, to be able to receive Christ in the Eucharist, to be able to receive Christ's forgiveness through the sacrament of penance—these are true treasures that we should take full advantage of.

Three Sacraments

Instead of systematically examining all the sacraments, let's just look at three that heavily influence the day-to-day spiritual life of Christians: the sacraments of baptism, reconciliation, and the Eucharist.

THE SACRAMENT OF BAPTISM

Many of us don't recall our own baptisms—just as we most certainly don't remember our births. The greatest gift of our entire lives—liberation from sin and adoption into God's family as his beloved sons and daughters—is offered to us as a completely free, unrequested gift. This mirrors the beginning of our human existence. We did nothing to earn it, nothing to deserve God's divine life, nothing to win over his love and care. How well this reflects our entire relationship with God! How free he is with his love and his gifts!

What actually happened that day, when we were immersed in the river or had water poured over our heads? Several things all at once. We were freed of the guilt of humanity's rebellion against God, often called "original sin," and we became God's children, brothers and sisters of Jesus and heirs to his kingdom. We also became temples of God, as the Holy Trinity took up his dwelling within us and made us sharers in his own divine life. Finally, we also became members of God's family, the Church, and brothers and sisters of believers everywhere, even those who have gone before us into the heavenly kingdom.

As remarkable as this sacrament is, you may be wondering: *What does it have to do with our spiritual lives now? Why include these reflections in a book on the spiritual life?* In the first place, baptism illustrates God's initiative in our spiritual lives and inspires a love suffused with gratitude. At the Last Supper, Jesus reminded his apostles: "You did not choose me, no, I chose you" (John 15:16). Our faith is first and foremost a gift. When we are tempted to see our spiritual lives simply as personal decisions, free choices for Christ against the secular currents of

Baptism illustrates God's initiative in our spiritual lives and inspires a love suffused with gratitude.

the modern world, baptism reminds us of God's pursuit of man. Even if we converted to Christianity at a later age and requested baptism, a sincere look at our personal history suffices to recognize God's action and initiative—like an impassioned suitor wooing the object of his love. God loved us *first*, and our love is a response to his.

Second, our baptisms weren't onetime ceremonies when we dressed up in white garments and then returned home to continue business as usual. Baptism initiated in us a new life, the life of grace, that we are called to nourish and protect. The life of grace is the indispensable base for the entire spiritual life. At the time of our baptism, our friendship with Christ was but a seed, but that seed is called to grow into a plant and eventually into a tree. It requires water, sunlight, and attention. That is what the spiritual life is all about.

Third, baptism not only opened the door of our spiritual lives, it continues to strengthen us to be faithful to our commitments.

Baptism, like faith itself, is a gift that keeps on giving. We live immersed in the graces of this sacrament, not just the day of our baptism, but every day of our lives. Even when we are unfaithful to God, he is faithful to his promises and, as the Good Shepherd, continues to call us back to himself when we stray.

Our baptisms were not simply a nice ritual, pressed between the yellowed pages of childhood scrapbooks, but a sacrament that continues to embolden us every day of our lives. How beautiful to recall in prayer that Christ has already claimed us for himself and made us his own in this sacrament. We are not strangers, but friends, indeed brothers and sisters of Christ and members of his body.

THE SACRAMENT OF RECONCILIATION

In his epistle to the Christian community, James wrote: "Confess your sins to one another, and pray for one another, and this will cure you" (5:16). Under various forms, this outward confession of our failings has been a practice in the Christian Church from the very beginning. Our willingness to admit our own faults helps us avoid judging others and assures us of God's pardon.

For Catholics, the confession of sins assumes the form of a sacrament. According to John, the first act of the risen Christ when he appeared to his apostles was to entrust them with the forgiveness of sins. He said to them: "Peace be with you. As the Father sent me, even so I send you." And in what does this sending consist? "And when he had said this, he breathed on them, and said: 'Receive the Holy Spirit. If you forgive the sins of any, they are forgiven; if you retain the sins of any, they are retained'" (John 20:21–23 RSV). The very first fruit of Christ's Passion and resurrection was the forgiveness of sins, and this is made immediately concrete through the institution of this sacrament.

Jesus couldn't wait to confer the power to forgive sins on his apostles, and this beautiful ministry of Christ's mercy has been passed down to every new generation of Christians by the laying on of hands. For Catholics, when a priest tells us in confession: "I absolve you from your sins in the name of the Father, and of the Son, and of the Holy Spirit," he does not forgive in his own name, but in God's name. It is not a man who forgives, but God.

What a blessing it is to hear those words and know that they are true! Despite our best intentions and resolutions, we do not live perfect lives. And not just "Oh, yeah, there was that time back in 1984," but every day. We need Christ's forgiveness, not just once, but over and over. As John wrote, "If we say that we have no sin, we are deceiving ourselves and the truth is not in us. If we confess our sins, He is faithful and righteous to forgive us our sins and to cleanse us from all unrighteousness" (1 John 1:8–9 NASB). It is relatively easy to say we are sinners in a general, comprehensive way but much tougher to recognize on a practical level our concrete failings and lack of generosity day by day.

The most frequent complaint about confession (besides how hard it is to say our sins out loud!) harkens back to our initial discussion of outward signs of inward grace. Many ask: "Can't God forgive my sins without the help of a priest? Why can't I just tell God I'm sorry?" And again, the answer is that God can forgive sins without this sacrament, and he surely does. But he instituted this sacrament for our good, not for his. He gave us a surefire way to experience his mercy, to know that we are heard, and to physically *hear* the words of absolution the way the paralytic heard them: "My child, your sins are forgiven" (Matt. 9:2). A sincere examination of conscience, a humble confession of our failings, the counsel the priest offers, our firm purpose of amendment, our act of contrition, the words of absolution—all of these help us to experience the mercy that the sacrament confers, and the joy and peace that reconciliation with God invariably brings.

Some think confession is a cop-out. They think that it furnishes Catholics with an excuse to keep on sinning, knowing that they can always go back to confession and be forgiven. They think that once converted to Christ, a person should never sin again. All of this has some truth to it. Some undoubtedly abuse the sacrament. And it's true that we shouldn't sin at all. But we do. Jesus left us an important lesson when Peter asked him how often he must forgive his brother who has offended him. Peter made what he thought to be a generous offer and asked Jesus whether he ought to forgive him "up to seven times?" But Jesus surprised Peter by demanding much more. "I do not say to you, up to seven times," Jesus told him, "but up to seventy times seven" (Matt. 18:21–22 NASB). In fact, Jesus went further still: "And if he sins against you seven times a day, and returns to you seven times saying, 'I repent,' forgive him" (Luke 17:4 NASB).

Stop for a moment and think what this means. Jesus wasn't just telling us how indulgent we were to be with those who offended us, he was giving us an important lesson about the mercy of God himself. If God expects us to be so magnanimous in extending forgiveness to others—"seventy times seven" times—how much more graciously does God deal with us? If over and over again we are required to pardon our neighbors' faults, will our Lord ever deny us his merciful love when we return to him in sorrow?

For Christians, in confession we are not acquitted of our sins; rather we are found guilty. We don't approach Christ in this sacrament to *excuse* ourselves but to *accuse* ourselves. But Jesus has already taken upon himself our guilt and won our redemption through his death on the cross. Confession involves more than a mechanical, pro-forma listing of our sins. Part of a good confession is repentance and the sincere intention to avoid sin in the future. As with the woman caught in the act of adultery, Jesus looks at us with compassion and tells us: "Neither do I condemn you; go, and do not sin again" (John 8:11 RSV). This intimate experience of our Lord's love and patience, of a mercy that knows no bounds, leads us to a deeper love and gratitude of God. As Jesus tells us, the one who has been forgiven much shows much love (Luke 7:47).

Though this sacrament is necessary for the forgiveness of grave sins, frequent confession even of "smaller" sins and imperfections helps us grow in our spiritual life by leaps and bounds.

It helps us grow in humility, by obliging us to recognize our failings and to utter them aloud. It helps us know ourselves more deeply as we examine our consciences under the light of the Holy Spirit. The experience of God's mercy helps us grow in gratitude and in love for him. Knowledge of our own need for forgiveness helps us to be more merciful toward those who offend us.

Frequent confession also aids in overcoming bad habits and pulls us out of spiritual mediocrity by helping us pay more attention to "little things" in our friendship with Christ. In confession, we receive not only the gift of forgiveness, but also the grace and strength to resist sin in the future and to grow daily in our love of God. No wonder so many holy people through the centuries have recommended frequent confession as a privileged means of growing in union with God!

In confession, we receive not only the gift of forgiveness, but also the grace and strength to resist sin in the future and to grow daily in our love of God.

THE SACRAMENT OF THE EUCHARIST, OR COMMUNION

The sacrifice of Jesus Christ on the cross, which is the very same sacrifice offered in the Eucharist, is the holy and perfect sacrifice of God himself. Human works themselves, in fact, take on their value by virtue of being united with Christ's sacrifice on the cross, and that union takes place perfectly in the celebration of the Lord's Supper. The value of the Eucharistic celebration is consequently infinite and becomes the focal point of all Christian worship, and of the Christian life itself.

This being the case, we cannot treat the Eucharist as just one more pious practice, to be taken or left according to one's spiritual fancy, but the nucleus of Christian worship. It is the new Passover, instituted by Christ himself, and he is the Paschal Lamb of God "who takes away the sin of the world" (John 1:29). It was Jesus who commanded us to "do this in remembrance of me" (Luke 22:19 NASB). It was he who said, "He who eats my flesh and drinks my blood abides in me, and I in him" (John 6:56 RSV). Christians have always taken our Lord's words to heart. Acts tells us that the early Christian community dedicated themselves "to the breaking of bread" (2:42). From the very beginnings of Christianity, the Eucharist formed the heart of Christian worship and allowed believers to share in the benefits of Jesus' death and resurrection by partaking of his body and blood.

The Greek origins of the word *Eucharist* speak of thanksgiving, and the eucharistic celebration is the Church's thanksgiving to God *par excellence*. Remember the words of the psalmist, searching for the proper way to thank God for all his gifts: "What shall I render to the LORD / For all His benefits toward me?" And he hit upon the following answer to his own question: "I shall lift up the cup of salvation / And call upon the name of the LORD" (Ps. 116:12–13 NASB). This "cup of salvation" Jesus referred to as the cup of his blood, shed for men and women for our salvation and the forgiveness of sins. And as Paul adds, "For as often as you eat this bread and drink the cup, you proclaim the Lord's death until he comes" (1 Cor. 11:26 RSV).

In the Eucharist—Christ's own perfect sacrifice—we have the prayer we are looking for.

We Christians, like the psalmist before us, often fumble about looking for prayer and worship that is worthy of so good a God. We want the right words, the right gestures, the right actions to give him the praise and thanksgiving that he so abundantly deserves. In the Eucharist—Christ's own perfect sacrifice—we have the prayer we are looking for. We have a way of rendering our good Father a truly perfect prayer, so that in the midst of all our imperfections and impurities, one thing may be exactly right.

How many Christians have reaped untold spiritual fruit from their fervent and frequent participation in the Eucharistic sacrifice! It provides a sure source of grace, a well where we can always find "living water" (John 4:10). Thankfully, the value of Communion cannot be gauged by the spiritual feelings it produces in us. Our faith testifies to its power, regardless of our feelings. The Eucharistic celebration may not be the most "thrilling" spiritual activity we can engage in, but then again it promises no thrills, only limitless grace.

Eucharistic devotion is critical to our spiritual life. It brings all our acts of love together into one common offering, the offering of Christ himself to the Father. In obedience to the Father, Jesus sacrificed himself for the forgiveness of sins and left us a memorial to be celebrated in his name. When we participate in the Eucharist, we share in Christ's sacrifice and are present on Calvary. When we receive Jesus in Holy Communion, we eat "the living bread which has come down from heaven" (John 6:51) for the life of the world. We are joined to Christ and to all Christians in his family meal, the Lord's Supper. Our communion with one another in faith—the bond of all believers—is strengthened and in Christ we are made one.

Eucharistic devotion reaches its apex in the celebration of the Lord's Supper, but it doesn't end there. Once the bread is consecrated it becomes Jesus' body, and so it remains even after Communion is over. We can visit him whenever we like, adoring and worshiping him as the apostles did after his resurrection. We accompany him, and he accompanies us. Just being in his presence transforms us, as our skin is warmed and bronzed under the sun's rays. Under Jesus' gaze we learn to love the Father as he did. Since *Eucharist* means "thanksgiving," our prayer to Jesus should especially emphasize how grateful we are for this gift. "Lord, thank you for being here for me. Thank you for dying for me and offering yourself to the Father for my redemption. Thank you for giving me your body and blood to be my food and drink. I love you."

Under Jesus' gaze we learn to love the Father as he did.

The sacraments of God's grace are means that Christ left us to encounter him and to experience his love. They are channels of his grace and strength, guarantees of his abiding presence among us. Each helps us in a particular way to grow day to day in our love for God and one another. Just as water, sunlight, and fertilizer help small plants to grow strong and healthy, our spiritual lives increase in depth and vitality by taking advantage of these gifts.

How many times in my own life I have experienced God's love in a truly exceptional way through participation in the sacraments! How often I have experienced his merciful love, his gentle power, his abiding friendship! True, often these experiences take place deep within, with no thunderclaps or mighty wind. The sacraments touch our souls like a soft, refreshing breeze that assures us of Christ's presence and love.

The sacraments touch our souls like a soft, refreshing breeze that assures us of Christ's presence and love.

From where do these sacraments draw their astounding effectiveness? What force is behind them, making ordinary signs into extraordinary channels of grace? It is the Holy Spirit himself, the third person of the Holy Trinity. It is he who gives the sacraments their efficacy and he who makes all our spiritual work bear fruit. We will now examine his key role in the spiritual life of a Christian.

CHAPTER 8

You've Got a Friend

How the Holy Spirit Can Make You a Saint

When the Spirit of truth comes he will lead you to the complete truth, since he will not be speaking as from himself but will say only what he has learned; and he will tell you of the things to come.

John 16:13

When I was ten years old or so, my younger brother Mike, who was eight, used to love to accompany my father in his household tasks. At the time we had a six-hundred-pound 1956 Gravely lawn mower that cut a six-foot swath, perfect for the expansive lawn outside our house. My father was—I was convinced—the strongest man in the world. He maneuvered that great behemoth with the same ease that you would swing an empty shopping cart through the aisles of the supermarket. Mike often traipsed along behind my father, back and forth along the length of the lawn as my dad piloted the unwieldy machine.

One day, after much insistence, my father allowed Mike to grip one of the red handles as they walked along. Once the job was done, Mike was beside himself with joy and came rushing into the house to announce to my mother: "I helped Dad cut the lawn!"

Of course, as far as the effective "help" goes, there was little or none. In fact, my dad probably had to work twice as hard to keep one eye on the task at hand and another on keeping Mike out of harm's way. Yet, in its own way, Mike's description was accurate. He really did participate in cutting the lawn, even though the force that moved things didn't come from him but from my father.

On occasion God gives us that same thrill, that same sense of accomplishment, in our spiritual lives. There was the time, for example, when Jesus sent out seventy disciples before him, two by two, to the towns he intended to visit. The disciples returned from their first mission bursting with enthusiasm: "Even the demons are subject to us in your name!" (Luke 10:17 RSV). True, the power to cast out demons didn't come from them but from God, yet the sense of achievement was still awesome.

God calls us as partners in his mission of redemption. He wants us to work alongside him, to actively cooperate with his grace rather than passively receive it. His mysterious choice to make use of human collaboration to bring about his plan of salvation for the world astounds us. He could just have easily—in fact, more easily—done everything himself. More often than not, his human partners don't do much more than get in the way. Yet that was his choice. He so respects our freedom that he doesn't force salvation on us, and he even makes use of our free cooperation to channel his grace to others.

He even makes use of our free cooperation to channel his grace to others.

This same divine-human cooperation takes place in our spiritual lives as well. We become saints by working together with him. The challenges of the Christian life can seem daunting, even overwhelming. God often asks of us more than any person could reasonably expect to achieve. But this is where the Holy Spirit kicks in. Like my brother Mike walking along behind the lawn mower, the force comes from Someone Else.

Power from on High

The night before his Passion, Jesus promised to send the Holy Spirit to his disciples. This Spirit would teach and console, strengthen and encourage, enlighten and fortify the fledgling Christian community. Jesus made an astonishing prediction that must have seemed like nonsense to his disciples. "It is for your own good that I am going because unless I go, the Advocate will not come to you, but if I do go, I will send him to you" (John 16:7). How could Jesus' departure possibly be in the disciples' best interests? How could they possibly be better off without him? How often do we wish that Jesus were still around today, walking the earth as he did two thousand years ago? Yet Jesus insists: "It is for your own good that I am going." What must this Holy Spirit be that Christians are better off now than when Jesus was on earth?

Jesus' promise was fulfilled on Pentecost Sunday, often called the "birthday of the church." The eleven apostles were gathered in the Upper Room and suddenly they heard a sound like a mighty wind that filled the house. They saw something like tongues of fire dancing over their heads, and they were filled with the Holy Spirit and began to speak in languages they had never learned (Acts 2:1–4). The next thing they knew, they were out on the streets of Jerusalem, prophesying and bearing witness to Jesus' resurrection.

We've seen that the change wrought upon the apostles was astounding. The timorous little band huddled away behind locked doors suddenly burst out preaching Christ with a courage and eloquence no one could refute. One minute they were cowering in fear, the next they were boldly proclaiming the Good News—and the difference was the Holy Spirit.

Isn't that what we desperately need in our own spiritual lives? Isn't that courage, enthusiasm, and confidence what we most lack? How often have we failed to say or do what we should because of fear of what others might think or say about us? The Holy Spirit filled the apostles with joy even in suffering for Christ and made all their work fruitful. He let them experience the truth of the words, "With God all things are possible."

The Saint-Maker

People don't make saints, God does. Sanctification is not a human endeavor that we can achieve with goodwill and hard work alone. Along with being the Consoler, the Holy Spirit is also the Sanctifier. He is the Saint-Maker. Like a sculptor, he chisels us like marble and molds us like clay. It sometimes hurts, but he knows the result he is looking for, and he won't be satisfied until he gets it just right. He never gives up on us.

And at the same time our sanctification isn't solely a divine project, either. It requires our free and loving cooperation. Saint Augustine's celebrated saying—"He who made you without you will not save you without you"—could be slightly reworked without losing any of its force: he who made you without your help will not make you *holy* without your help. Sanctification is the happy result of a divine-human partnership, a joint venture that produces a remarkable yield. God works genuine wonders in a soul that cooperates generously with his grace.

Sanctification is the happy result of a divine-human partnership, a joint venture that produces a remarkable yield.

The key is getting the hierarchy right. He is first, we are second. He doesn't help *us* achieve *our* plans, we help *him* accomplish *his*. That is why in prayer we ask for his will to be done, rather than our own. The Holy Spirit's action is not a supplement or appendix to our own efforts. We are not to work hard and then pray "just in case," or as a last resort, when all else fails. He is the Provider, and our work is a complement to his work. Our prayer reminds us who is in charge, who gives the fruit.

An Unequal Partnership

What does it mean, then, to work together with the Holy Spirit? What is his role and what is ours? God's "providence," which refers to the way he takes care of and governs the world, can be understood in different ways. One form, called *providentialism*, leaves everything up to God. We pray; God acts. We put everything in his hands, stay out of the way, and he solves our problems. This notion means that God expects us to sit around, arms crossed, waiting for him to do something. Taking action ourselves could seem like distrust, as if we didn't think God could take care of things on his own.

The opposite extreme is Pelagianism, named after the fourth-century British monk Pelagius, who denied original sin and downplayed the need for God's grace. Pelagianism exaggerates *our* importance. God put the world in our hands, and we are ultimately responsible for making things work and for our own destiny. Pelagianism holds that we are competent to do things ourselves without God's help. We call on him for the really tough jobs, but the regular, day-to-day stuff we can take care of ourselves. Pelagianism denies man's fundamental weakness and the need for God's grace.

Although these two approaches are diametrically opposed to one another, they reflect the same error. They both pit human action against divine intervention, as if some natural antagonism split the two. Our actions and God's would be fundamentally separate and distinct. God does his part and we do our part. According to these views, the Christian challenge consists in hitting on the right proportion between God's share of the work and our own.

Yet if we examine the Gospels, neither one of these attitudes reflects Jesus' way of working. Jesus seems to prefer to work together *with us*, rather than without us. Much of his training of the apostles consisted of engaging them. He sent them out and actively involved them in his mission.

God's most impressive miracles are not when he says, "Step aside and watch what I can do" but rather when he says, "Get into action and watch what I can do *through you*." This evangelical approach to providence is perfectly mirrored in Paul's pithy saying: "I can do all things through Him who strengthens me" (Phil. 4:13 NASB). Saint Ignatius of Loyola offered the following wise counsel: "Act as if everything depended on you and pray as if everything depended on God." Again, this isn't to get just the right mix of God's part and ours—like a seventy-thirty or eighty-twenty ratio—but to realize that in a certain way everything *does* depend on us and *does* depend on God at the same time.

True, God can and often does work alone. Sometimes he shows us our powerlessness and simply asks us to believe in him, to have childlike trust. But this is his choice, not ours, and our

He chooses *to need us.*

attitude should be one of active availability to cooperate with him as directed. He *chooses* to need us.

The prophet Isaiah offered a beautiful expression of this interdependence in his canticle to the Lord: "It is you who have accomplished all we have done," or, as rendered in another translation, "LORD, You will establish peace for us, / Since You have also performed for us all our works" (Isa. 26:12 NASB). Even when we work hard and achieve the results we were looking for, we are still correct in thanking God who has made our efforts fruitful. Even when we are generous, he has given us the strength to be generous. In this way, we can honestly thank him for all things. Again, this takes nothing away from our personal responsibility—we are truly the authors of our actions. But in acting, we are never alone.

The perfect model of this intermingling of the human and the divine is Jesus himself, both God and man. If we look at his actions, we cannot distinguish where God leaves off and man starts, because the union is perfect. As our model, Christ expresses where our own relationship with God is to tend: to union. With the psalmist we pray, "Confirm the work of our hands" (Ps. 90:17 NASB). That is, I put all my talents and qualities to work for good, and I trust in God to make my efforts bear fruit. I know full well that God could do this without me, but he chooses to do it through me, as a divine-human partnership. Such freely chosen collaboration pleases God, and he makes it prosper.

Despite this intimate union of the human and the divine in the spiritual work of a Christian, we can still look at what the Holy Spirit provides and what sort of response we are called to give. He is our grand Ally, our Defender and Guardian. He works in us and through us: opening our minds, softening our hard hearts, strengthening our wills, and healing our souls. The better we recognize his activity, the better we are able to cooperate with it.

The Holy Spirit's Part of the Partnership

THE HOLY SPIRIT TEACHES US

At the Last Supper, Jesus promised to send his Spirit, who would "teach you all things, and bring to your remembrance all that I have said to you" and "guide you into all the truth" (John 14:26, 16:13 RSV). Rather than a new teaching, the Spirit confirms what Jesus himself taught, since "he will take what is mine and declare it to you" (John 16:14 RSV).

The Holy Spirit teaches, then, not so much by offering new material as by opening our minds to understand what Jesus taught. The Bible tells us that the Spirit of the Lord is "a spirit of wisdom and understanding, a spirit of counsel and might, a spirit of knowledge and the fear of the LORD" (Isa. 11:2 RSV). These "gifts of the Spirit" center on his role as Teacher and Guide, the One who takes us by the hand and leads us to the truth. Like an experienced trail guide, who knows the territory perfectly, he guides us surely even when we can't see around the next bend.

THE HOLY SPIRIT INSPIRES AND ILLUMINATES

The Christian God is not the disinterested clockmaker god of the deists, who creates the world and then sits back to watch how things transpire. He is a passionately involved, interested, loving Father. *Inspiration* literally means "breathing into," and this is the characteristic work of the Spirit. When we don't know what to say (or whether to say it), the Holy Spirit gives us the right words and makes them effective (see Luke 12:11–12). The wind blows where it will—Jesus tells us—we see its effects without knowing where it comes from or where it is going. "That is how it is with all who are born of the Spirit" (John 3:8). Like the wind to which he is compared, the Holy Spirit whispers, suggests, and moves. As divine Fire, he also provides both warmth and light and illuminates even the remotest corners of our existence.

THE SPIRIT URGES US

We see this clearly in Christ's life. Jesus, the Son of God, was led by the Spirit of God in all he thought, willed, said, and did. After his baptism in the Jordan, Jesus, full of the Holy Spirit, was immediately *driven* by the Spirit into the wilderness.

The Spirit urges us, as well, above all to love. In fact, Paul wrote that it is the love of Christ that urges us on (2 Cor. 5:14) and reminds us that "God's love has been poured into our hearts through the Holy Spirit which has been given to us" (Rom. 5:5 RSV). By this love poured into our hearts, we in turn are *enabled* to love. When we find it hard to love, hard to forgive, it is the Holy Spirit that urges us to do so and likewise enables us to do so.

THE HOLY SPIRIT MAKES OUR WORK FRUITFUL

As Paul says, we are called to plant and to water, but we do not produce the yield, God does (1 Cor. 3:6–8). The Holy Spirit is the One who makes our efforts bear fruit. If we are working like crazy with only mediocre results, we should ask ourselves whether we are trying to work alone or in union with the Holy Spirit. Where the Spirit is, fruitfulness is evident. Paul contrasted the "fruit" of the Spirit with the "works" of the flesh. What are these "fruits of the Spirit"? Paul enumerated them as follows: "love, joy, peace, patience, kindness, goodness, faithfulness, gentleness, self-control" (Gal. 5:22–23 RSV). Under the impulse of the Holy Spirit, and in Christ's name, we can expect an abundant yield.

THE HOLY SPIRIT CONSOLES US

Notice that two of the "fruits" of the Spirit are joy and peace. He does not bring anxiety and internal division. Rather he fills us with God's own peace and joy and reminds us that everything is all right. In moments of sorrow and trial, the Holy Spirit comes to assuage our suffering and relieve our pain. He strengthens our conviction that "if God is for us, who can be against us?" (Rom. 8:31 NASB). In moments of doubt or discouragement, the Holy Spirit is for us the peace that the world cannot give. Jesus himself "rejoiced in the Holy Spirit" (Luke 10:21 RSV) and taught us to do the same.

THE HOLY SPIRIT STRENGTHENS US

He steels our resolve and bolsters our convictions so that we stand firm even in difficulties. The natural weakness we experience finds its remedy in the power of the Spirit, and with him we can surmount even the toughest obstacles.

THE HOLY SPIRIT HELPS US PRAY

When we do not know what to say, he gives us the words and even prays in us. That is why Paul urges us to "pray at all times in the Spirit, with all prayer and supplication" (Eph. 6:18 RSV) and reminds us that "the Spirit also helps our weakness; for we do not know how to pray as we should, but the Spirit Himself intercedes for us with groanings too deep for words" (Rom. 8:26 NASB). How consoling to know that the Spirit of God intercedes for us and prays in us and with us!

We speak much these days of "character formation." The great Character-Former is the Holy Spirit. He is the one who forms Christ in us and makes us like him. But this beautiful process involves our active participation and commitment as well.

Our Part of the Partnership

From the foregoing look at the Holy Spirit's role in our spiritual lives, it is clear that he has taken the lion's share! Compared to his, our work is really quite simple. The human element of the partnership consists especially in three key virtues: attention, docility, and prompt implementation.

Attention

The Spirit speaks. He inspires and suggests, but he often does so in a subtle way. The Spirit of God often passes—as in the case of Elijah on Mount Horeb—not as a hurricane or fire or earthquake, but as a gentle breeze, perceptible only to the attentive.

Our generation suffers from an unhealthy phobia of silence. We feel a need always to be surrounded by noise, music, and conversation. We flee silence, and yet it is in silence that the voice of the Spirit is heard. We need to cultivate a contemplative spirit able to hear the soft whispers and inspirations of the Holy Spirit, who rarely shouts to be heard or announces his coming with a blare of trumpets.

Silence has both external and internal dimensions. External silence means eliminating the noise around us. It involves the ability to recollect ourselves, mastering curiosity and retiring into quiet. It doesn't come easily but is a habit to be formed. Strange as it may seem, we really don't need noise all the time. The next time you get into your car, instead of instinctively reaching to turn on the radio, make the decision to spend some time in silence with the One who loves you. You won't regret it.

Internal silence means silence inside us as well as outside. We need to calm the voices of our passions, memories, imaginations, and affections. Internal silence means imitating the sea, which on the surface may be dynamic, active, even agitated yet down deep is peaceful and serene. Cultivating this interior and exterior silence, we will be surprised how much the Holy Spirit has to say to us.

Silence allows us to connect to the presence of God through-out the day—that habitual awareness that we are never alone, never abandoned, never simply left to fend for ourselves. He is with us al-ways. What an immense consolation and source of strength to walk with the Spirit. Talk with him, cultivate your friendship with him, thank him, ask him for counsel.

As regards inspirations of the Holy Spirit, a couple of doubts may assault us. The first concerns his activity—or *inactivity*—in our lives. Though at first blush it may not be evident, the Holy Spirit is just as active today as he was two thousand years ago. Though we see few prophets walking the street speaking in tongues, he continues to stir up projects and movements and to invite people to holiness.

This happens at the personal level in your life as well. Sometimes you may think that he speaks to everyone *but* you. With you he may seem at best a silent partner. Yet he is more present in your life than you realize. His actions are subtle, but real. Sometimes the thinnest of veils separates us from recognizing his activity, which simmers beneath the surface. Our attention to him, suffused with a living faith, often suffices to draw back that veil and contemplate his work.

Another doubt concerns the origins of our inspirations. *How can I distinguish between an inspiration of the Holy Spirit and a temp-tation? Or how can I tell whether a given "inspiration" comes from the Holy Spirit speaking in my heart or simply from my overactive imagination? Maybe I just want to hear him so much that I project my own desires on my mind.*

Three simple means can help us overcome this doubt. First, we should examine the content of the inspiration. *Does it lead me to a more perfect living of the gospel? Does it lead me to live my duty with greater perfection and love?* If so, chances are it comes from God. *Does it distract me from what God is already asking of me?* Chances are it doesn't come from God. We ought to be especially suspicious of "inspirations" that happen to coincide with our natural preferences and inclinations. The right road, on the contrary, often leads uphill.

Second, we need to recall that the Holy Spirit also speaks through natural events, through our consciences, and even through our imaginations. So we needn't worry so much about discerning whether our imagination is involved, but rather whether such ideas come from God. The better we know God, the easier it becomes to recognize his stamp on the ideas that come to us. In the gospel Jesus assures us that his sheep recognize his voice and follow him whereas "they do not know the voice of strangers" (John 10:5 NASB). The more time we spend with Jesus, the more easily we recognize the voice of his Spirit.

Third, an objective third party can often help us see God's action more clearly in our lives. Despite our best intentions, our subjective desires often cloud our discernment in spiritual matters. An experienced third party can help us sort through our events of our spiritual lives and to more clearly see what God is doing for us and asking of us.

Attention to Holy Spirit, then, means the awareness that God is always active in our lives and an earnest effort to pay attention to his presence. Turning an open ear to the voice of the Sanctifier helps us perceive his action and cooperate more effectively with it. "Speak, Lord, for your servant is listening!" (see 1 Sam. 3:10).

DOCILITY

Docility is the ability (and willingness) to let oneself be taught and led. The Holy Spirit offers his guidance but doesn't impose it. He may suggest that you make an act of kindness toward a person you meet, he may inspire you to pray a little more, he may invite you to swallow your pride and forgive a friend when she offends you, but he will never *compel* you to do so. He respects our freedom and proposes yet imposes nothing. Much of our role in dealing with the Holy Spirit consists in allowing him to lead us. Luis María Martínez wrote in *The Sanctifier*, "What is devotion to the Holy Spirit but a loving and constant cooperation with his divine influence, with his sanctifying work?"

Yet when you do follow his lead, you advance quickly on the road to holiness. In fact, for those who want to conform their lives to the will of the Father, docility to the leadership of the Holy Spirit becomes the key to success. Remember, he is the Guide: he knows the trails, he understands the terrain, and he has already mapped out the best route for us. He knows what he is doing.

Docility is closely wrapped up with trust. The Holy Spirit will never steer you wrong, but sometimes he asks difficult, even unpleasant things. Just look at the example of Jesus in Gethsemane, where God was asking him to make the supreme sacrifice for the salvation of the world. Though Jesus' human nature resisted, he entrusted himself to the Father's will. If he had doubted God's goodness, he could never have gone through with it. In the same way, the more you trust the Holy Spirit, the easier it will be to follow his cues.

Following the Holy Spirit makes us like the Son since, as Paul taught, "all who are led by the Spirit are sons of God" (Rom. 8:14 RSV). Obedience to the Spirit was the path Jesus chose for himself. When the Holy Spirit urged him to leave Nazareth and begin his public ministry, Jesus acted. When the Spirit led him into the desert,

Jesus obeyed. His underlying disposition to always say yes to God's will led to an absolute docility to the Holy Spirit.

We, too, are invited to docility in our daily lives. Again, rather than impose our wills on God or bring him around to our way of seeing things, we are called to follow his lead and conform our lives to his program. His invitations to greater generosity with our brothers and sisters, a closer attention to our duty, greater self-control, and a more patient attitude with others will bear much fruit in our lives if we are docile to his lead.

PROMPT IMPLEMENTATION

Cooperation involves still more than attention to his voice and docility to his leadership. It also means the generosity to immediately put into practice the inspirations and lights of the Holy Spirit. Sometimes these inspirations bear little fruit because, though we don't reject them outright, they never translate into positive action. We may stop at the point of accepting and admiring them without taking the necessary measures to make them practical. The Holy Spirit plants seeds in us, seeds destined to grow into virtues and habits of goodness. But this requires a prompt, generous response.

As one example from the gospel, look at the way Jesus' mother, Mary, responded when the angel Gabriel, in the midst of many other important things, told her that her elderly cousin Elizabeth was also pregnant. Despite her own concerns and consternation on discovering that she herself was to be the mother of the Messiah, Mary took the angel's message as a cue from God and left like a shot to take care of her cousin. Saint Luke tells us that she "went as quickly as she could" (Luke 1:39) to the Judean hill country to visit Elizabeth and there she remained until Elizabeth gave birth to John the Baptist. This was a prompt, generous response to the Holy Spirit.

Our implementation of the inspirations and suggestions we receive from the Holy Spirit convert our attention and docility into action and good habits. The prompter we are to respond—not just with good intentions but good actions—the more we advance on the road to holiness.

And speaking of Mary, she accompanied the eleven apostles in their constant prayer awaiting the Holy Spirit and was almost certainly in the Upper Room with them on Pentecost to receive the Holy Spirit. Much confusion swirls around Mary's role in the Church. Who was she to Jesus? Who is she to those who follow him? To her our thoughts now turn.

CHAPTER 9

Honor Thy Mother

What Mary Has to Do with the Christian Life

Of all women you are the most blessed, and blessed is the fruit of your womb. Why should I be honored with a visit from the mother of my Lord?

Luke 1:42

I t's time for a pop quiz. What was the first miracle Jesus worked? Was it something poignant, like healing a leper or raising a dead girl to life? Was it something deeply spiritual, like forgiving the sins of a paralytic or welcoming a reformed prostitute into his band of disciples? Or was it something dramatic and spectacular, like calming the tempestuous sea or walking on water? Answer: none of the above. According to the Gospels, Jesus' first miracle took place at the unlikely setting of a wedding reception and consisted in the seemingly banal act of producing wine to make up for the miscalculations of the wedding planners.

More important than the type of miracle worked, however, were the circumstances. On reading the text, one gets the impression that Jesus wasn't planning to work any miracles that day. He was a guest like any other. As you will recall, it was his mother's intervention that provoked Jesus to perform this unusual act of viniculture, even though his "hour [had] not yet come" (John 2:4 RSV). Mary had apparently perceived the need and thought it appropriate to take her concerns to her son.

The whole scene is rather extraordinary. For the Jewish people, a wedding feast without wine is a terrible thing. Wine is the life of the feast. We read in the book of Sirach: "What is life to one who is without wine? It has been created to make people happy" (31:27). Mary's heart went out to the young couple at Cana when she realized that the wine had run out. She appealed to Christ as only a mother could. She didn't need to ask, she merely informed: "They have no wine" (John 2:3 RSV).

This maternal-filial custom of informing works both ways. When my brothers and I were little, we sometimes informed my mother of things and she would understand: "Mom, we have no more milk," or "Mom, I can't find my blue oxford-cloth shirt." This method of informing clearly intended more than a mere data transfer and looked for a practical outcome. My mother, too, sometimes informed us of household situations: "The garbage needs to go out tonight" or "The back walk is covered with ice." We also understood, though sometimes more slowly than she would have liked.

At Cana, Mary informed Jesus that the young couple had no more wine. She didn't make any requests ("Jesus, honey, could you run out to the wine shop and pick up two five-gallon jugs of some inexpensive wine?"), yet Jesus understood. Though his response seems to be a put-off ("O woman, what have you to do with me? My hour has not yet come"—John 2:4 RSV), the next thing we know Jesus was ordering the servants to fill huge jugs with water, which he subsequently turned into wine. The mother had her way.

The Problem with Mary

Despite Mary's interesting—albeit limited—role in the Scriptures, many Christians find her problematic. Some think that she has assumed too prominent a role in traditional Christian piety, with the risk of overshadowing her Son, and others accuse their confreres of abandoning her altogether. Where does the truth lie? What is Mary's role for a Christian, and for our spiritual lives?

Some fear that devotion to Mary will somehow separate them from Christ. But if we stop and look at the gospel, we find that instead of leading people away from her Son, Mary always led them *to him*. Mary is the true *Christophora*, the "Christ-bearer," who carries Christ to the world. Even before Jesus was born, Mary carried him in her womb to visit her cousin Elizabeth. When Elizabeth heard her greeting, the unborn John the Baptist leapt for joy and Elizabeth blessed her: "Blessed are you among women, and blessed is the fruit of your womb!" (Luke 1:42 NASB). After Jesus' birth, the wise men and the shepherds came to pay him homage in Bethlehem, and where did they find him? In Mary's arms (Matt. 2:11). She stood faithfully by him beneath the cross and after Jesus' ascension accompanied the apostles in prayerful expectation of the Holy Spirit.

Where could we possibly find an obstacle in this humble maiden who did nothing but give Christ to the world? And if we look at our own lives, we find the same thing. How grateful we are to those people who showed us how to pray, who told us about Jesus, who taught us right from wrong—without ever fearing that their mediation in our lives detracts in the least from Christ's unique mediation or could upstage his singular place in our hearts. Mary is the apostle *par excellence*, the Queen of Apostles. Her last recorded words in the gospel, her final testament, exhort us to follow her Son: "Do whatever he tells you" (John 2:5 RSV). She will never separate us from Christ but always lead us to him.

In the last days of his life, Christ gave his apostles many precious gifts. At the Last Supper he left them his body and blood as a perpetual memorial of his death; he left them his new commandment of love; he gave them his Holy Spirit; and from the cross, he gave them his mother. When Jesus looked down from the cross and saw his mother and the disciple he loved, he said to his mother: "Woman, behold, your son!" and then to John: "Behold, your mother!" (John 19:26-27 RSV). In the person of John Catholics have always seen the figure of all Christians, to whom Christ gives his own mother to be ours.

How does Mary help us love God more? Her role for the Christian Church is double: intercessory and exemplary.

How does Mary help us love God more? Her role for the Christian Church is double: intercessory and exemplary. Let's look at each separately.

Mary's Intercession

One of the most important ways that Christian believers support one another is through prayer. We intercede for each other and entrust our own needs to our brothers' and sisters' prayers. In writing to the Christians at Ephesus, for example, Paul exhorted them to prayer for all the brethren and to pray also for him (6:18–20). How often do we find ourselves spontaneously asking others to pray for us, to pray for a sick relative or friend or a person especially in need? This binds us together and allows us to exercise true charity even toward those far away from us.

If this is how we treat our brothers and sisters on earth, how else would we treat those who have gone before us? Do we imagine that their intercession means less now than before, or that they are less interested in us now than when they were with us on earth? Now that they are united to God in heaven and "see him just as he is" (1 John 3:2 NASB), how much more fervent and effective must their prayer be!

From the earliest centuries of Christianity, believers felt a special devotion to Mary and entrusted their intentions to her with the confidence of a child with its mother. One of the oldest formal Christian prayers that we possess is actually a prayer addressed to Mary and goes by the Latin name of *Sub tuum praesidium*. This ancient prayer, the oldest known version of which is found on an Egyptian papyrus from the third century, reads as follows: "We fly to thy patronage, O holy Mother of God; despise not our petitions in our necessities, but deliver us always from all dangers, O glorious and blessed Virgin. Amen."

Before the painful divisions among Christians began splitting the Church into more and more splinters, when Christians were just Christian and not divided among denominational lines, believers invoked the assistance of Christ's mother, Mary. Long before John Wesley broke from the Church of England to found the Methodist Church and penned his famous hymns; before King Henry the Eighth split from Rome and declared himself the head of the Anglican Church; before Martin Luther nailed his Ninety-five Theses to the door of the Wittenburg church; and even prior to the Great Schism of 1054, when Pope Leo IX and the Eastern Patriarch Michael Caerularius mutually excommunicated one another, Christians—the Church—were offering this prayer to Christ's mother, Mary.

To highlight Mary's role, Christians throughout history have come up with beautiful titles for her drawn from scriptural references and reflecting her mission in the Church. Some of her titles include Consolation of the Afflicted, Refuge of Sinners, Queen of Apostles, Help of Christians, and Ark of the Covenant. In the Marian litany, after each invocation, we respond: "Pray for us!" How natural for children to spontaneously turn to their mother, to ask for her prayers, her counsel, her tender care. Prayer is always directed to God, and the expression "praying to the saints" must always be understood as asking them to pray for us. That is why we ask Mary to "pray for us," just as we ask one another the same favor.

How natural for children to spontaneously turn to their mother, to ask for her prayers, her counsel, her tender care.

Devotion to Mary helps us grow in our devotion to Christ. The prayer of the rosary, for instance, involves meditating on the mysteries of Christ's life, while asking Mary to pray for us sinners "now and at the hour of our death." In the beautiful words of Pope John Paul II: "To recite the Rosary is nothing other than to contemplate with Mary the face of Christ."[1] Mary knew Christ as no one else did and wants nothing more than for us to get to know him and to fall in love with him.

I will end this section with a short poem composed by Mary Dixon Thayer that was popularized in the 1950s by Archbishop Fulton Sheen.[2] It sums up in the simplest of terms who Mary is for Christians.

Lovely Lady dressed in blue,
    Teach me how to pray!
God was just your little boy,
    Tell me what to say!

Did you lift Him up, sometimes,
    Gently, on your knee?
Did you sing to Him the way
    Mother does to me?

Did you hold His hand at night?
    Did you ever try
Telling stories of the world?
    O! And did He cry?

Do you really think He cares
    If I tell Him things—
Little things that happen?
    And do the angels' wings

Make a noise? And can He hear
  Me if I speak low?
Does He understand me now?
  Tell me—for you know.

Lovely Lady dressed in blue,
  Teach me how to pray!
God was just your little boy,
  And you know the way.

Mary As the First Disciple

True devotion to Mary consists especially in the imitation of her virtues. All of us ecognize our need for role models. We point to histor-ical figures and even contemporaries who shine for their excellence in their field. How often do we Christians search for role models among pop stars and athletes to offer young people as someone to look up to? For Christians, the saints are principally role models, friends of Jesus who show us how Christianity is done. They are not saviors (there is only one Savior) or teachers (there is only one Teacher), but exceptionally good *learners*, outstanding *disciples* of Jesus.

> *True devotion to Mary consists especially in the imitation of her virtues.*

Isn't Jesus enough? we may ask. Of course he is enough. But this isn't the question, is it? Jesus gives us a superabundance of gifts, and who are we to judge some necessary and others excessive? An un-fortunate minimalism sometimes creeps into Christianity whereby *less* always seems better than *more*. We want to strip everything down to a bare minimum, as if that somehow purified our faith and worship. Yet Jesus is offering us much more.

As we saw in the last chapter, Jesus chooses to share his mission with human coworkers. He doesn't jealously guard every action for himself. He wants us to boost each other, encourage each other, pray for each other, emulate each other, and even correct each other. This is part of what it means to be called not only as individuals, but as a *church*. We are all members of the body of Christ, the Church, and we are responsible for one another.

Paul understood this very well when he enjoined the Christians of the Church at Corinth to "be imitators of me" (1 Cor. 4:16 RSV). Paul wasn't trying to usurp Christ's place. He wasn't setting himself up as a rival redeemer. He was providing an example of what it means to follow Christ, and generations of Christians afterward have been grateful to him for it. In fact, Paul explicitly recognized that the ultimate point of reference for all imitation is Christ himself and said: "Be imitators of me, *as I am of Christ*" (1 Cor. 11:1 RSV). Moreover, this appeal to imitation isn't limited to Paul alone. The author of the Letter to the Hebrews held up Abraham as an example for all to follow and invited his readers to be "imitating those who have the faith and the perseverance to inherit the promises" (Heb. 6:12). The tradition of exemplary witnesses of faith and virtue is as old as Christianity itself.

Among all Christian heroes held up for our imitation, Mary has always held a special place. In the early centuries of Christianity the fathers of the Church referred to her as the "New Eve." Where Eve had been disobedient, falling into Satan's wiles and leading Adam into sin, Mary was the perfect "yes" to God, and not just once but over and over again.

I have heard quite a few women say that they can't identify with Mary. She is too perfect, too submissive, too pure, too untroubled to serve as a model or even to understand their problems. Yet I think that this separation from Mary often stems more from unrealistic myths created around her person than from the real Mary. We picture her like those television moms of the 1950s and 1960s: ever unruffled, all done up in pearls, even in the kitchen. At some point women look at this image and say: "Enough! I can't do that."

Yet that isn't the real Mary. Sometimes we may think that Mary had it easy, while we have to stumble through life amidst uncertainties, compromises, and darkness. What could she possibly know of our temptations, our weakness, and our doubts? But a closer look reveals that her struggles remarkably resemble our own. Mary was anything but the gauzy, prim ingénue that we sometimes imagine.

Mary was anything but the gauzy, prim ingénue that we sometimes imagine.

True, Mary presents a lofty model of discipleship. Although she had a tough job to do, she did it beautifully. Her faithfulness and humble response to God's grace should challenge us rather than put us off. Her mission was hard and the list of trials seems endless. First there was the small-town gossip, as friends and neighbors discovered she was pregnant (but not married). Joseph himself was ready to leave her and would have done so were it not for a dream where God set things straight. Then there was the long trek to Bethlehem for the census in the last days of her pregnancy, only to find that there was no place at the inn to have her child. No room in the world for her Son, and consequently, no room for her!

Later, in the temple, the elderly Simeon took Jesus in his arms and turned to his mother, predicting that her son would be a sign of contradiction, and that a sword would pierce her soul as well (Luke 2:34–35). Hard words for a young mother to hear! Next King Herod wanted to kill her baby and she had to flee her country for Egypt, where she knew no one and didn't even speak the language. We can only imagine what went through Mary's heart the day Jesus announced that he was leaving home to begin his public ministry. Not long after, as hostility began to mount against Jesus, Mary saw storm clouds forming on the horizon but could do nothing for her son but pray and trust in God. Through all of this, Mary continued to say yes to God the way she had at the Annunciation.

Qualities of Mary's Devotion

Her devotion to her Lord displayed itself in a number of virtues that merit our attention.

HUMILITY

First, Mary exemplified humility. The reason she so naturally obeyed God's word stemmed from her understanding of who God was and who she was. That explains why her two sentences flow together as a single response: "Behold, I am the handmaid of the Lord; let it be to me according to your word" (Luke 1:38 RSV). When we conceive of ourselves as God's servants, we readily obey his loving commands. He has the right to ask us whatever he wants. Humility and obedience merge into a single attitude of openness to God and his will.

Mary's God-centeredness, exemplified so perfectly in her words "My soul magnifies the Lord," allowed her to serve without thinking of herself. Look at the way she receded into the background during Jesus' public life, knowing that the Son must establish a new family. Her hour, like Christ's, would come only with the cross, when she would accompany Jesus in his Passion.

A WOMAN OF GOD'S WORD

Mary also showed herself to be a *woman of God's word*. Her canticle of thanksgiving that we know as the Magnificat paints a portrait of her soul.

> It is entirely woven from threads of Holy Scripture, threads drawn from the Word of God. Here we see how completely at home Mary is with the Word of God, with ease she moves in and out of it. She speaks and thinks with the Word of God; the Word of God becomes her word, and her word issues from the Word of God. Here we see how her thoughts

are attuned to the thoughts of God, how her will is one with the will of God. Since Mary is completely imbued with the Word of God, she is able to become the Mother of the Word Incarnate.

(Pope Benedict XVI, encyclical letter
Deus Caritas Est, December 25, 2005, 41)

FAITH

Mary is, moreover, a woman who lives by *faith.* "Blessed is she who believed," Elizabeth says to her (Luke 1:45 RSV). For Mary, believing carried with it the same struggles and darkness that it does for us. How could she possibly understand what God was asking of her—that she was to be at the same time virgin and mother, that her son was going to be both God and man? How could she understand, as she watched her Son die on the cross, how God would fulfill his promise that "of his kingdom there will be no end" (Luke 1:33 RSV)? It seemed that her whole world was crashing down.

And yet, even without understanding, she accepted what God revealed to her in the "obedience of faith." Mary trusted absolutely, unconditionally in God. For Mary, God was God and she was his creature, his little girl. Whatever he wanted was fine with her, because she was all his. Her faith led her to see God's providential hand in everything and to praise him for having done "great things" for her, for showing his mercy to Israel, and for lifting up the lowly while confusing the proud (Luke 1:46–55).

> *For Mary, God was God and she was his creature, his little girl.*

CHARITY

Mary also exemplifies for us her son's commandment of *charity.* We have already seen this manifested in her sensitivity to the needs of the young couple at Cana. In the Gospel of Luke we find her engaged in a service of charity to her cousin Elizabeth, with whom she remained for "about three months" (Luke 1:56) so as to assist her in the final phase of her pregnancy. Mary is a woman who loves. How could it be otherwise? As a believer who in faith thinks with God's thoughts and wills with God's will, she cannot fail to be a woman who loves.

In Mary God shows us what grace can do in a soul, in the life of a human being. When we look at Mary, it's as if God were challenging each one of us: "See what I am capable of doing when a person is generous and trustful? Just imagine what I could do in you and through you if you would give yourself to me the way Mary did!" Think for a moment of who in your life has led you closest to God. Whose example of virtue has had the greatest impact on your life? In the same vein, which of Mary's virtues inspires you the most? I have always been taken with her humility, her ability to get out of the way and let Christ shine. All she wanted was for God to be glorified, "magnified" in her. What a beautiful model for today's Christian!

With these thoughts in mind, let us now look at our response to God's grace. He has given us so many gifts, so many means to draw near to him, among them prayer, the sacraments, his Holy Spirit, and his own Mother. What virtues should we be cultivating in order to respond to so much love?

Part III

WHAT WE ARE TO DO

Much of what it means to be a Christian involves making choices. God created us free so that we could love him and follow him not out of compulsion, but spontaneously. For all Christians, there comes a time when we realize that we no longer believe in and follow Jesus "because our parents say so," but because we have personally embraced the faith and accepted Jesus as Lord and Savior. For many this fundamental decision comes around the time of adolescence, the initiation into adulthood, and for many Christians it is even accompanied by a sacrament called Confirmation. For others, this personal decision comes at another moment in life, perhaps well into adulthood.

Along with this crucial choice to be a Christian come many occasions to ratify or in some way mitigate our Christian commitment. A crisis of faith can sometimes make us rethink our beliefs and often we come out with our faith either weakened or purified. Sometimes, too, we realize that our Christian faith languished in mediocrity, because we have allowed other concerns to slowly invade our hearts and become more important than our love for Christ. Other times, a good example of fervor from a fellow Christian or insistence from the Holy Spirit moves us to ratchet up our spiritual and apostolic energy.

We have examined Christ's words that without him we can do

nothing and also looked at the relationship between God's initiative and our cooperation. We have seen how the two go so closely together that it is hard, and at times even impossible, to discern where God's action leaves off and ours begins. Nonetheless, in this next section we will pay special attention to the part we are called to freely play in following Christ and growing in our love for him. Every day we have countless opportunities to say yes or no to his advances, to either grow or slacken in our Christian commitment.

Sometimes we wish that our Lord would be less "respectful" in dealing with us. We wish that he would take us by the scruff of the neck and forcibly make us better: more generous, more loving, more prayerful, more patient. Yet though he unfailingly promises his grace and companionship, he also refuses to impose his love or to move our wills without our consent. Love to be love must be free, and he desires our freely given love more than anything else in the world.

In the next three chapters we will examine a key part of our response to Christ. We will look at three fundamental pillars that form the foundation of the spiritual edifice whose crown is charity: faith, humility, and generosity. These quintessential Christian virtues complement one another and together enable us to respond as we should to God's loving initiative in our loves. Faith opens the door to God's action by saying yes to his self-revelation and by accepting the message of salvation that he offers us in Jesus his Son. Humility dislodges us from the center of our hearts and recognizes Christ as the sovereign Lord of our lives, and our brothers and sisters not as means to be subordinated to our desires, but dear fellow pilgrims to be loved and served in Jesus' name. Finally, generosity moves us to give beyond our comfort level and to die to ourselves in order to live for Christ alone.

Clearly even these virtues are in many ways gifts of God. Yet each requires a free response. Jesus assures us: "Behold, I stand at the door and knock; if anyone hears My voice and opens the door, I will come in to him and will dine with him, and he with Me" (Rev. 3:20 NASB). Jesus already stands at the door of my heart and knocks. Let us together look at how we can open wide the door to him.

CHAPTER 10

Becoming a Believer

Faith As Gift and Choice

Now faith is the assurance of things hoped for, the conviction of things not seen.

Hebrews 11:1 NASB

Few things slowed Jesus down. Whenever he put his mind to something, he did it. He overturned tables (when necessary), walked on water, calmed storms, and stood up to the scribes and Pharisees. He feared nothing and let nothing—almost nothing—get in his way. The one thing that did stop Jesus in his tracks was disbelief.

The gospel reports that when Jesus was in his hometown of Nazareth "he could work no miracle there" *because of their lack of faith* (Mark 6:5). And the Gospel writer adds: "He marveled because of their unbelief" (Mark 6:6 RSV). Disbelief did to Jesus what kryptonite did to Superman: it left him powerless.

Faith, in fact, seemed to have much to do with many of Jesus' miracles. When he cured the centurion's servant at Capernaum, he did so as "you have believed" (Matt. 8:13 RSV). When the woman who had been suffering from hemorrhages approached him and touched his cloak, she was immediately healed, and Jesus said to her: "Daughter, your faith has made you well" (Mark 5:34 NASB). When two blind men came calling after him, asking to be cured, Jesus first asked them: "Do you believe that I am able to do this?" (Matt. 9:28 RSV). Only after their affirmative response did Jesus perform the cure. And on healing Bartimaeus, the blind beggar of Jericho, Jesus assured him: "Your faith has made you well" (Mark 10:52 NASB). Over and over again Jesus attributed the effects of his miracles to the faith of those whom he cured.

Faith was not only instrumental for those looking to be healed; it also affected the apostles' *ability* to heal. Jesus had given them authority over unclean spirits and the power to heal, but faith was necessary too. There was, for instance, the case of a man who brought his epileptic son to the disciples but they were unable to cure him. In their consternation, the disciples asked Jesus privately why they hadn't been able to effect the healing, and Jesus soberly replied: "Because you have little faith" (Matt. 17:20). Later, at the Last Supper, he assured them that "whoever believes in me will perform the same works as I do myself, he will perform even greater works, because I am going to the Father" (John 14:12). Faith not only allows God to work *in* us, it also allows him to work *through* us.

> *Faith not only allows God to work in us, it also allows him to work through us.*

Does this mean that God cannot act in our lives unless we have faith? Does our disbelief bind his hands? Mercifully, many times he blesses us *despite* our lack of faith. But he clearly does often *choose* to act or refrain from acting according to our faith. Faith gives God the green light to work miracles in our lives. Jesus affirmed that "all things are possible to him who believes" (Mark 9:23 RSV) but likewise finds his action hampered by our lack of faith.

How many times do you suppose God has wanted to do amazing things in our lives but gets held up by our unbelief? How many times do we doubt his love for us, his power to bring us through crises, his interest in our problems? Faith is so important for our spiritual lives that many times our growth in friendship with Christ depends directly on our willingness to believe and trust in him.

Faith Is Our First "Yes" to God

Faith is the response God is waiting for. It is the first and most important "act" that the Christian is called to carry out. When the Jews asked Jesus: "What must we do, to be doing the works of God?" Jesus answered them, "This is the work of God, that you believe in him whom he has sent" (John 6:28–29 RSV). Our first means of collaborating with God is to believe in him. He reveals himself to us, initiates a conversation, and wants most of all for us to believe in him. Our faith gives God a permission slip, an "informed consent" to work freely in our lives.

Of course "believing in him" means more than just believing he *exists*—as when we say: "I believe in God." Faith in God means believing in his presence in our lives and his interest in everything that befalls us. It means believing in his faithfulness and reliability. Above all, it means believing in his love for us. When we really believe these things, then we also trust in him. More than mere intellectual assent, faith also means a loving trust and confidence in the One who reveals himself.

When you look at salvation history—all the things God did for the Israelites leading up to the time of Jesus and all the things God revealed about himself *through* Jesus—it's as if God were shouting at us with every new action how much he loves us and how anxious he is for us to believe in him. And that same divine activity goes on in a smaller scale in each of our lives. He shows himself again and again and begs us to believe.

Imagine that you were madly in love with another person and did everything in your power to prove it to him or her—flowers, chocolates, love letters, fine dinners—and at the end the person said: "I don't believe you really love me." That is what our disbelief is like for God: it crushes him. As God says through the prophet Isaiah, "What more was there to do for my vineyard that I have not done in it?" (5:4 NASB). Yet still he respects our freedom, because he wants our belief to be a free choice. So he doesn't bowl us over. He is more subtle than that. Still, he longs for our belief.

In the Gospels' narrations of Jesus' life, we find some of his most passionate responses—both negative and positive—evoked by people's belief or lack of it. On several occasions he reprimanded the apostles for their "little faith," always exhorting them to believe more and to trust absolutely in him. When they couldn't cast out a devil, he exclaimed in exasperation: "O faithless generation, how long am I to be with you? How long am I to bear with you?" (Mark 9:19 RSV).

Then again, when Jesus did meet up with faith, he practically couldn't control his joy. When the Canaanite woman insisted with him despite his put-offs, Jesus exclaimed: "Woman, you have great faith. Let your wish be granted" (Matt. 15:28). When the Roman centurion expressed his belief that all Jesus had to do was say the word and his servant would be healed, Jesus was "amazed" and said to his followers: "Truly, I say to you, not even in Israel have I found such faith" (Matt. 8:10 RSV). If you really want to make Christ happy, show him how much you trust in him. Don't ask for signs or entertain the doubts that assail you.

This isn't always easy. Believing in Christ sometimes demands heroism. He asks for our unconditional belief, not only on sunny days when all is going well, but on dark days, too, in the midst of sorrow and apparent contradictions. It is relatively easy to believe in God (and his goodness) when you are doing well in school, thriving in your personal relationships, and coasting along in your career. It's much tougher—but also more meritorious—to believe when everything points in the opposite direction. How hard to continue trusting in a loving God after the death of a child, the betrayal of a spouse or close friend, or a long, painful illness.

Believing in Christ sometimes demands heroism.

Jesus' words to Thomas were clearly meant to encourage *us*: "Have you believed because you have seen me? Blessed are those who have not seen and yet believe" (John 20:29 RSV). The reward for belief stems, in the first place, from finding out that our trust was not misplaced. God really is good and holds us in the palm of his hand. Believing in Christ sometimes demands heroism.

A Different Way of Knowing

Faith—believing—has different meanings. Sometimes belief can express a minimum degree of sureness. It can mean "I don't *know*, but I believe so." When you are asked where Susan is and you respond, "I believe she is at the library," you are using belief in this sense. It would be a less-than-knowing, a non-knowing, even though you have *reasons* for thinking so. Belief of this sort is—at best—an approximate knowledge.

This belief as less-than-knowing has nothing to do with Christian faith. Faith reflects not probability but certitude, even though empirical knowledge is lacking. When my mother tells me something, I have no doubt whatever that what she says is true. I believe what she says, because I believe in her. Belief of this sort has reference to a person and becomes a question of trust and confidence.

Supported by nothing less than God's truthfulness, Christian faith offers a certainty that leads us to construct our lives around the truths that God reveals, and on God himself. How many practical choices do we make based on our belief in God? Look at the martyrs, who gave up their lives rather than betray their beliefs. Perhaps more than anyone else, they present a glorious witness of a titanic faith, more precious and certain than life itself. Peter wrote that faith is "more precious than gold" (1 Pet. 1:7).

One of the most common errors in the spiritual life comes from associating faith with "feeling God." When we feel God's loving presence in prayer, we are happy and think our prayer is going well. When our prayer is dry or we experience desolation, we assume that somehow we have lost God's favor. Sometimes we even prefer to follow our feelings rather than what we *know* to be true and good through faith. How many have gone so far as to switch churches for another where they "felt" more welcome or "fed" or even where the singing was better?

Yet faith means much more than feeling good. Faith means knowledge of the truth God reveals. It assures us that God loves us always, whether we feel him or not. It lets us discern what is true, what has value, and where to place our treasure. Jesus says that "your eye is the lamp of your body; when your eye is sound, your whole body is full of light; but when it is not sound, your body is full of darkness" (Luke 11:34 RSV). The "eye" of faith differentiates true from false, and precious from worthless. Like the expert eye of the jeweler who quickly distinguishes a precious diamond from a cheap trinket, faith distinguishes the real thing from a sham. This clarity of vision far surpasses "good feelings."

Jesus likens faith to *sight*, considered the surest of our senses. Whoever believes in him has light to see where he is going, whereas the absence of faith makes us stumble about, as in darkness. "I have come as light into the world," he says, "so that everyone who believes in me will not remain in darkness" (John 12:46 NASB).

Imagine walking through an unfamiliar house in pitch-black darkness. We tentatively grope along, never sure where we are going. Such is human existence without faith. Faith provides the flashlight, or better still, the light switch, which allows us to see where we are.

Those who accept faith reject the idea that physical seeing, hearing, and touching comprise the totality of what we can know. Faith provides a second mode of access to reality, a mode that enlarges our whole view of the world. In this sense, faith is an option, the deliberate acknowledgment of the immaterial world. The invisible is no less real than the visible. This view recognizes that at the very center of human existence there is a core that cannot be nourished and supported on the visible and tangible but needs a deeper reality imperceptible to the senses.

It isn't that knowledge gained from faith goes *against* our reason or contradicts the knowledge we get from our senses. Rather, it surpasses that knowledge. Faith is not *irrational*, but superrational. Faith simply enables us to know more than we can discover by our natural powers, because it opens the door to accepting knowledge from another person who is both more knowledgeable and trustworthy.

Faith and reason are two different ways of knowing that complement each other. Reason comprehends or grasps certain truths, by which they then become our possession. By reason we can then control facts, disassemble and reassemble them, relate them to other propositions, employ them to construct arguments or syllogisms. Information enters our heads and becomes *ours*. We dominate it.

Faith, unlike reason, draws us into a mystery where we no longer have the upper hand. We are no longer in charge. Faith does not amass data to be used at its good pleasure but enters into the mystery of God, commending itself to the One who is faithful and true. In other words, by reason, information and data enter into us; by faith, *we* enter into a mystery that is larger than us and encompasses us.

Thus Christians defend the value of reason but reject rationalism—the dogma that everything that can be known, we know by reason alone. Rationalism and materialism go hand in hand and together deny the possibility of a spiritual world transcending the visible world. Rationalism feeds our pride, because it gives us a false sense of control, ruling out a world bigger than the world we can see and touch. Faith works hand in hand with reason by illuminating and confirming it, and reason in turn helps us understand what we believe and to see how it relates to the rest of our experience.

Faith is not only a different kind of knowing but also a clearer kind of knowing. Many times I have been on the Sorrentine Peninsula in the south of Italy and looked out over the blue waters of the Gulf of Naples. Often in the morning a translucent mist hangs over the gulf and visibility is minimal. But then the sun appears and burns away the mist, and the island of Ischia appears on the horizon, shining clearer and clearer. The beautiful island was there the whole time but invisible without the cleansing power of the sun. Faith is like that. It allows us to see what before was invisible. It gives us the certitude of the reality of God's grace and providence in helping us live our Christian lives. Like the sun, faith clears away the morning smog and haze and allows us to see what is really there all the time.

> *Faith is not only a different kind of knowing but also a clearer kind of knowing.*

It is faith that has moved the saints to embark on great tasks that human calculations deemed impossible. This is the faith that moves mountains. It is not just compatible with reason but is in fact the deepest reason, because, for the person who has faith, trusting in God is the most reasonable and indeed rational thing to do.

Believing in God and Believing God

Christian faith has two complementary dimensions. Faith is first of all a personal adherence to God. Joseph Ratzinger wrote in *Introduction to Christianity*: "Christian faith is more than the option in favor of a spiritual ground to the world; its central formula is not 'I believe in something,' but 'I believe in Thee.' It is the encounter with the human being Jesus, and in this encounter it experiences the meaning of the world as a person."

At the same time—and inseparably—it is a free assent to the

whole truth that God has revealed. As adherence to God, Christian faith is essentially personal. It finds its most authentic expression in the words: "I believe in you." Faith is not just assent to this or that truth, or even to a whole, integrated bundle of truths. Christian faith means, in the first place, to accept Jesus Christ as *the Truth*, with all that that entails for our personal lives. Accepting Christ as Truth itself means submitting ourselves totally to that truth and allowing him to be the uncontested Lord of our lives. In this way Jesus becomes our norm and standard, the center, model, and point of reference for every facet of our existence.

This faith differs from our belief in any human person. It is right and just to entrust oneself wholly to God, whereas it would be futile and false to place such faith in a creature. As the prophet Jeremiah said: "Cursed is the man who trusts in man and makes flesh his arm," but "Blessed is the man who trusts in the LORD, whose trust is the LORD" (Jer. 17:5, 7 RSV).

Thus faith, more than just intellectual assent, entails entrusting ourselves to God. He doesn't explain what will happen later, where we are going, what he will ask of us in the future. All we have to bank on is him: his faithfulness, his love, and his truthfulness. I may not know where he is leading me, but *he* knows, and that will have to suffice for me.

This attitude of faith is very costly to our human nature. We would prefer a clear contract with everything spelled out in black and white, and instead Christ merely says, "Sign this blank sheet." He invites us to "Come, follow me," without spelling out where we are going. Even if we ask, he won't tell us what is coming. He *wants* us to walk by faith.

Gift and Choice

Faith is first and foremost a *gift*. In baptism we receive this theological virtue that makes belief natural and allows us to know God. Ours is a hidden God, and we see him not with our material eyes but with the eyes of faith. Yet besides being a gift, faith is also a *choice*, and involves an act of the will, a decision to believe. Thus Paul could say: "I know whom I have believed" (2 Tim. 1:12 NASB). The gift of faith allows us to believe, but the act of believing goes beyond the gift. Only through the *exercise* of faith, through *acts* of faith, does this virtue transform our way of seeing life. We are born with muscles in our arms and legs, but only by our exercising them do they become strong enough to walk. We receive the *power* to believe, but the *act* of belief depends on us.

On the other hand, faith isn't a toggle switch with only two positions—off and on. Faith also admits of degrees. We can have more or less faith, a deeper or more superficial faith, a wavering or steadfast faith. So it's not merely a question of believing or not believing, but believing more and more. Faith means seeing, rather than feeling, but more often than not it means seeing dimly, as in a cloudy mirror (1 Cor. 13:12).

Sometimes it is terribly difficult to believe. Though we want to trust in God, we recognize that we need his help even for that. And in these cases, with great humility, we must imitate the father of the boy with an unclean spirit, who brought his son to Jesus to be healed. When Jesus reproved him for his unbelief, the man replied: "I do believe; help my unbelief!" (Mark 9:24 NASB). The disciples, too, recognizing their little faith, begged Jesus: "Increase our faith" (Luke 17:5). This heartfelt prayer acknowledges that faith comes from God first of all. It is good for us to pray every day: "Lord, preserve my faith; Lord, strengthen my faith; Lord, increase my faith!" Christ himself promised his prayers for his apostle Peter in much the same vein: "I have prayed for you that your faith may not fail" (Luke 22:31 RSV).

Faith is a gift unlike any other gift, since it gives meaning to everything we do. Without faith, where would we be? What sense would all our work and effort make? Everything—struggles, projects, sorrows, trials, pleasures, beauty, and even love itself—would lose its meaning and become simply a hollow, passing experience. Faith is a gift more precious than life itself, because it gives us a reason to live. It reveals to us the eternal truth behind earthly existence and gives us the assurance that things ultimately make sense. Above all, it assures us that we are loved from all time.

At the same time, faith is an adventure. It is a voyage we undertake together with the One who created us and who leads us by sure yet tortuous paths to our complete human fulfillment and eternal happiness. He repeats over and over throughout our lives: "Trust in me and stay by my side. I made you and know what will make you truly happy." Even so, at times we wander off, trusting more in our supposedly better judgment or seduced by the sirens of the world that promise a cheaper, quicker, more immediate happiness. In these occasions, far from abandoning us to our senselessness, he sets out looking for us, the true Good Shepherd for whom every soul is precious. He hoists us gently upon his shoulders, binds our wounds, and dries our tears. Like our entire spiritual lives, faith springs from a relationship rather than from a solitary project we carry out on our own.

Like a timid hiker setting out over a frozen lake, we take baby steps, unsure of whether or not the ice will sustain our weight. As we move forward, our confidence grows and our fear diminishes. Every act of trust in Christ, as we acknowledge his faithfulness, leads us to a greater trust in him. We must not be afraid to take those first steps and even to venture out farther than we have ever dared before. He will sustain us! He will be our strength if we but allow him!

Faith and Love

Early on in this work, we set out to show how love—charity—is the goal of the spiritual life, and the content of Christian holiness. Faith, like the whole spiritual life, is ordered to love. It is bound up with love and finds its fulfillment of love. Knowing God through faith leads us to love him. Thus Thomas Dubay can say, referring to Saint John of the Cross: "John always considers faith as vivified by love, never as a mere intellectual assent devoid of charity. His concept of faith is a loving knowing, a knowing loving" (*Fire Within*).

Belief, as James reminds us, is essential, but without works of love it is dead. Even the demons believe—he adds—and they fear God and shudder, but they do not love (James 2:17–20).

You've no doubt heard the expression "To know her is to love her." We use it to describe a person who is so good, so kind, so generous that all those who meet her cannot help but like her. This saying is never truer than when applied to Christ. We can be absolutely sure that if we aren't madly in love with him, it is simply because we don't yet know him well enough.

Faith unveils the face of Christ. It penetrates his thousand disguises and allows us to discover him, and to know him.

Imagine a little child growing up with every good thing provided for her by an anonymous benefactor. She has lovely clothes to wear, delicious food to eat, and she takes wonderful trips to exotic places—all thanks to her unknown provider. Imagine, too, that every day as she walks to the market she passes a poor beggar by the side of the road who silently holds out his tin cup. What will be her utter surprise the day she finds out that the poor beggar and the anonymous benefactor are really the same person? With how much joy, gratitude, and tenderness will she invite him into her home? Such is Christ for us. Faith unveils the face of Christ. It penetrates his thousand disguises and allows us to discover him, and to know him. It grants us access to him. It opens a window to his heart where we can learn what he is really like. But faith also reveals that Christ is often where we least expect him, especially in the least of our brothers and sisters. This is where faith and charity meet in an especially poignant way.

Shortly before his Passion, Jesus told a story about the Last Judgment to come at the end of the world. In it he said that at the end of time all the peoples of the earth will assemble before the Son of Man, who will separate them into two groups, on his left and his right, the way a shepherd separates sheep from goats. To those on his right the King will say: "Come, O blessed of my Father, inherit the kingdom prepared for you from the foundation of the world." To those on his left, he will say: "Depart from me, you cursed, into the eternal fire prepared for the devil and his angels." Yet the reason he gives in both cases—for reward or condemnation—is the same: "As you did it to one of the least of these my brethren, you did it to me" (Matthew 25:34, 40-41 RSV).

We don't need to look far to find Jesus. We don't need to be extraordinarily ingenious to love him. He is before us, identifying with each person we meet. He identifies especially with the "least": the unpleasant ones, the smelly ones, the ignorant and uneducated, the petty and the rude, the poor and forgotten, the ones from whom we can derive no benefit.

To make room for the faith that leads to such love, we must clear out space in our hearts. We must clear out space in our world that revolves around ourselves, our problems, and our concerns. We must open our eyes to others—to their needs and their desires. In other words, we must become humble. Humility—the bedrock of the spiritual life—will be the topic of our next discussion.

CHAPTER 11

Discovering Your Best Self

True Humility in a World of Vanity

What I have come to understand is that this whole groundwork of prayer is based on humility and that the more a soul lowers itself in prayer the more God raises it up.

Teresa of Ávila

In many churches, at the beginning of Lent, the priest or minister smudges ashes on the foreheads of the faithful in a sign of penance. As he does so, he may remind the person of God's words as they appear in the book of Genesis, "Remember you are dust and to dust you shall return" (see Gen. 3:19). This is a symbolic gesture, evocative of days when public penitents sat in sackcloth and ashes in repentance for their sins.

But all poetry aside, the short phrase contains a profound truth. The key word to be noted here is "remember." The priest doesn't say, "Let's pretend that you are dust" or "Act as if you were dust" but "*Remember.*" It's as if God himself were saying to us, "Remember the truth about yourself that you are so prone to forget, that you were *nothing*, not figuratively but literally, and I called you into existence because I loved you."

The word *humility* comes from the Latin *humus* (soil or ground) and recalls the fact that we humans are very much "of the earth." Throughout history the greatest thinkers have wrestled with the truth of the human person. Man is at once so great and yet so frail, capable of astounding creativity and sensitivity, yet also of the most vile abasement and cruelty.

And what is true of the human race is true of each of us as an individual. We are capable of kindness and self-sacrifice, but also of incredible selfishness and sin. Humility is the virtue that sifts through the many paradoxes of human existence in search of the truth. It peels off the layers of vanity and self-deception to reveal us to ourselves, as we really are. And it does so not by comparing us to other people to see how we stack up in the rogues' gallery of humanity but by placing us before the throne of God. Only in the refulgent light of God's truth and love

The truly humble person sees himself as he really is, since he sees himself as God sees him.

can we see the whole truth about ourselves, without exaggeration or subterfuge. Before him we see who we are, and who we are called to be. The truly humble person sees himself as he really is, since he sees himself as God sees him.

It was the great Spanish mystic and reformer, Teresa of Ávila, who offered the simplest and most direct definition of humility: humility is truth. The devil loves distortions and deception. He doesn't much care whether we think too much of ourselves and become overconfident or think too little of ourselves and become timid and desperate: "The wiles of the devil are terrible; he will run a thousand times round hell if by doing so he can make us believe that we have a single virtue which we have not. And he is right, for such ideas are very harmful" (*Interior Castle*). If we tend toward one error, he will push us in that direction, if toward the other, that's fine too. Humility avoids fictions of any sort and plants our feet firmly on the solid ground of the truth.

Knowledge of the truth about ourselves, however important, does not suffice. We all know, at least in theory, that we are poor sinners in need of God's mercy, and that everything we have we have received from him. Humility goes one step farther. It not only instills in us a *knowledge* of the truth, but also the ability and indeed the habit of *living in the truth*. This means thinking, speaking, and acting according to the truth of who we are. It's one thing to admit our dependence on God in the abstract and quite another to live with him as the center of our lives.

Our spiritual lives must be grounded in the truth in order to grow. If we compare the Christian life to an edifice, faith is the *foundation* and humility is the *bedrock* on which it is laid. Therefore, the first step is: Dig! Dig deep! Because the deeper you go, the surer your footing and the higher you can build. The deeper the roots of a tree sink into the earth, the higher its branches can stretch toward heaven.

Counterfeit Humility

As we have done with other concepts of the spiritual life, so, too, with humility we should begin by weeding out false notions that obscure the truth. Among all Christian virtues, humility seems to lend itself especially to misinterpretation. Often our ideas of humility stray so far from its true character that it hardly seems a virtue at all. Often, too, distortions of humility are really sophisticated expressions of pride.

HUMILITY IS NOT FALSE MODESTY
We have all met people who can't take a compliment. When faced with praise for their accomplishments (or good looks, or intelligence, or whatever) they deny what seems evident to everyone else. "My performance wasn't really very good." "I am the worst skater." "I am so fat." Often we chalk such behavior up to humility, as if humility were

the ability to deny our positive qualities or attributes. We logically assume that if pride is expressed in boastfulness, humility must show itself in self-effacement. But if humility really is *truth*, then there must be something fundamentally distorted about this idea of humility.

Sometimes of course, people act this way in order to fish for more compliments. They want others not only to praise them, but to *insist* in their praise despite polite refusals. But others reject compliments because they honestly believe that this is the Christian thing to do. They believe that humility compels them to debase themselves whenever possible and even to try to make themselves believe that they are less than they are. Here, too, can lurk a subtle pride. After all, only a very "good" person would have to invent false defects, because there aren't enough real ones. A humble person sees enough real faults without needing to invent more.

True humility recognizes the truth—good and bad. Moreover, it recognizes the *whole* truth. It knows: *Yes, I may be pretty, but I did nothing to earn that, and one day I will surely not be so pretty. Yes, I may be intelligent, but that is a gift from God for which I am accountable, and which I am called to use for his service and that of my brothers and sisters. Yes, I may have done well here, but I also know in my heart that many times I don't do so well.* True humility rounds out the truth of our existence by keeping everything in its proper perspective and especially by acknowledging God as the origin and Giver of all good things. Far from denying his gifts, it moves us to praise and thank him, and to use the gifts we have not for our own self-aggrandizement, but for the good of all.

HUMILITY IS NOT WEAKNESS OF CHARACTER

Some see humility as the absence of backbone and passion, opposed to boldness, confidence, and strength of will. It would lead us to hang our heads and avoid demanding enterprises. Yet while humility's opposite, pride, often manifests itself in excessive self-assurance and independence, humility does not therefore lead a Christian to become a wallflower or a milksop. Humility hardly induces us to quiet acquiescence in the face of spiritual challenges. The greatest saints have been persons of intense conviction and burning love, not fickleness and inaction.

Sacred Scripture calls Moses "the humblest man on earth" (Num. 12:3). That is a lot to say. Yet when this humble Moses came down from Mount Sinai and found the Israelites worshiping the golden calf, he burned with righteous anger and didn't hesitate to hurl the stone tablets to the ground, pulverize the golden calf, and make the Israelites drink water laced with its dust. In standing up to Egypt's pharaoh and in the arduous years trekking through the desert to the promised land, Moses showed more than a little backbone.

Or look at the example of Christ himself. He declared himself to be "meek and humble of heart" but Jesus was no wimp. This Jesus, meek and humble of heart, is the same one who gave the scribes and Pharisees a dressing-down that they never forgot, calling them "blind guides," "whitewashed tombs," "hypocrites," and a "brood of vipers" (Matt. 23:24–33). When this same humble Jesus entered the temple and found money changers and vendors, he proceeded to make a whip out of cords and to drive them all out, overturning their tables. As gentle as he was, Jesus was a man of passion and decisive action, a leader in every sense of the term.

Sometimes out of a mistaken sense of humility we avoid taking positions of responsibility or preaching Christ to others. After all, who are we with all our faults to be telling others what to do? We can even tamp down our natural leadership abilities, believing it to be the "humble" thing to do. Yet Jesus gave us our faith and our talents for a reason, to build up his body and not to atrophy. In a spirit of service rather than superiority, we are called to put all we have and are to work for the good of society and of the Church.

It is often a well-disguised pride that tempts us not to act. We know full well that we can't do everything we would like to do. We cannot solve all the world's problems. Pride would suggest to us that in this case we might as well do nothing. Humility, on the contrary, impels us to do *something*, even if that something is small and imperfect, for the good of others. It recognizes that if each of us were to add his or her grain of sand, soon the world itself would change for the better.

HUMILITY IS NOT ABDICATION OF THE TRUTH

Many today, thinking they are practicing intellectual humility, refuse to take a firm position on religious or moral questions. They mistakenly think that by doing so they are being "open-minded" and humble. An unambiguous religious faith would leave them in the awkward position of affirming that people who disagree with them are . . . wrong. We think it judgmental and discourteous to proclaim our religious or moral beliefs as absolutely true, as if such religious conviction could only be the fruit of arrogance.

Yet humility doesn't mean intellectual waffling. We can be convinced without thinking that we are better than others. We can possess the truth without using the truth as a weapon to beat others down. After all, a position of agnosticism is no less dogmatic or absolutist than Christian faith and conviction. The statement "We cannot know whether God exists" is no less absolute than the statement "I am certain that God exists" or even than the simple statement "God exists." None of itself implies greater humility than the other.

True, if our Christian faith makes us feel smug, superior, and self-complacent, we are hardly practicing humility, but these attitudes don't come from our faith but from our pride. Growing more humble does not mean abandoning our certitudes or entertaining unreasonable doubts but recognizing that our faith came to us as a free gift that we did nothing to merit and has nothing to do with any supposed tribal superiority. With gratitude and confidence we profess the faith that we received and in which we live by the grace of God.

In humility and gratitude we need to examine the gifts we have received from our Lord. What are my particular talents? How can I better put them to use for the good of the community and especially those closest to me? An honest, humble evaluation of the many blessings we have received is often the first step to a more generous engagement with the world, and a precious witness to the faith we have received.

An Eminently Christian Virtue

Humility is a quintessential Christian virtue. The great Greek philosophers Plato and Aristotle didn't include humility in their lists of virtues. The Stoics and Epicureans had no place for humility either. It was Christianity, building on the tradition of Judaism, that elevated humility to the rank of a virtue. What original sin distorted—namely the truth of who we are before God—humility puts right again. Humility provides the remedy to a wounded nature in need of mending, especially as regards our relationship with God and with our neighbor. Our exaggerated self-importance needs correcting in order for us to grow in our love for God and one another.

Humility provides the remedy to a wounded nature in need of mending, especially as regards our relationship with God and with our neighbor.

Of Christ's many virtues, the only one he specifically showcases for our imitation is his humility: "Learn from me, for I am meek and humble of heart." His example of humility is truly impressive. Jesus is the King of Heaven who chose to be born, not in a palace, nor even in a respectable hospital, but in a stable, surrounded not by satin sheets and an attentive court but by smelly hay, shepherds, and farm animals. "Learn from me." He does not assert himself but empties himself for our sake, taking on our human condition and dying in our place.

Yet Jesus' command to imitate his humility also contains a blessed promise: "And you will find rest for your souls. For my yoke is easy, and my burden is light" (Matt. 11:29-30 RSV). Much unrest and anxiety assail the proud, who cannot know the peace of heart enjoyed by humble souls. Letting God be God and happily taking our place as his sons and daughters is an immensely liberating experience and allows us to taste "a peace the world cannot give" (John 14:27).

Deposing a Tyrant

Humility restores God's place as sovereign Lord of our lives—but at a price. In order to enthrone Christ in our hearts, we must first *dethrone* the reigning tyrant: ourselves. Our fallen nature clings desperately to the self-centeredness that sees all reality in terms of self. Each of us is like the sun of our own little galaxy, with all the other planets revolving around us. Like Julius Caesar, we would rather reign supreme in a small province (our own lives) than settle for second place in Rome (God's kingdom). We buck at the idea that God's will is more important than ours and cling to our independence.

We easily fall into the myth of "rugged individualism" or the "self-made man." This myth paints absolute autonomy—that recognizes no other authority but itself—as the supreme human achievement. It embraces independence from others as the greatest good; we depend on no one and no one depends on us. Yet recall that the only perfect rugged individualist was Satan, and look what it got him. He stood up to God and declared, "I will not serve!" It won for him an eternity of misery, serving no one but himself and hating God for it. Among humans as well, this unwillingness to serve—the unwillingness to love and be loved—destroys the person and stunts his ability to reach affective and moral maturity.

Though rarely does our pride manifest itself in such crude and rebellious terms, we find it lurking behind many of our attitudes and reactions. Our unwillingness to forgive, our resentment toward others, the subtle disdain we feel toward those who are less sophisticated or clever than we are: all of these conceal pride simmering just beneath the surface. Often, too, we mask our pride in many guises of supposed virtue: "responsibility," "independence," "not wanting to burden others."

> A civilized age is more exposed to subtle sins than a rude age. Why? For this simple reason, because it is more fertile in excuses and evasions. It can defend error, and hence can blind the eyes of those who have not very careful consciences. It can make error plausible, it can make vice look like virtue. It dignifies sin by fine names; it calls avarice proper care of one's family, or industry; it calls pride independence; it calls ambition greatness of mind; resentment it calls proper spirit and sense of honour, and so on.
>
> (John Henry Newman, *Homily at St. Chad's Cathedral*, 1848)

In the end, the essence of pride is the centripetal force of self-reference and self-importance, where everything else acquires value only in its relation to me.

Although pride is only one of the seven capital sins (the others are greed, anger, lust, gluttony, laziness, and envy), in a certain way *all* sin depends on pride.

> From the moment a creature becomes aware of God as God and of itself as self, the terrible alternative of choosing God or self for the centre is opened to it. This sin is committed daily by young children and ignorant peasants as well as by sophisticated persons, by solitaries no less than by those

who live in society: it is the fall in every individual life, and in each day of each individual life, the basic sin behind all particular sins: at this very moment you and I are either committing it, or about to commit it, or repenting it.

(C. S. Lewis, *The Problem of Pain*)

The implicit assumption that we somehow have a right to act contrary to God's will finds its way into all our sins. The truly humble person knows that God's will is more important than his own preferences and submits to that will.

Humility, then, opens us to a grand revelation: *It isn't all about me. Life, even my life, doesn't revolve around me,* or at least it shouldn't. Back in 1972, when I was in fifth grade, a popular book circulated among my friends called *I Am Third*, the autobiography of Chicago Bears running back Gale Sayers. The provocative title comes from Sayers' credo: "The Lord is first, my family and friends are second, and I am third." Here is humility in a nutshell. By exiting from center stage, we are able to focus on God, and on the needs of our brothers and sisters. We are able to love. Moreover, we experience the peace and happiness he promised. It's no coincidence that Jesus-Others-You spells JOY.

No Love Without Humility

True love—the core of holiness—is necessarily humble and self-forgetful. If we are full of ourselves, we will have no room for God or others. Only by looking away from ourselves for a moment can we acknowledge the importance of others. A humble person listens to others. Humility takes others seriously and realizes that they are a gift. A humble person knows he has something to learn from everyone, and that the person he has before him is precious in God's eyes. As important as my plans and projects may be, the other merits my attention and my interest. Isn't this why humility is such an attractive virtue? Isn't this why we naturally gravitate toward the company of humble persons and avoid the proud?

God invites us to be humble so that we can be like his Son. He doesn't command humility in order to see us grovel in the dust before him, or because he is jealous of his authority, but in order to lift us up. He wants us to be everything we were created to be. He knows that our greatness does not consist in exalting ourselves but in joyfully living according to the truth of our being, which includes the truth of our absolute dependence on him and our interdependence on our brothers and sisters.

We are created for love, for communion with God and with our fellow men. Pride encases us within ourselves and makes this communion impossible; we stand on principle, on our reason, on our way of seeing things, and let the rest be damned. Yet this leads nowhere but to the loneliness of hell. Where pride isolates, humility provides the necessary humus for communion.

Humility and Trust

God hates pride, because pride separates us from him and from one another. At least that is what one gleans from sacred Scripture. "God opposes the proud but he gives generously to the humble" (James 4:6; see also Prov. 3:34; 1 Pet. 5:5). As you can see, this proverb is referenced three times in the Bible—and numerous times by Saint Augustine in his *Confessions*. The proud person trusts in himself, the humble in God. It is as simple as that.

Nothing blocks the sanctifying power of God's grace as effectively as the impermeable shell of pride. As Thomas à Kempis wrote, "Know that your love of self hurts you more than anything else in the world." God and the proud are like oil and water—you can shake them up but they will never blend or unite. If holiness implies "blending with God," then pride hampers holiness in a way no other sin can.

Remember all Jesus' diatribes against the pride of the Pharisees. While he showed indulgence toward the weak, he was tough on the self-assured. Think, too, of his frequent warnings to the rich. What is it, really, that hinders the rich man from "entering the kingdom of heaven"? Is it the abundance of material things, or is it not rather the almost overwhelming temptation to place his trust in his riches rather than God?

Humility and trust go hand in hand. God wants us to place our trust in him alone: not in riches or intelligence, not in power or connections, not in personal abilities and know-how. None of these will save us. None of these stands faithfully by us when the going gets tough. All of these things will eventually fail. Humility assures us of our absolute need for God. We need his grace, his mercy, his strength, and the salvation that only he can provide. In the spiritual life, no one picks himself up by his own bootstraps. It is Christ, the Good Shepherd, who lifts us up, places us on his shoulders, and carries us home.

Humility and trust are related in another way too. Humility tempers trust and in turn needs to be tempered by trust. Humility without trust leads to despair. Trust without humility leads to presumption. If we are painfully aware of our sinfulness and misery but unaware of God's overpowering love for us, we have no choice but to despair. We are, in point of fact, much more wretched than we know.

Yet the contrary is also true. If we have absolute trust in God but no knowledge of our own sinfulness and weakness, we easily fall into presumption and take God's goodness for granted. Pride incites us to believe in our own strength in the face of temptation, whereas humility reminds us of our weakness and leads us to a healthy distrust of our own ability to do good. Pride whispers in our ears that we are beyond that—we are "mature" and don't need to exercise the caution of a mere beginner. A healthy distrust of self combined with an even more sturdy trust in God is the recipe for steady growth in the spiritual life.

God's Penchant for Littleness

Our vocation to greatness as sons and daughters of God could appear as contrary to the humility he asks of us. Even our desire for holiness (and humility!) itself could be seen as a form of ambition. Yet not all ambition is evil, and Jesus does not squelch our desire for excellence. He does, however, gently *channel* and *purify* our ambition. He shows us where true greatness lies.

One day Jesus caught the apostles arguing among themselves as to who was the greatest. Jesus did not reprimand the apostles for their ambition; he merely nudged them in the right direction. He placed a little child in their midst and invited them to be like him. "If anyone wants to be first, he must make himself last of all and servant of all" (Mark 9:35). In other words, if you really aspire to greatness—true greatness—learn to serve. If you want to be great, learn to be small. Smallness is not an end in itself, but the means to true greatness.

Over and over again in the Bible God exhibited a special predilection for the little people, a preference to work through the weak. When the Philistine giant Goliath challenged the Israelite camp to send out its finest warrior to face him alone on the battlefield, who went but the shepherd boy David, who could not even handle wearing Saul's heavy armor? When God wanted to castigate the Israelites for their infidelities, he sent a youngster named Jeremiah, who, by his own admission, was just a boy and knew not how to speak (Jer. 1:6).

Moses was a stammerer, Bethlehem, the smallest of the clans of Israel, and Jesus Himself was born in a stable and grew up in the despised hamlet of Nazareth, son of a poor, young girl married to a carpenter. In his public life Jesus chose for apostles twelve coarse, uneducated men and sent them out two by two, like sheep in the midst of wolves, stripping them of even the barest necessities for such a mission: a walking stick, sandals, or a few coins in their pockets.

My own personal favorite is found in the book of Judges and involves a fellow named Gideon (of hotel Bible fame). God sent the poor man out on a nearly impossible quest to muster an army and defeat the occupying Midianites, who held Israel in a reign of terror. To start with, Gideon himself was no military man, but a farm boy, from the weakest clan in Manasseh, and the least in his family (Judg. 6:15). Through great personal effort Gideon managed to mobilize an army of thirty-two thousand men and prepared to do battle.

But God looked at the Israelite army, shook his head, and informed Gideon that they were *too many*. With so many, God said, Israel would take the credit for the battle as if it had won without God's help. So Gideon harangued the army, underscoring the difficulties of the ensuing battle and inviting the weak of heart to go back to their families. In this way, the ranks were cut to only ten thousand soldiers. Still unsatisfied with the large size of the army, God devised a further plan to diminish the troops. He had them drink water from a stream and told Gideon that any who lapped the water like a dog could stay while the rest were to return home. In this way, God whittled the Israelite army down to a mere three hundred men, who subsequently destroyed the immense army of Midian.

This is God's MO. He likes long odds. An even race doesn't seem to present enough of a challenge for him, so he prefers to stack the deck against himself. By tipping the playing field, God reminds us that it is by his strength, not our own, that battles are won. Paul summed up this divine proclivity for littleness in his well-known expression: "God chose what is weak in the world to shame the strong" (1 Cor. 1:27 RSV).

Once we accept Christ's invitation to follow him, we must accept his conditions and expect an uphill battle. That is simply the way God wants it. We will have to work hard. We might as well eliminate the expression "That's not fair!" from our vocabulary right from the get-go, because the Christian life isn't fair and doesn't claim to be. Innocence crucified is hardly the icon of fairness. The playing field will never be level but will always be skewed to our apparent disadvantage. This is God's choice, and we would do well to accept it from the start. The final victory is all the more splendid.

> *The playing field will never be level but will always be skewed to our apparent disadvantage.*

Humility with Others

In the first place, then, humility binds us to the truth of who we are before God. Yet it also deeply affects the way we see and treat other people. If humility with God is tough, humility with others is harder still. It doesn't take much to acknowledge our defects in private to ourselves, but woe to the one who dares to contradict us! Our hackles go up immediately and we defend ourselves tooth and nail.

As we have seen, pride isolates while humility unites. Pride leads us to distrust others, to see them as rivals and to work against rather than with them. One particular expression of pride is our tendency to judge others. We can be remarkably perceptive of others' faults and limitations and just as obtuse when it comes to recognizing our own. Moreover, we are soft on ourselves, always ready to excuse our own faults, and severe with others, attributing the worst possible motives to their actions.

Here the Christian message enjoins us to attend first to ourselves. Jesus warned that I mustn't dare try to remove the speck from my neighbor's eye while I have a log in my own. And he added: "First take the log out of your own eye, and then you will see clearly to take the speck out of your brother's eye" (Matt. 7:5 NASB).

The more aware we are of our own limitations, the more indulgent we will be toward others. Who am I, with all my faults and sins, to judge another? When an adulterous woman was dragged before Jesus for his judgment, he famously invited the one without sin to throw the first stone (the penalty for adultery was death by stoning). Everyone walked away with his tail between his legs. Humility teaches us to look first at our own sins before rushing to judge others'.

Obviously Jesus' indictment against judging others does not preclude judging actions as good or bad. Jesus welcomed prostitutes, but he never welcomed prostitution. He was soft on adulterers, but unyielding on adultery. After forgiving the adulterous woman, in fact, he added: "Go and sin no more." Jesus never welcomed cheating, but he did welcome reformed cheaters. This is not just a matter of semantic hairsplitting. Jesus came to call sinners but to condemn sin, much as a doctor heals sick people but eradicates sickness.

Human nature impels us to seek solutions to our difficulties by having *others* change. How typical in the case of marital difficulties that both spouses are absolutely convinced that the problem lies with the other. And yet the only one I can change is myself, and when I am judged by God it will not be in comparison with other people ("Compared with the bulk of humanity, I am a pretty good person"), but according to what he has given me and what he is asking of me.

Always incisive about such things, this is what Augustine had to say: "But men are hopeless creatures, and the less they concentrate on their own sins, the more interested they become in the sins of others. They seek to criticize, not to correct. Unable to excuse themselves, they are ready to accuse others."

What, after all, was Adam's spontaneous response when caught red-handed eating the forbidden fruit? "It was the woman you put with me; she gave me the fruit, and I ate it" (Gen. 3:12). Not only did Adam quickly shift the blame to his wife, he even insinuated that perhaps God himself had some responsibility in the matter, since he was the one who put her in the garden. And once the spotlight moved to Eve, she, too, quickly passed the buck: "The serpent tricked me, so I ate it." Instead of looking around for someone else to blame, true humility keeps the focus on self and recognizes that we simply haven't lived up to God's love.

We have been disobedient, shallow, self-centered, and cowardly. And in humility we must acknowledge our fault and repeat time and time again with the publican: "Lord, be merciful to me, a sinner." This attitude pleases God, and he immediately comes to our aid. Remember: "God resists the proud and gives his grace to the humble."

Vanity of Vanities

Pride has a little sister named Vanity. She, too, needs to be curbed by humility. We all love to be praised. We love to be recognized for our accomplishments. Yet Jesus invites us time and time again to refer all glory to God. In our good works—fasting, almsgiving, prayer—Jesus warns us to avoid the subtle temptation of impurity of intention, acting "in order to be seen" (Matt. 6:1 RSV).

The Greek word meaning "to be seen" is *theathénai*, from which comes our English word "theater." The theater is where one stands up on stage "in order to be seen." The Greek word for actor is *hypocrités*, from which we take our English word "hypocrite." The hypocrite turns life into a stage, where what matters is to be seen. Jesus warned us sharply to avoid converting our good actions into a stage spectacle looking for applause and recognition. By so doing, we sap our good deeds of their value before God.

Jesus used a very suggestive metaphor to express this sort of humility. He suggested "not to let your right hand know what your left hand is doing" (Matt. 6:3 RSV). He contrasted that with those who parade their good works before others. These "have had their reward" (Matt. 6:2). On the other hand, Jesus was not asking us not to do good but to do good *with the right intention.* Recall that Jesus also invited us to "let your light so shine before men, that they may see your good works and give glory to your Father who is in heaven" (Matt. 5:16 RSV). In other words: do good, but do it for the glory of God, and not in order to be thought well of.

Vanity's preoccupation with others' opinions has two different dimensions, one active and the other passive. Vanity's *active* dimension makes us seek attention and praise, recognition and esteem. It guts the value of our good works through self-seeking. Vanity's *passive* dimension makes us worry about what others will say and think and often keeps us from doing the good we ought to do. This passive dimension—sometimes called "human respect"—stifles the action of the Holy Spirit in our lives and truncates our Christian growth.

Humility serves as a remedy for both dimensions of vanity. By placing us in the presence of God and directing us to please him alone, we avoid both the impure intentions of self-seeking and the fear of ridicule. "The truly humble person will have a genuine desire to be thought little of, and persecuted, and condemned unjustly, even in serious matters. For, if she desires to imitate the Lord, how can she do so better than in this?" (Teresa of Ávila, *Way of Perfection*).

What Jesus asks of us—not just doing the right thing, but doing the right thing for the right reason—is much tougher than a merely external observance of a juridical code. Humility means letting go of our concern for what others think, for their esteem and appreciation. It helps us recognize that everything we have is from God and urges us to direct all our actions to God's glory and not our own.

John the Baptist had a beautiful motto in this regard. "He [Christ] must increase, but I must decrease" (John 3:30 RSV). Above all things, John wanted Christ to shine. He wanted Christ to be loved. He didn't use the gospel for personal profit but in order to help people find their salvation and happiness in Christ. Therefore when his disciples started leaving him to follow Christ, he rejoiced. "The bride is only for the bridegroom," he said (John 3:29). Our role as Christians is to lead souls to Christ and then to humbly step out of the picture. "The friend of the bridegroom, who stands and hears him rejoices greatly because of the bridegroom's voice So this joy of mine has been made full" (John 3:29 NASB).

Getting Small

So if this is the task set before us, how do we get started? How can we become more humble? The first, and perhaps most important step, involves recognizing our need to change. The terrible fact is that we need humility in order to grow in humility. We need to acknowledge our imperfection, and this acknowledgment sets us on the right track to become more humble.

In the 1970s the comedian Steve Martin had a clever little skit called "Let's Get Small," as if getting small were like doing some sort of drug. "Growing" in humility means "getting small," shrinking in importance in our own eyes. The following means may help in this challenge.

PRAYER

As in the case of most things, the most effective means of growing in humility comes through prayer. God can help us become humble if we allow him to, and he is happy when we ask. On the other hand, we had better be ready for his response. In answer to a prayer for humility, God sometimes sends *humiliations* to help us put our lives in perspective. Like a good doctor, he knows the best remedies for what ails us. The key here is to cooperate with his grace rather than resist it. If we recognize God's loving hand in these opportunities, it will help us to accept the prescriptions he offers.

As in the case of most things, the most effective means of growing in humility comes through prayer.

We can exercise humility when we are treated badly, accused of things we did not do, or made to look foolish. Instead of jumping to our own defense in the name of "justice" and "setting the record straight," we can imitate the example Christ left us in his Passion, when "like a lamb that is led to the slaughter, and like a sheep that before its shearers is dumb, so he opened not his mouth" (Isa. 53:7 RSV).

Along with asking for God's intervention, the very act of putting ourselves in God's presence helps us become humble. It's enough to think for a moment with whom we are speaking and who we are before him, to grow in this virtue.

Meditation on God's goodness and our own sins also helps us become more humble. When in the presence of God we contemplate our own nothingness, our weakness and inconstancy in doing good, we obtain a more objective view of ourselves. Who we are before God becomes clear in prayer: we are his children, his handiwork, debtors, and worse still, often ungrateful sinners. Yet we are also precious in his eyes, infinitely loved and cared for. Meditation on the goodness of God and his mercy toward us fills us with admiration and gratitude and inspires us to treat others with the same magnanimity with which God has treated us. The soul that contemplates God and savors him in prayer will never be proud.

REALITY CHECK

When we are tempted to lord it over others, or judge their actions, three simple exercises may help us take a more humble attitude. First, I can remind myself: *If this other person had received the graces I have received, he or she would be much better than I am. After all,*

I have received so much and give back so little. Then again, there are many things I don't know about him/her. Probably if I were in that person's situation, I would handle it much worse. By these reflections, we can teach ourselves to give others the benefit of the doubt and to cut them a little slack.

Another similar exercise also produces good results. If we recall how patient God has been with us, and how many times he has forgiven us, we cannot help but recognize our duty to treat others in the same way. *God has exercised infinite patience with me, how can I deny that to my neighbor?* Christ's parable of the unforgiving debtor makes me shudder. There he spoke of a servant whose immense debt was written off by his master, but who was in turn unable to pardon a far smaller debt of one of his fellow servants. If we are to expect mercy from God, he requires that we be merciful with others. Jesus' words should give us pause: "The amount you measure out is amount you will be given" (Matt. 7:2).

A third reality check can also help us adopt a more humble attitude toward our neighbor, especially those whose goodness is not immediately evident. The exercise consists in trying to look at my neighbor as Christ sees him. Where I see a small-minded, fault-ridden individual, what does Christ see? When Christ gazes on this fellow specimen of humanity that I am tempted to judge or disdain, what thoughts fill his heart?

I know the answer to that question. He looks on my neighbor with intense love. He wants my neighbor—yes, that unpleasant one—to be a saint and to share his life forever in heaven. How can my attitude be any different?

GRATITUDE

Some people are naturally optimistic and always see the "glass half full," where others may see the glass half empty. While our temperaments surely color our view of things, we can also freely choose to focus on the negative or the positive. Focusing on the positive, especially on God's abundant gifts to us, serves as an excellent means of growing more humble.

A fixation on our own struggles and personal endeavors can fuel the myth of the "self-made man." We attribute our successes to smart planning and hard work and feel entitled to the good things we have. There is plenty of truth to this, but it doesn't tell the whole story. Personal responsibility is a good thing and teaches us to be accountable for our actions and their consequences. At the same time, we wouldn't be where we are without God; in fact we wouldn't "be" at all. Even our good actions bear the seal of God's grace.

The habit of gratitude—thanking God for the good things in our lives—helps tip the center of our lives toward God. From an individualistic one-man show, we can shift to a more balanced awareness of God's action in our lives, as well as the important role other people have played in our endeavors. Sincere gratitude toward parents, family, and friends leads to a more humble worldview.

CHRISTIAN LOVE

Humility does not so much consist in thinking less of ourselves as in thinking of ourselves less. We don't become more humble by imposing a negative self-image on ourselves but by forgetting about ourselves entirely. Thus, one of the more effective remedies to pride consists in actively focusing on others and their needs. We have said that humility leads to love, but love also leads to humility. When we apply our creative

Humility does not so much consist in thinking less of ourselves as in thinking of ourselves less.

energies to loving others, the ego is necessarily displaced from the center. Attention to others crowds out our excessive attention to self.

Christian love, or charity, encourages humility in another way too. Since for the proud person "it's all about me," and others are rivals and competitors, rejoicing in others' successes helps us become more humble. Referring to the Christian Church as Christ's body, Paul remarked: "If one member suffers, all suffer together; if one member is honored, all rejoice together" (1 Cor. 12:26 RSV). Charity urges us to lavish praise on others, to lift them up and see them recognized. This spirit of communion, so characteristic of Christian charity, helps us grow in true humility.

SOME PRACTICAL POINTERS FROM MOTHER TERESA

In one of her precious letters to her Missionaries of Charity (October 31, 1966), Mother Teresa of Calcutta offered a few practical tips for growing in humility that are every bit as useful to us as to her own sisters. She remarked that it is our emptiness and lowliness that God needs and not our plenitude and suggested the following simple ways of emptying ourselves:

- Speak as little as possible of oneself.
- Mind one's own business.
- Avoid curiosity.
- Do not want to manage other people's affairs.
- Accept contradiction and correction cheerfully.
- Pass over the mistakes of others.
- Accept blame when innocent.
- Yield to the will of others.
- Accept insults and injuries.
- Accept being slighted, forgotten, and disliked.
- Be kind and gentle even under provocation.
- Do not seek to be specially loved and admired.
- Never stand on one's dignity.
- Yield in discussion even though one is right.
- Choose always the hardest.

(Letter of 31 October 1966)[1]

These simple suggestions hardly require commentary. She wrote them specifically to religious sisters living in community, but they can help any Christian seriously interested in becoming more humble. Again, how easy to see the value of these measures, but how difficult to practice them with any consistency!

As we have seen, humility and faith provide the bedrock and the foundation for our spiritual lives. An unshakeable belief in God combined with a healthy distrust of self gives us a firm grounding upon which to build. This honest assessment of who we are and especially who God is emboldens us for the work that lies ahead. Now only one thing is necessary: a willingness to set out.

Christ calls us and sends us. He calls us out of ourselves, as he called Abraham to leave behind his comfortable homeland of Ur of the Chaldeans and to set out for a new land he had never seen. Moreover, he sends us out to others as apostles, as the Father sent him.

Our response to these challenges demands another eminently Christian virtue: generosity. Our success in this venture depends upon our readiness to give and our courage to go beyond our comfort zones and to embrace the Christian enterprise that Christ holds out to us. What generosity means and how we can attain it is the topic of our next chapter.

CHAPTER 12

Letting Go

Generosity As a Christian Virtue

Give, and there will be gifts for you: a full measure, pressed down, shaken together, and running over, will be poured into your lap; because the amount you measure out is the amount you will be given back.

Luke 6:38

J esus dished out compliments sparingly in the Gospels, so when he did, we should pay close attention. One such occasion was the so-called widow's mite (Mark 12:41–44). Sitting opposite the temple treasury, Jesus and his disciples watched as many wealthy people deposited large sums. Yet none of this seemed to impress Jesus. When a poor widow dropped in a couple of pennies, however, Jesus sat up and took notice, calling the apostles' attention to her gift. She had put in more than all the rest—he said—since they had given from their *surplus* whereas she had given from her *want*. The materiality of the gift seems to matter less than the spirit with which it is given. "More," in Christ's eyes, transcends simple quantitative superiority and looks to the generosity behind the gift.

The word *generosity* comes from the Latin *genus* and speaks of one who is of good lineage. It means nobility, excellence, liberality, and magnanimity expressed especially in one's willingness to give what is one's own. Generosity is opposed to tightfistedness and miserliness, just as Bob Cratchit's openhandedness, even in his poverty, stood in stark contrast to Ebenezer Scrooge's stinginess. Generosity means ampleness in giving and even giving beyond one's means. It is lavishness, largesse, and a refusal to measure out one's offering.

Why does God like generosity so much? Because he likes love, and real love is generous. Love does not hold back and knows no limits. Saint Augustine famously said that the measure of love is to love without measure. Love does not calculate how much it can spare or what it can comfortably part with. It sees a need and meets it. It gives without counting the cost or calculating the personal price.

Generosity fails not when we measure out too little but in the *act* of measuring. When the widow threw two copper coins into the temple treasury, she didn't give two coins and keep the rest; she threw in all she had. They could have been two or two hundred, since she didn't count them out but simply emptied her purse of its entire contents. That is why the proper categories of love are not *little* or *much* but rather *all* or *nothing*. The widow, after all, didn't give *much* but she did give *all*.

> *Generosity fails not when we measure out too little but in the* act *of measuring.*

Saints throughout history have appreciated that a generous spirit matters more than the quantity of one's giving. Saint Thérèse of Lisieux, popularly known as the "Little Flower," stumbled upon this profound truth at a very young age. The value of a gift, she understood, comes not from its material price, but from the love it bears within. Hence her endearing motto: "The smallest things with the greatest love."

Mary of Bethany anointed Jesus' feet with costly perfume—pure aromatic nard—and dried them with her hair (John 12:1–8). To do so, she didn't count out a certain number of drops or even pour out a generous quantity into her hand. Rather than remove the top, she *broke the jar*, making it impossible to save any of the precious perfume, and simply poured the whole contents over his feet.

Judas, who was standing nearby, was scandalized. He quickly tallied the cost of this prodigality. An exorbitant sum—three hundred days' wages—was his experienced appraisal of the expense. For Mary, the calculus meant nothing, for there was never a question in her mind of how much to give and how much to hold back for herself. How starkly these two approaches contrast each other: the one who pours out, the other that stands and calculates.

Love deals only in terms of all or none. Love cannot hold back, cannot divide, cannot calculate, since by its nature it pours itself out entirely as a single, whole gift. For love, *little* and *much* have no meaning, since love deals only in terms of *all* or *none*. Anything else is not love.

Traits of Generosity

Generosity has four key characteristics that help explain its beauty: *abundance, gratuitousness, joy in giving*, and *self-emptying*.

1. ABUNDANCE

As in every other aspect of our Christian lives, in the area of generosity Christ is not only teacher but also model. Have you ever asked yourself why at Cana Jesus produced far more wine than the guests could possibly drink? Scripture scholars estimate that the quantity of wine (good wine!) that Jesus made exceeded six hundred bottles. Why, when multiplying loaves and fishes, did Jesus generate twelve basketsful of leftovers, above and beyond what the hungry crowds were able to consume? He is no God of measured love or exact fits; he is a God of lavishness and abundance.

Everywhere around us we see examples of God's abundant generosity. Why is it that God created an entire universe for mankind, when a single planet would have sufficed? Why this infinity of space and stars and galaxies? And what we observe in the material realm is also mirrored in the spiritual realm. God's rewards infinitely outweigh our merits, and his bountiful mercy washes away our sinfulness as the abundance of the sea washes away small drops of water. Paul exclaimed that "where sin increased, grace abounded all the more" (Rom. 5:20 RSV). Experience shows that God will never let himself be outdone in generosity and "gives him the Spirit without reserve" (John 3:34).

2. GRATUITOUSNESS

Generosity is not repayment for services rendered, or the just desserts merited by one who has done well. By its very nature generosity goes beyond obligation. As a quintessential Christian virtue, generosity transcends mere justice (giving what is due) and freely offers more than what is required. Jesus asked for this generosity from his disciples, reminding them that God treated them in the same way: "Freely you received, freely give" (Matt. 10:8 NASB).

God's goodness to us is always gratuitous. He created us, drew us out of nothingness into existence, before we had the chance to merit anything at all. Life was a free gift we did nothing to deserve. Yet we see this generosity still more in his mercy. Not only did we not merit his love, we have often merited punishment and death.

When God became man in the Incarnation, he came to a world that had rejected him. And he died for us while we were rebels. As Saint Paul reminds us, "Why, one will hardly die for a righteous man—though perhaps for a good man one will dare even to die. But God shows his love for us in that while we were yet sinners Christ died for us" (Rom. 5:7–8 RSV). He continues to hold out his hand to us, offering us reconciliation and friendship despite our frequent refusals and habitual backsliding. He calls us to exercise the same benevolence and patience not only with our friends and those who treat us well, but with our enemies.

3. JOY IN GIVING

The generous person does not grumpily part with his goods as if with each gift the dentist were extracting a molar. He gives joyfully, focused more on pleasing the receiver than on the personal cost. In fact, the personal cost can even augment his joy, as when a lover derives more pleasure in giving a precious gift than in giving a cheap trinket. Paul said, "Each one must do as he has made up his mind, not reluctantly or under compulsion, for God loves a cheerful giver" (2 Cor. 9:7 RSV). A "cheerful giver" pleases the recipient both with his gift and with the joyful attitude that accompanies it.

The relationship between generosity and joy doesn't end here. Generosity not only connotes joy, it also *causes* joy to those who practice it. Selfishness and greed close the soul upon itself and bring anxiety and sadness. Remember the rich young man who went away sad when Christ asked him to sell his possessions and follow him.

On the other hand, openheartedness and munificence beget lightness of spirit and joy. Jesus himself said that "there is more happiness in giving than in receiving" (Acts 20:35). Why is there so much sadness in the world, even among those who lack no worldly goods? Many times the reason can be sought in the selfishness that turns us in on ourselves and closes us to the needs of others.

4. SELF-EMPTYING

For the generous, mere giving becomes *self-giving*. What is generosity if not the willingness to give beyond what is comfortable or pleasant? Generosity cuts deep and draws not from our surplus, but from our necessity, from our very selves. The widow's gift meant self-denial, since she was depriving herself in order to give to others. The generous person is always prepared to share what he or she has, be it little or much.

Jesus' greatest testimony of generosity is not found in his many miracles, as wonderful as they are. It is found in the Incarnation and in the Cross. Though he was God, Jesus "emptied himself, taking the form of a servant, being born in the likeness of men. And being found in human form he humbled himself and became obedient unto death, even death on a cross" (Phil. 2:7–8 RSV). Unwilling to send a messenger in his place, to "give from his surplus," God himself took on our humanity.

And since love can never be satisfied until it has given everything, Jesus could not be satisfied until he "showed how perfect his love was" (John 13:1). Only when he had poured out his very life could Jesus exclaim: "It is finished!" His gift of generous love in offering his life for us became salvific love and won for us eternal life. The manifestation of God's generosity continues in the sending of the Holy Spirit, where God reveals himself not only as giver but as *self-gift*.

What Do You Give a God Who Has Everything?

As beautiful as generosity is when we see it in others, it scares us. It easily gets out of control and we don't know where it will end. A God who demands all is not easily satisfied. If we give a little, he will undoubtedly ask for more. We are afraid that if we open the door a crack, he will move in like an intrusive mother-in-law and start rearranging everything in our lives, and our comfortable, ordered little worlds will be thrown into complete disarray.

As beautiful as generosity is when we see it in others, it scares us.

Remember the parable of the talents (Matt. 25:14–31). The servant who buried his one talent in the ground offered his master this excuse: "I was afraid of you, because you are a *severe man*; you take up what you did not lay down, and reap what you did not sow." And the master did not deny the accusation; in fact he used it as evidence against the servant's action. "You knew that I was a severe man. . . .

Why then did you not put my money into the bank, and at my coming I should have collected it with interest" (Luke 19:21–23 RSV, emphasis mine). Yes, God is terribly demanding. He doesn't want a lot; he wants everything.

Why does God ask this of us when he has everything already? It hardly seems fair. He could get along perfectly well without our gifts. As he said in the Psalms, "I shall take no young bull out of your house nor male goats out of your folds. For every beast of the forest is Mine, the cattle on a thousand hills . . . If I were hungry I would not tell you, for the world is Mine, and all it contains" (Ps. 50:9–10, 12 NASB). If God does not need our gifts, why does he ask?

Moreover, sometimes he can be incredibly tactless in his requests. He frequently doesn't ask in the most opportune moment. Many times he makes requests when we least feel like giving, or after he has already asked so much that the last thing we feel like is giving more. The saying "When it rains, it pours" seems especially applicable in our relationship with God. It has often seemed to me that God has been most demanding with me when I am sick, or tired, or have already pushed myself as far as I think I can go. Here, both my faith and my generosity are tested, but how beautiful the fruit when I am able to say yes!

We may wonder at God's "severity" seen throughout the books of the Bible. Why did God rejoice in a gift of two small coins that meant life or death to a poor widow but would only be lost in the temple administrative bureaucracy? Why ask Abraham to sacrifice his only son, Isaac, whom he loved, the son of the God's own promise? (Gen. 22:1–8). Why demand of the indigent widow of Zarephath that she give bread and water to the prophet Elijah, when she didn't have enough for herself and her son? (1 Kings 17:8–16). Why deprive a boy of his lunch—a few loaves and fishes—when they clearly are insufficient for a huge crowd? (John 6:5–13).

I don't want to seem disrespectful, but God's actions almost seem to fit the prophet Nathan's description of the unjust rich man, who was unwilling to take a sheep from his plentiful flocks to prepare for a visitor and instead took his poor neighbor's only little lamb, which meant everything to him (2 Sam. 12:1–4). Isn't God like the rich man who has everything yet demands from poor humans that they give up the little they have?

God is undoubtedly very generous, but again, he is also very demanding. He gives, but he also takes. And he not only takes, he takes the best: the firstborn male, without blemish, the firstfruits of the harvest, the first place in our hearts. Why?

The answer can be found only by remembering our conclusions in chapter 4 regarding God's will. God is love, and everything he does proceeds from love and manifests his love. If God asks it can only be because he loves us. He desires us to flourish and shows us the path to do so.

1. God Asks in Order to Give

Remember Christ's meeting with the Samaritan woman at the well? Rather than offer her all sorts of good things, Jesus opened their exchange with a request. He asked her for a drink. Only after engaging her interest did he announce to her: "If you knew the gift of God, and who it is that is saying to you, 'Give me a drink,' you would have asked him, and he would have given you living water" (John 4:10 RSV). He often asks in order to reward us. He longs to give us heaven, and he offers us opportunities to choose it and be worthy of it. As Paul wrote in 2 Corinthians 9:6, "Thin sowing means thin reaping; the more you sow, the more you reap."

Moreover, sometimes we discover the value of what is offered to us only once we have given ourselves. Often children recognize the value of their parents' sacrifices only when they become parents themselves. When we give love, we overcome our selfishness and become more able to receive and appreciate love.

2. GOD WANTS TO BE OUR TREASURE

He wants us to discover for ourselves how much his friendship is worth. As long as many "loves" clutter our lives, God remains just another book on the shelf, another pastime

He doesn't want to be our pastime, but our passion.

among many. And he doesn't want to be our pastime, but our passion. Again, this does not stem from some divine megalomania, but from *our* need for God in order for *us* to be truly happy. We are made for him and only he can truly and fully satisfy us.

In the Gospels Christ used strong language to convey this: his disciples must leave everything, turn their backs on father and mother, brothers and sisters, and even on themselves to become his followers. But through this generosity and detachment from created things, these very things cease to be obstacles and take their rightful places in our lives.

3. GOD WANTS OUR HEARTS

God asks us for things not because he wants these *things* (for which he has no need whatsoever), but because he wants our *hearts*, he wants *us*. Remember the eloquent words of Jesus as envisioned by Thomas à Kempis in *The Imitation of Christ*: "What more do I ask than that you give yourself entirely to Me? I care not for anything else you may give Me, for I seek not your gift but you. Just as it would not be enough for you to have everything if you did not have Me, so whatever you give cannot please Me if you do not give yourself." The more we give of ourselves to God, the more we find ourselves and the reason for our existence.

4. GOD WANTS US TO LEARN TO LOVE

Finally, God asks for our generosity so that we learn to love. His request—and our response—stretches our hearts and makes them capacious, able to receive the gifts he has in store for us and more able to love. But love does not come naturally, because love means dying to ourselves, and we naturally tend to self-preservation; love means preferring others to ourselves, and we naturally prefer ourselves to others. God's requests for generosity teach us what love is about, and once we have experienced it, we begin to understand the joy that only selfless love can bring.

Though God wants everything, he accepts our fumbling attempts at generosity and patiently leads us, little by little, to higher degrees of self-giving. By seeing for ourselves that there *is* more happiness in giving than in receiving, we are encouraged to climb the ladder of generosity, rung by rung.

The Degrees of Generosity: the Divine Beggar

Many high schools host yearly fund-raising auctions and some poor students receive the unsavory charge of collecting items to be auctioned off. They go from store to store, asking for donations to benefit their schools, with varying degrees of success. Christ, too, comes knocking at the door of our hearts, as a beggar asking for a handout—more time, more attention, more care for the "least of his brethren." He doesn't commandeer, he asks. He doesn't compel, he invites. I imagine that the different responses Christ receives from souls resemble those received by students asking shopkeepers for auction prizes.

Responses vary, but they can be broken down into four basic categories. Some shopkeepers give a peremptory "No" and shoo prospective beneficiaries away. Though they may not slam the door, their reply leaves little room for doubt that this is their meaning. And even when the response is couched in more genteel forms or accompanied by explanations about the flagging economy, low liquidity, or poor fiscal timing, the end result is the same, and the beggar still goes away with empty hands.

Sadly, God's advances have often been unwelcome. When Jesus was to be born in Bethlehem, there was no room for his parents at the inn. Later in the Gospels Christ spoke of invited guests who made excuses for absenting themselves from his banquet. One had bought some land, another had acquired several yoke of oxen, and a third had just gotten married. For one reason or another, none accepted the Master's invitation. All of us have had the unfortunate experience of saying "no" to Christ on one occasion or another. Yet, happily, Christ often persists in his requests instead of writing us off after a first refusal. Despite our stubbornness and spiritual lethargy, he pursues us, like a good shepherd tracking down a beloved stray.

A second response to the Lord could be likened to throwing a bone to a whining dog to keep him quiet. When approached for a donation, some shopkeepers will look about for a worthless bauble or a piece of unwanted merchandise that has been sitting around collecting dust for years and dispatch the fund-raiser with this trifle. The shopkeeper can congratulate himself on clearing his store of an unsightly item while simultaneously taking a tax deduction for his donation.

How often our responses to Christ resemble this attitude! He wants a lot, and we give him a little. We ease our consciences by avoiding a direct "no" while getting off with as little personal cost as possible. To keep God at bay, we often give him a little something and demand that he take it or leave it.

A third sort of response moves farther up the generosity scale. Instead of tossing the beggar a worthless knickknack, some shop clerks will make an effort to offer something truly worthwhile. They look about for a decent, moderately priced item and bequeath it to the auction. Maybe it's not the most expensive item in the emporium, but the donation represents a sincere desire to support the fund-raising effort. If this were the typical response, our fund-raiser would quickly complete his task and fill the auction hall with worthy articles.

Sometimes we treat Christ's requests in this fashion. We sincerely strive to give him something worthwhile and pleasing. We don't offer our leftovers but choose from among our best stock: our time, our love, our work. Perhaps Christ and his interests don't occupy the first place in our lives, but he is important to us and we endeavor to take our friendship with him seriously.

A fourth and final type of response takes generosity to a whole different level. A rare sort of shop keeper, perhaps in a transport of generosity, may simply grant *carte blanche* to the one seeking donations and allow him to choose whatever he wants from the store. Imagine the look on the student's face when the shopkeeper says: "Go ahead. Take whatever you want." This level of generosity requires tremendous trust and tremendous detachment. We trust that we will not be cheated in our offer. We are detached in that anything—no holds barred—that the student chooses, we are willing to give.

How rare this attitude is in man's dealings with God! We almost always put conditions on our offers. We prefer to be the ones to decide what he can take and what he must leave. Few are willing to sign a blank check and place it in his hands!

Yet above and beyond these four levels of generosity stands a still higher level, one of a different sort. How can there be anything higher that an open offer to take *any* item in the store? Imagine that when the shopkeeper receives his young student, on looking closer he realizes that it is really the shop owner's son. On offering him the run of the store the shopkeeper knows that he is giving nothing, since the young man has a right to whatever he wants. The shopkeeper is just a steward, the manager of the business, but he doesn't own the merchandise.

Something like this happens when we come to grips with our own status as stewards who owe everything to God. We don't feel like *benefactors* but *beneficiaries*, since he owns the store and we just work there. When we give to him, we are returning what he gave us. He could simply take, but he prefers to ask and be given.

Where the Rubber Hits the Road

Important as it is, this theoretical discussion about generosity and its degrees doesn't tell the whole story. We are left with the pressing questions: *What does all this mean for me on a practical level? How am I supposed to live out the generosity that God asks of me?* One thing is to want to be generous, another thing is to succeed in being generous in a concrete way.

The answer could take many directions, but I would like to underscore three key areas of generosity toward God and others. We are called to be generous especially with our *treasure*, our *talents*, and our *time*.

1. OUR TREASURE

Even though God doesn't need our possessions, we've seen that he identifies with "the least of his brethren," who do have very real material needs. Christ's words at the Last Judgment couldn't be clearer: "I was hungry and you gave me food. I was thirsty and you gave me drink" (Matt. 25:35 RSV). Sharing with those less fortunate than ourselves offers a practical channel for our desire to be generous. Just as love cannot be reduced to good intentions, so our benevolence must be expressed in *beneficence*: active assistance to those in need. After all, we are all stewards of the goods we possess, and our surplus is meant to supply for others' want. See 2 Corinthians 8:13–15 (RSV), where Paul wrote:

> I do not mean that others should be eased and you burdened, but that as a matter of equality your abundance at the present time should supply their want, so that their abundance many supply your want, that there may be equality. As it is written, "He who gathered much had nothing over, and he who gathered little had no lack."

An ancient tradition recommends the practice of tithing, of giving a tenth of our income to the Church for its upkeep and to meet the needs of the poor. Paul told us that a "laborer deserves his wages" and that "the Lord commanded that those who proclaim the gospel should get their living by the gospel" (1 Tim. 5:18 RSV; 1 Cor. 9:14 RSV). Our pastors and those who work full time in the service of the people of God deserve our active support, both in our prayers and in our material contributions.

2. OUR TALENTS

Generosity extends beyond writing checks and taking old clothes to the shelter, however. Along with our material possessions, each of us has received many talents and qualities that are useful not only to ourselves, but to the whole community. Sharing our abilities and expertise with others furnishes another outlet for Christian charity and opens up a broad horizon where generosity can take shape. As Paul wrote, "Having gifts that differ according to the grace given to us, let us use them: if prophecy, in proportion to our faith; if service, in our serving; he who teaches, in his teaching; he who exhorts, in his exhortation; he who contributes, in liberality; he who gives aid, with zeal; he who does acts of mercy, with cheerfulness" (Rom. 12:6–8 RSV).

Along with these spiritual qualities, the abilities of draftsmen, attorneys, dentists, seamstresses, and chefs all have practical utility for many people who cannot always afford professional rates.

3. OUR TIME

A third area for active generosity is the gift of our time. Time is perhaps the most precious commodity we have, since it is so very limited. Yet it is also what people desperately need. A willing ear to listen to another's woes, stopping to smile or exchange greetings rather than hurrying by, calling someone on the phone to wish him or her a happy birthday, visiting a sick person in the hospital—all of these and many other selfless gifts of time change the world for the better, one gesture at a time. Though it is often the most costly of gifts, it is also the most appreciated.

Generosity with our time applies to our relationship with God as well. How often the hour we give him for Sunday worship seems like a heavy burden, when we easily spend many hours a week lounging in front of the television, reading the newspaper, or surfing on the Internet. We always have time for our own projects and hobbies, yet we measure out time for God with an eyedropper! A practical way to be generous with God is to make more room for him in our lives: more room for prayer, more attention to his inspirations, more gestures of love and gratitude.

To sum up these practical suggestions, generosity leads us to make a firm resolution never to say "no" to God: Whatever he may ask, no matter how tough or unpleasant, I will never deny him anything. No matter what guise he comes dressed in—a homeless person, an irritable in-law, or a simple grocery clerk—I will have time for him and be attentive to his needs.

Most often generosity makes itself present not in the once-in-a-lifetime martyr moments, but in the daily constancy that our Christian life demands, and in the barely perceptible, incremental increases in self-abandonment that God tends to ask of us as life progresses.

Part IV

GETTING DOWN TO BRASS TACKS

I f you have read this far, chances are that you are champing at the bit, ready to get to work on your spiritual life. In fact, no doubt as you have been reading you have thought a lot about your own experience and where you want to go with your life. The challenges and adventures of the spiritual world open up new perspectives on the focus our lives should take. Now it's time to model your life on Christ's and shape your decisions according to the scale of values and priorities offered by your Christian faith.

The big question now is: where do you go from here? Obviously one way to respond involves applying the insights you may have gleaned from your reading thus far. Readjusting objectives to center more on holiness of life by imitating Christ especially in his charity and attention to God's will; opening yourself to the grace of God through prayer, the sacraments, and the inspirations of the Holy Spirit; cooperating more effectively with his grace by practicing faith, humility, generosity, and self-denial: all of these resolutions will contribute effectively to making your life more Christian, and immensely more fruitful and satisfying.

Getting more concrete still, we need to recognize the obstacles and enemies we will face in our spiritual work and also take stock of other specific tools that can help our good intentions become realities, and our aspirations become achievements. They will help coordinate and orient your spiritual work to make it more effective. This final part of the book first addresses the issue of our spiritual enemies, calling them by name and sizing them up.

The following three chapters examine practical tools that make our spiritual work accessible and effective. The first deals with a concept called *spiritual direction* (also known as *discipleship*), the centuries-old practice of enlisting an experienced person to guide you in your spiritual work. The second chapter explains another helpful exercise, that of drafting a personalized spiritual program to help you concentrate your spiritual efforts in a single direction, to avoid dispersion and maximize results. The third chapter takes a slight outward turn and focuses on the active *apostolate* as a necessary complement to your work at personal holiness, and a channel to make your love for others more real and dynamic.

In describing the different virtues that come into play in the spiritual life, I have often employed the expression "spiritual work," and

Holiness is not for the faithhearted.

work it is. Despite its attractiveness, holiness is not for the fainthearted. It demands a real commitment and active desire. Dilettantes may swoon with admiration and wax rhapsodic about the wonders of the Christian life, but they will never leave the starting gate. Only those prepared to change what needs to be changed and to labor with constancy—despite the inevitable falls and setbacks—will make real progress in the spiritual life and enjoy its fruits.

The measures described here provide a useful structure to bolster our willpower and support us in moments of disorientation or despondency. No one can go it alone for long in the spiritual life. Thankfully the Church offers a wealth of resources to accompany and strengthen us in our spiritual pilgrimage. Let's examine them.

CHAPTER 13

Enemy at the Gates

A Dose of Christian Realism

For our struggle is not against flesh and blood, but against the rulers, against the powers, against the world forces of this darkness, against the spiritual forces of wickedness in the heavenly places.

Ephesians 6:12 NASB

The spiritual life is not just about you and God. It's not even just about you, God, and other people. The reason we so often fail to live up to our good resolutions, the reason holiness seems like an uphill battle, the reason even good people so easily sour to the spiritual life, is that we have enemies working against us.

Now before you close the book, thinking I have crossed the threshold of conspiratorial ravings, I would invite you to consider what Christ said about this. Recall his very first parable (Matt. 13:1–9). He compared himself to a sower going out to scatter good seed, yet by his own admission, most of that seed bore no yield. Some of it fell on a footpath, where birds carried it away, which Jesus compared to the devil snatching away our good intentions before they could bear fruit. Other seed fell on rocky ground and failed to penetrate the soil—this Jesus likened to an initial enthusiasm that withers in the face of difficulties. Some seed, he said, fell in a thorn patch and began to grow, but the thorns and weeds choked it, just as the worries and cares of our busy agendas can suffocate our spiritual lives.

Why all this failure? Obviously the seed was good; after all, Jesus compared it to God's Word. Many times the intentions of the hearers were also good, and they sincerely wanted to know what God was offering and to make room for him in their lives. True, we could simply say that they didn't want it badly enough. They didn't work hard enough. Yet neither does this explanation tell the whole story.

Christian tradition speaks consistently of three enemies that beset man's efforts to become holy. These are the devil, the flesh, and the world. These "enemies" of God did not spring up as medieval myths but are all found in the New Testament. Any serious effort to grow in the spiritual life needs to take them into account, since we are called not only to work, but to warfare (Eph. 6:11–13). This chapter will look at these enemies a little more closely and propose some means of overcoming them.

We are called not only to work, but to warfare.

The Enemies of Holiness

The Devil

According to published surveys, most people today don't believe in the devil. At best he would be an abstract personification of evil; at worst, an invented bogeyman foisted on past generations to keep them in line and now fully superseded in a less-gullible time. Modern men and women like to consider themselves more "mature" than their forbears and think that denial of the devil and acceptance of personal responsibility for one's life necessarily go hand in hand.

No matter what your personal thoughts may be concerning the devil, one thing is clear: Jesus believed. He spoke of Satan as "a liar and the father of lies" and a "murderer" (John 8:44 RSV). The Gospels describe Jesus being tempted by the devil to deviate from the mission the Father had given him (Matt. 4:1–11; Mark 1:12–13; Luke 4:1–13). Many of Jesus' teachings include references to the devil, and the existence of both the devil and other demons is taken for granted throughout the New Testament.

Now that fact alone will not convince everyone, but for most Christians it will be decisive. Over the centuries the Christian Church has never doubted the existence of the devil and the reality of his work in the world.

Though popular representations of the devil often depict him as a red-clad man with horns and tail, lurking about with pitchfork in hand, Christian tradition understands him to be a spiritual being, a fallen angel. Together with other angels, Lucifer (the name means "light-bearer") rebelled against God and was condemned to hell. The very first pages of the Bible speak of the devil as a tempter, the ancient serpent that seduced Adam and Eve and led them to distrust and disobey God (Gen. 3:1–15). As God's enemy, he constantly strives to separate human beings from their Creator and to win them over for himself.

The devil continues to work to foil God's plans. He hates God and all that God loves. In Peter's words, "Your adversary the devil prowls around like a roaring lion, seeking some one to devour. Resist him, firm in your faith" (1 Pet. 5:8–9 RSV). Though we must reckon with his destructive activity in our lives, we can take consolation from our knowledge that he is merely a creature whose actions are limited by God. In this regard the Catholic Catechism states:

> The power of Satan is . . . not infinite. He is only a creature, powerful from the fact that he is pure spirit, but still a creature. He cannot prevent the building up of God's reign. Although Satan may act in the world out of hatred for God

and his kingdom in Christ Jesus, and although his action may cause grave injuries—of a spiritual nature and, indirectly, even of a physical nature—to each man and to society, the action is permitted by divine providence which with strength and gentleness guides human and cosmic history. It is a great mystery that providence should permit diabolical activity, but "we know that in everything God works for good with those who love him."

He can do no more in our lives than God allows, and God's grace is always superior to the devil's influence.

Moreover, the devil may tempt, but he cannot make us sin. Christian realism invites us to avoid two extremes: attributing an almost divine power to the devil and thus living in constant fear, and going about our business as if the devil didn't exist and wasn't active in the world.

In his book *The Screwtape Letters*, the Christian apologist C. S. Lewis masterfully described the workings of the devil and the nature of his temptations. The better you know what the devil hopes to achieve in your life, the better you can unmask his activity and take the proper steps to resist him. He lives in lies and darkness and hates the light. Shining light on his works and temptations already strips them of much of their effectiveness. What does the devil hope to accomplish in your life? If you know that, you can work against him. In a nutshell, the following are five of the devil's greatest aims in dealing with human beings.

The better you know what the devil hopes to achieve in your life, the better you can unmask his activity and take the proper steps to resist him.

1. *Sin*. The devil's final objective is always the definitive loss of souls. He wants you separated from God on earth and in eternity. Sin leads to spiritual death, whereas Christ is life (see Rom 6:23;

James 1:15). What poison is to the body, sin is to the soul. The devil wants you to try the poison, become addicted to the poison, and eventually to die from a lethal dose. And even if he can merely keep you sick and infirm, he will have you always a step away from death. If somehow he can make you a "dealer" to share the poison with others, all the better. All his other wiles and seductions have this as their final aim: your spiritual destruction and the destruction of as many others as possible.

2. *Mediocrity and complacency.* We are called to be very holy—saints, in fact—so the devil likes nothing more than to convince us that we are good enough already, maybe even "too good." He tries to convince us that we are already better than most people and cautions us not to overdo it. He seduces us into lowering our guard, relaxing our efforts, and "taking it easy." *Why all this strenuous climbing? Sit down and enjoy the view!* He endeavors to paint a life of holiness as boring, unattainable, unbearably difficult, and an all-around drag. Especially when he sees you enthusiastic and motivated, he will try to lessen your fervor and induce you to follow an easier road.

3. *Discouragement.* Nothing saps spiritual energy like discouragement. It leads to inactivity and ultimately to despair, two results that the devil delights in. Especially after a fall, the devil persuades us to wallow in self-pity, like a boxing coach telling his man to stay down in the ring. The devil paints everything black and instead of looking to God's mercy and grace, he makes us focus on our own misery. He wants us to throw in the towel and give up the fight, as Maximilian Kolbe writes: "Whenever you feel guilty, even if it is because you have consciously committed a sin, a serious sin, something you have kept doing many, many times, never let the devil deceive you by allowing him to discourage you" (*Stronger Than Hatred: A Collection of Spiritual Writings*).

Being a consummate liar, the devil often employs a thoroughly underhanded tactic. Before we sin he downplays its importance and emphasizes how attractive sin is. Once we have ceded to the temptation, however, he changes his tune and becomes our accuser, pointing his finger and telling us how wretched we are and how unforgivable our sin. Anything to keep us away from God and focused on ourselves!

4. *Self-righteousness.* The devil loves extremes and will always push us to exaggerate. If he cannot convince us to wallow in our misery, he will flatter us into thinking we are better than we are. He minimizes our faults and exaggerates our virtues. He would love for us to fall into self-righteousness, the certainty of our own moral superiority. The less aware we are of our own need for mercy, the less likely we are to exercise mercy with others. Self-righteousness is a daughter of pride and leads us to be indulgent with ourselves and severe with others. Suddenly everything seems so clear to us, and everyone else appears incompetent. We start lamenting that our Church leaders are a useless bunch of dolts and the minister a well-intentioned but hopelessly backward fellow. If only we were running the show!

5. *Apostolic inactivity.* A wise, anonymous maxim, often misattributed to the British political philosopher Edmund Burke, reads: "All that is necessary for the triumph of evil is that good men do nothing." That is certainly the case with Christianity, and the devil knows it. What would have happened if, after Christ's resurrection, Peter, James, and John had simply packed it in and returned to fishing in Galilee? No one would have faulted them for this omission, but the spread of Christianity would have jerked to a near-halt.

Again, in his love for extremes, if the devil can't make you fall into self-righteousness he will push you toward false humility, so that you don't dare share your Christianity with others. "Be good, but keep it to yourself." "Who are you to preach?" All those graces, all those talents you have received, the devil wants to see barren and atrophied.

If these are the devil's plans for you, what can you do to counteract them? As we've seen, Jesus told his disciples in the garden of Gethsemane, "Watch and pray that you may not enter into temptation; the spirit indeed is willing, but the flesh is weak" (Matt. 26:41 RSV). The dynamic duo of vigilance and prayer are the best defense against Satan's ploys. Never think you are strong, but then again, never doubt the infinite strength

Never think you are strong, but then again, never doubt the infinite strength of God's grace.

of God's grace. Alone you can do nothing; with Him you can do anything (Mark 10:27; Luke 18:27; Phil. 4:13). Remember, too, that the devil isn't the focus of your spiritual work, Christ is.

THE FLESH

Critics often accuse Christianity of hating the human body. This unfair criticism is based in part on a popular misinterpretation of Paul's writings regarding the opposition between the "flesh" and the "spirit." "Flesh" here does not simply mean the human body but refers to the downward pull of our baser instincts. Despite the length of the text, it is worth quoting Paul in full:

> But I say, walk by the Spirit, and do not gratify the desires of the flesh. For the desires of the flesh are against the Spirit, and the desires of the Spirit are against the flesh; for these are opposed to each other, to prevent you from doing what you would. But if you are led by the Spirit you are not under the law. Now the works of the flesh are plain: fornication, impurity, licentiousness, idolatry, sorcery, enmity, strife, jealousy, anger, selfishness, dissension, party spirit, envy, drunkenness, carousing, and the like. I warn you, as I warned you before, that those who do such things shall not inherit the kingdom of God. But the fruit of the Spirit is love, joy, peace, patience, kindness, goodness, faithfulness, gentleness, self-control; against such there is no law. And those who belong to Christ Jesus have crucified the flesh

with its passions and desires. If we live by the Spirit, let us
also walk by the Spirit.

(Galatians 5:16–25 RSV)

Christians affirm that all created reality is good, and the human
person—body and soul—is especially good. God made all things
good, and good they are. At the same time, man's first sin disrupted
God's plan for man and brought disorder to the original harmony
existing in man's interior. Heirs to original sin, we are broken beings. This disorder profoundly influences every aspect of our spiritual and moral lives. As a result of original sin, all of human life has
become a dramatic struggle between good and evil, between light
and darkness. As Paul says, we find ourselves inclined to do things
we are ashamed of and avoiding what we know we should do.

Perhaps the most significant contribution of the idea of original
sin to our spiritual lives comes from the bracing realism it imposes
on our spiritual work. Both our knowledge and our freedom were
darkened by the sin of our first parents. Man is still good, indeed
very good, yet he is not Jean-Jacques Rousseau's *bon sauvage*, cor-
rupted only by the external influence of society. He bears the seeds
of corruption within himself. Because of original sin, all of us tend
toward inordinate self-love and virtue often feels foreign to us.

In our spiritual and moral lives we must come to grips with our
condition as fallen creatures, taking inventory of strengths and weaknesses. We must not behave or theorize as if we were not fallen, did
not tend "naturally" to sin, due to concupiscence. Indeed, we are
weaker than we think. A program of diet and exercise designed for a
healthy person differs substantially from a regimen drafted for the ill
or infirm. In the same way our spiritual work must take into account
the inordinate pull of the "flesh" away from what God intends for us.

That giant of the spiritual life, Saint Paul, described in vivid detail the interior division he experienced in his own life. In this well-

known passage he speaks of the frustration of not being able to accomplish the good that he wills because of another law "at war with the law of my mind."

> We know that the law is spiritual; but I am carnal, sold under sin. I do not understand my own actions. For I do not do what I want, but I do the very thing I hate. Now if I do what I do not want, I agree that the law is good. So then it is no longer that I do it, but sin which dwells within me. For I know that nothing good dwells within me, that is, in my flesh. I can will what is right, but I cannot do it. For I do not do the good I want, but the evil I do not want is what I do. Now if I do what I do not want, it is no longer I that do it, but sin which dwells within me. So I find it to be a law that when I want to do right, evil lies close at hand. For I delight in the law of God, in my inmost self, but I see in my members another law at war with the law of my mind and making me captive to the law of sin which dwells in my members.
>
> (Romans 7:14–23 RSV)

Despite his brutal realism, Paul never lost hope, never doubted for a minute Christ's promise that his grace would be sufficient. Paul's evident frailty did not keep him from staunchly moving forward with his hope firmly placed in Christ.

THE WORLD

The final enemy facing the Christian comes not from his interior, but from without. Yet when speaking of "the world" as our enemy, we must be very careful to avoid still more misunderstandings. After all, "For God so loved *the world*, that He gave His only begotten Son, that whoever believes in Him shall not perish, but have eternal life." And again, "For God did not send the Son into *the world* to judge *the world*, but that *the world* might be saved through Him" (John 3:16–17 NASB, emphasis mine). Aren't we, after all, part of the world? Aren't we called to be engaged with the world and, like God, to "love the world"?

On the other hand, at the Last Supper Jesus employed some rather sober language to speak of this reality. "If the world hates you," he said, "remember that it hated me before you. If you belonged to the world, the world would love you as its own; but because you do not belong to the world, because my choice withdrew you from the world, therefore the world hates you" (John 15:18–19). The "world" here refers not to planet Earth nor to the global community of persons, but to an overarching materialism and secular spirit. Those who live rooted in the things of the earth, with their hearts set only on health, money, and the fleeting pleasures the world can offer, are blinded to the greatest truths of human existence.

In this sense, the world not only hates the Christian, but the Christian is enjoined to actively resist the allurement of the world. In his first epistle Saint John wrote to the early Christians: "Do not love the world or the things in the world. If any one loves the world, love for the Father is not in him. For all that is in the world, the lust of the flesh and the lust of the eyes and the pride of life, is not of the Father but is of the world. And the world passes away, and the lust of it; but he who does the will of God abides for ever" (1 John 2:15–17 RSV).

The world becomes our enemy when it threatens our scale of values and challenges God for our allegiance. The criteria of hyper-efficiency, profit, image, exploitation, and pleasure that predominate in the world oppose the gospel values of humility, truth, and self-giving. Though we claim to be Christians, all of us are affected by the seductive criteria of the world. We should regularly ask ourselves: *Up to what point are my priorities those of Jesus Christ? How much do I value being loved by the world and how fearful am I of seeming different from others? Have I truly let the gospel values of mercy, humility, patience, and self-giving take hold in my life?*

The world and everything in it were created to be signposts pointing beyond themselves. The Christian, sacramental view of reality invites us to transcend what we see and touch so as to reach the deeper truth of things. The beauty and artistry of the created world were meant to lead us to God, not to compete with him or to become an end in themselves. Our hearts cannot find enduring satisfaction in things that are destined to pass away, but only in God who is eternal. Therefore the secularism that rejects transcendence and treats the concerns of this world as if they were the whole of reality cannot but hinder us in our quest for holiness.

> *The beauty and artistry of the created world were meant to lead us to God, not to compete with him or to become an end in themselves.*

A hurdler focuses on the finish line as the object of his pursuit but also takes into account the obstacles placed along his path. Our spiritual work focuses on Christ and his kingship over us as the goal of our endeavors, yet to be effective we must also bear in mind the enemies that seek to hamper our progress. The devil, the flesh, and the world describe real enemies that resist the triumph of grace and holiness in our lives, and a sober consideration of their action can help us avoid some unpleasant surprises. With this Christian realism as a starting point, we can now turn to two very helpful supports to assist us in our work: spiritual direction and a spiritual program.

CHAPTER 14

Your Own Personal Trainer

Many, many souls would have become holy if they had been properly guided from the very start.

Thérèse of Lisieux, *Story of a Soul*

K ing David was a bright man. Well versed in God's law and with a keen sense of justice, he competently governed the kingdom of Israel and led his armies with unparalleled military prowess. Thus when Nathan the prophet laid out a hypothetical case of an unjust man who takes his poor neighbor's ewe lamb to serve it up to visiting friends, David quickly sized up the situation and issued a summary judgment. Seized by righteous anger, David proclaimed: "As Yahweh lives, the man who did this deserves to die!" (2 Sam. 12:5).

And although the analogy to his own situation was plain as the nose on his face, David just didn't get it. He had recently seduced his neighbor's wife, Bathsheba, and on discovering that she was pregnant, had had her husband, Uriah the Hittite, killed in battle to avoid a compromising situation. Speaking for God, Nathan declared: "You are the man" (2 Sam. 12:7 RSV). For all David's intelligence, when it came to his own moral and spiritual situation he was remarkably obtuse.

An old Latin adage reads: *Nemo est iudex in sua causa*, that is, "No one is a good judge of his own case." We can understand many things in the abstract and see things clearly when we are called upon to give advice to others, but this clarity doesn't necessarily carry over to our own situations—there moral myopia easily sets in. This is where a spiritual guide proves especially helpful.

When investing, we consult experts to help build a profitable portfolio; to streamline our accounting, we contract an external audit; and even advanced athletes hire personal trainers to improve their performance. How much more important is it to have an advisor when the most significant enterprise of our lives is at stake? Saint Francis de Sales queried, "Why do we want to be our own teacher in spiritual things, when we don't in regard to our bodily health? Don't we know that when doctors fall sick, they call other doctors to determine what remedies to apply?" And Saint Bernard of Clairvaux wrote that from his own experience, "it is much easier for me to direct many others than to direct myself."

Why do we want to be our own teacher in spiritual things, when we don't in regard to our bodily health?

Certainly God can guide us without the need of human mediation—just as he can communicate his grace without the mediation of the sacraments—but he has chosen to call us and sanctify us not just as individuals, but as a community of believers, which we call the Church.

We can easily be blinded by our instincts, preferences, and personal inclinations. Some tend to be too severe with themselves and need a director to temper natural rigor and scrupulosity. Others—the majority—are too indulgent with themselves and hesitate to apply the measures necessary to advance along the path of holiness. Jesus told us that the devil is the prince of darkness, whereas we are called to be children of light. To bare our souls to an experienced director—

the lights we receive, our doubts, our temptations, our triumphs, and our falls—is a practical way of coming out into the light. God cannot fail to reward this sincere effort to seek his will above all things.

We see over and over again how God wills that we be led and sanctified through the mediation of others. Though the Virgin Mary received the announcement of her divine maternity directly from the angel Gabriel, from then on she received all instructions through her husband, Joseph—regarding their flight into Egypt, when to return to Palestine, and their eventual settling in Nazareth. When Saul converted on the road to Damascus, Jesus didn't tell him what to do directly but had him go see Ananias to receive instructions. Throughout the history of Christianity, spiritual mentoring has been a mainstay of those who have sought to follow Christ more closely.

The practice of spiritual direction has been a constant tradition in monastic and religious orders, and throughout the centuries it has also been practiced with great fruit by laypersons as well. Saint John Climacus in his *Stairway to Paradise* compared a spiritual director to a Moses who acts as guide in the spiritual journey from Egypt to the Promised Land. Just as Moses helped the Israelites find their way through the hostile desert, so spiritual directors—also known as disciplers or mentors—can give us sure guidance on our own road to holiness.

> *Just as Moses helped the Israelites find their way through the hostile desert, so spiritual directors . . . can give us sure guidance on our own road to holiness.*

What Exactly Is Spiritual Direction?

If we wanted to define spiritual direction in a single sentence, we could say that it is *the ongoing orientation of one person by another along the path of God's will.* A spiritual director is a person who meets with others in a one-on-one setting to help them discover what God is doing in their lives and what he expects from them as a response. Spiritual direction helps people to become holy, since it aims primarily at helping them find and follow God's will. The very act of seeking spiritual direction helps us grow in the virtue of humility, since it means putting aside self-sufficiency and acknowledging our need for spiritual assistance.

Since every soul is different, spiritual direction must be personalized to fit individual needs and situations. A good spiritual director will not apply a rigid, cookie-cutter mold to every person but tries to guide each one according to his or her situation and idiosyncrasies to a greater knowledge, love, and imitation of Jesus Christ. Friendship with Christ, like all friendship, is an intimate and singular affair and develops along unique lines. Spiritual direction can help this friendship grow deeper and deeper, without violating its uniqueness or intimacy.

Why Seek Spiritual Direction?

Spiritual direction bears much fruit in a person who makes use of it with good dispositions. In the first place, it can help you sort through your own subjectivity to reach a more objective *knowledge of God's will*. It helps you see more clearly what God is doing in your life and what sort of response he would like from you. Often God's will can be tough, and we can be tempted to interpret it according to personal preferences. A spiritual director helps us sort through our subjective reactions in order to discern what God really wants. In life's big decisions, like a call to the ministry or priesthood or persevering through a difficult period in a marriage, spiritual direction furnishes a moral compass that reminds us where we are headed and what it takes to get there. In key moments of my own life, notably when discerning my call to the priesthood, spiritual direction has been an invaluable help in knowing what God was asking of me.

Similarly, in your day-to-day efforts to respond to the inspirations of the Holy Spirit, a wise spiritual director can help you distinguish between God's will and an overactive imagination or scruples. Over the years I have met people who deeply love our Lord but who are afflicted by a scrupulosity that causes them anxiety, since they constantly worry whether or not their actions offend God. How helpful it is for these people to have a spiritual guide to help them sort through their doubts and live with greater peace and spiritual freedom!

Second, spiritual direction yields increased *self-knowledge*. Not only do we learn what God desires from us, we also come to a deeper understanding of ourselves: our temperaments, inclinations, virtues and vices, strengths and weaknesses, and dominant tendencies. When we are starting out in the spiritual life, we are often surprised by our failure to live up to our good resolutions and wonder why we act the way we do. A prudent spiritual director will help us recognize the forces at work in us, our allies and enemies, and the role of our emotions, intellect, will, and affections in the spiritual life. This heightened self-knowledge in turn leads to humility, since humility is truth, especially regarding our self-perception.

Third, beside these good fruits that flow from increased knowledge, spiritual direction also helps *motivate our spiritual work*. Regular spiritual direction keeps us in a state of healthy spiritual tension or "tautness" and helps us avoid spiritual laziness and neglect. The very act of examining our souls and preparing for our meetings with our spiritual director keeps us attentive to our spiritual work. Thinking over our behavior since the last spiritual direction, evaluating the fulfillment of our resolutions, and examining our faithfulness to our spiritual program obliges us to honestly confront our effort and progress.

> *The very act of examining our souls and preparing for our meetings with our spiritual director keeps us attentive to our spiritual work.*

Though in the end the one we are responsible to is God himself, rendering an account of our work to another human being offers an added incentive to keep pushing forward. How helpful to know that not only can we rely on the assistance of the Holy Spirit, but also on another person who knows us interiorly, prays for us, counsels us, and roots for our spiritual progress and union with God!

A final fruit of spiritual direction, similar to the previous one, is the *encouragement* it offers in our spiritual battles. Since discouragement undermines God's plans for us, we need to be reminded that things are not as gray as they seem, even in moments of slow progress and spiritual slumps. A good spiritual director will offer consolation and hope in times of despair and remind us of the power of God's grace in our lives to overcome even inveterate enemies and seemingly insurmountable obstacles.

Often the spiritual director will not reveal new spiritual lights that we had never considered before but will remind us of things we already know but that somehow get swept under the carpet in our day-to-day relations with God. This encouragement will sometimes take the form of a good spiritual kick in the behind. When we are tempted to sit back and laze even though God expects more from us, a spiritual director will help rouse us from our comfortable spiritual seat on the bench and put us back in the game.

Choosing a Spiritual Director

Once one has decided to seek out spiritual direction, where should he turn? The person we choose to help direct our spiritual work can have a profound effect on our lives, so this decision should not be taken lightly. According to Saint John of the Cross, the person wishing to advance toward perfection should "take care into whose hands he entrusts himself, for as the master is, so will the disciple be, and as the father is so will be the son" (*The Living Flame of Love*).

Though God is perfectly capable of making use of poor instruments to communicate his grace, just as fresh, clean water can flow through battered old pipes, generally the holier and more experienced the director, the more surely he will guide us along the path to holiness. I had a spiritual director for more than ten years who never led me astray. His simplicity and love for Christ was so genuine that his counsels bore a wisdom beyond his years.

The three main qualities of a good spiritual director, according to Saint Francis de Sales, are charity, knowledge, and prudence.

Spiritual directors can be ministers, priests, or laypersons, men or women. Priests receive special training for this work and often set aside time for this important apostolate, but more and more laypersons are working fruitfully in this area as well. The three main qualities of a good spiritual director, according to Saint Francis de Sales, are charity, knowledge, and prudence (*Introduction to the Devout Life*).

CHARITY

Charity here refers especially to an overarching, active desire for the good of souls that come to him/her, expressed especially in a desire for their sanctification. A good director-directee relationship rests on the solid bedrock of supernatural charity, not just on a natural friendship or a clinical client-patient agreement. Even more than his/her desire for the directee's financial solvency, social prowess, and soaring career, a good director looks for long-term success: holiness.

KNOWLEDGE

The second quality of *knowledge* refers to doctrinal soundness, a firm grounding in the moral teaching of the Church and experiential knowledge of the human person and the spiritual life. That is, a good theoretical understanding of Christian doctrine and the principles of the spiritual life must be wedded to a practical knowledge of the human heart, temperaments, and motivations, and of God's way of working in souls.

Jesus warned us that if one blind man leads another, both will fall into a pit (Matt. 15:14; Luke 6:39). A well-intentioned but ignorant spiritual guide can do great damage to souls, since his/her interpretation of God's activity and a person's responses will lack a solid foundation. Above all this person needs expertise in the supernatural realm. A spiritual director is not chiefly a psychologist or therapist, but a spiritual and moral guide, and the best guides are those who know the terrain. Directors with little care for their own spiritual lives won't be able to offer sound counsel to others.

PRUDENCE

Prudence means the ability to discern God's action in souls. Directors should understand themselves to be instruments of the Holy Spirit and rather than impose their own wills or programs, they must listen carefully to what God is saying and ask themselves: *What is God doing in this soul? Where is he leading her?* In this way they will guide the souls entrusted to them at God's pace, inspiring and encouraging them to greater generosity without overwhelming them.

Directors should constantly implore the Holy Spirit's gift of counsel as well as a deep humility to allow God to work. In the end, spiritual directors facilitate God's relationship with other people, but they should humbly stand back when their services are superfluous. The prudence required for spiritual direction entails discretion as well. Since this is a relationship based on trust and confidence, the director should respect the directee's intimacy and maintain absolute reserve with others regarding what has been discussed in the privacy of spiritual direction.

Remember that a good spiritual director is one who helps us progress in the love of God, which at times can be uncomfortable and even painful.

Remember that a good spiritual director is one who helps us progress in the love of God, which at times can be uncomfortable and even painful. For a director you shouldn't look above all for a person you get along with, but one who challenges you to be everything God wants you to be and effectively helps you along this path.

The Structure and Content of Spiritual Direction

There are many models for spiritual direction. Different directors employ different methods, and preferences among directees will also vary from person to person. Here I will explain a simple model that I have found to be effective and complete.

Before getting into the "meat" of the spiritual direction, a couple of other steps are necessary. First, begin with a prayer. When director and directee invoke the light and assistance of the Holy Spirit, they place the fruit of their encounter in God's hands and capitalize on Jesus' promise that where two or three gather in his name, there he will be in their midst.

Second, a brief look at the resolutions from the last meeting is in order. Resolutions are not made to be forgotten but to be fulfilled and checked. Whether you remembered to fulfill them or not, it is useful to render an account and to consider the results of your proposals. They provide continuity from one session to the next.

After these preliminary steps comes the body of the meeting. The core of spiritual direction consists of three main topics to be covered: *the prayer life, the moral life,* and *the apostolic life.*

These three categories basically encompass all the aspects of a Christian's spiritual life and its concrete manifestations in daily living.

1. THE PRAYER LIFE

The first matter to be dealt with is one's prayer life and personal relationship with God. This includes everything from one's deeper dispositions to love God and follow his will, to the structure of one's different prayer and devotional practices, to the sacramental life, to one's attention and generosity in listening to and putting into practice the inspirations of the Holy Spirit.

Here you can discuss the ways you pray, the times, and the fruit your prayer is yielding in your life. Difficulties in prayer also come into play here, as do particular questions or doubts concerning prayer. As with the entire spiritual direction, the focus should be essentially positive, with the aim not only of overcoming obstacles, but especially growth in union with God.

2. THE MORAL LIFE

The second main issue to be discussed is your moral life. This consists especially in your efforts to follow God's will in your own concrete situation, the particular temptations and obstacles you encounter, and the virtues you most need to acquire or strengthen. It is helpful to identify your dominant passion, or the tendency you most need to watch out for.

Again, this section aims at building virtue and growing in faithfulness to God and not merely at rooting out defects. If you have a spiritual program, all the better (see the next chapter), since this will keep your moral work on target.

It is helpful to identify your dominant passion, or the tendency you most need to watch out for.

3. THE APOSTOLIC LIFE

The third central topic to be addressed is your apostolic life. Since all Christians are called not only to live the faith but also to bear witness to it, this is an essential part of any spiritual direction. How can you live as an effective apostle in your family, work, and social settings? How can you integrate your particular gifts into the Church's evangelizing mission? How can you best express your love for God and other people, especially as regards sharing the faith? These and other questions will help focus your attention on practical ways of being an apostle in your daily life.

After tackling these primary issues (the time spent on each will vary with particular needs), you can also bring up other particular questions or difficulties. It is always helpful to bear in mind, however, that spiritual direction endeavors above all to provide guidance for one's spiritual life and moral decision making, and these aspects should remain front and center.

The session should end with the formulation of one or several practical resolutions spawned by the foregoing discussion. The more concrete the resolutions, generally, the more effect they will have on your life. After determining the resolutions, a closing prayer of thanksgiving to the Holy Spirit for his light and a petition for strength to carry out the proposals wraps up the session nicely and reminds us that all our spiritual work is, first and foremost, cooperation with his grace in our lives.

Qualities of a Good Spiritual Direction

Spiritual direction can produce abundant fruit in a Christian's life, but to do so, it requires certain dispositions on the part of the one seeking direction. To make our encounters truly profitable, four essential qualities are necessary: *sincerity, faith, continuity*, and *preparation*.

1. SINCERITY

The first quality of good spiritual direction is absolute *sincerity*. To be effective, a spiritual director must know the person he is guiding as well as possible. This knowledge should include the person's history, temperament, habits, lifestyle, tendencies, temptations, inspirations, qualities, dispositions, fears, and aspirations—in short, anything related to his or her Christian life. Obviously the director won't know this all at once but will discover it little by little.

Yet this knowledge always requires *transparency* and *objectivity* on the part of the one seeking direction. Some spiritual directees present only the favorable aspects of their moral and spiritual lives, as if they were submitting a résumé for a job application, highlighting qualities and sweeping defects and faults under the rug. Others do just the opposite: they paint everything as black and hopeless, without even a glimmer of light to suggest that somewhere in the midst of our human misery God just might be working some good. We should strive to present our situation as factually and objectively as possible.

The root causes of a lack of transparency and objectivity are manifold. Let's face it: most of us experience some degree of discomfort in speaking about our spiritual lives with others. Often vanity or human respect enters the picture, inducing us to try to make a good impression on the director so he doesn't think badly of us. Other times people simply don't know themselves very well, and thus they present a distorted image out of ignorance. Other times laziness may be the culprit. We may fear serious work in our spiritual lives, and so we don't get down to concrete details that would require attention. If all is rosy, after all, we expect nothing more than a pat on the back from our spiritual director and the admonition to keep on going just as we are. In the same way, if our whole spiritual lives are in shambles, why bother working at all? Pinpointing areas where we are not being generous with God yields the logical consequence of having to make a practical resolution in that area (and we often don't want to).

Imagine going to a doctor with a broken leg, and instead of explaining what happened to your leg you simply speak about your acne problem and a sore shoulder. Perhaps you

Why go to spiritual direction at all unless we are really looking to get to the root of our difficulties and conform our lives to Christ's?

would get a prescription for some Oxy-Ten and a good muscle massaging ointment, but the real problem—the broken leg—would still be as bad as ever. Would you leave the doctor's office smugly satisfied with yourself for having deceived the doctor? In the same way, a lack of sincerity with our spiritual director simply makes no sense. Why go to spiritual direction at all unless we are really looking to get to the root of our difficulties and conform our lives to Christ's?

2. FAITH

This absolute sincerity demands a good dose of *faith*. This would be the second necessary quality of a good spiritual direction. In our spiritual director we must see not only a wise, experienced guide or a friendly ear but also an instrument of the Holy Spirit. What distinguishes spiritual direction from a psychological counseling session is not only the subject matter but also the climate of prayerful attention to the action of the Holy Spirit and the realization that he is the primary actor in our dialogue and spiritual work. Rather than seeking out mere human wisdom to guide our steps, we seek God's guidance and light to better understand what he is doing in our lives and what he wants from us. Both the director and the one directed pray for light from the Holy Spirit to discern his actions and will.

This attitude of faith will help to draw attention away from the director's human qualities and defects to focus on God's action. Some directors naturally impress us with their eloquence and insights, while others can come across as more simple or even rough around the edges. If we maintain a good supernatural focus, we can overlook these human attributes in order to glean from the director's words and counsels what God wants to say to us. We shouldn't therefore compare our own intelligence or knowledge with our director's and continually second-guess his or her advice but rather accept and follow the director's good counsel with docility, faith, and humility. After all, we do not go to spiritual direction to receive a rubber stamp on our own ideas and projects but to open ourselves up to whatever God wishes to ask of us.

Even when the director's advice may not bear the seal of brilliance, we do well to follow it, barring serious reasons to the contrary. A good general rule of thumb is that even if the director makes a mistake, we will not be mistaken in obeying. This reflects Mother Teresa of Calcutta's saying that in obedience we are infallible.

> The good God has given you His work. He wants you to do His work in His way. Failure or success mean nothing to Him, as long as you do His work according to His plan and His will. You are infallible when you obey. The devil tries his best to spoil the work of God and as he cannot do it directly to Him, he makes us do God's work in our way and this is where the devil gains and we lose.
>
> (Letter of 20 September 1959)[1]

A good supernatural outlook also helps keep the flow of the spiritual direction on track and prevents it from deteriorating into chitchat. Even if our spiritual director is a friend of ours, the faith that permeates our spiritual direction obliges a certain respect for the person of the director as well as his or her time. Regardless of whether the director is a priest or a layperson, that person's role in our lives—at least in that context—invites us to treat him or her with particular regard. Getting down to the matter at hand is a good way to show our gratitude for this service as well as our appreciation for the importance of what we are doing.

3. CONTINUITY

A third quality of a good spiritual direction is *continuity*. Continuity— an unbroken flow in a single direction—can be divided into *chronological continuity, thematic continuity,* and *personal continuity.*

Chronological continuity means regular meetings with an established frequency to assure continuous spiritual work over time. Meeting three times in a single week but then not getting together again for another six months wouldn't bode well for a serious program of spiritual work. Likewise, a single three-hour session doesn't yield nearly as much spiritual fruit as three forty-five-minute meetings spread out over time. It is helpful to establish a regular periodicity (monthly, for example) and then stick to it as faithfully as possible.

Thematic continuity means the maintenance of a single program of work over time, with clear objectives and effective means to reach them. As we saw earlier, a good spiritual direction begins with a review of the resolutions and points of work agreed upon in the prior meeting, to see what fruits they have borne and pick up from there. As we will see in the next chapter, a simple, structured spiritual program also offers an excellent means of keeping on track in our spiritual lives.

Personal continuity means working with one spiritual director at a time and changing directors as seldom as possible. Once we have found a good spiritual director, we shouldn't go shopping around for opinions and spiritual advice from a variety of persons every time we have doubts. Part of the effectiveness of spiritual direction comes from sticking with a certain system and points of work over time.

Equally inadvisable is the practice of switching spiritual directors unnecessarily. Starting all over from scratch with a new director

entails a period of getting to know one another until settling into a regular rhythm
of spiritual work. Certain circumstances
could warrant changing spiritual directors, and absolute liberty of conscience
must be safeguarded in this area, but this
practice should be the exception rather
than the norm.

Some objective reasons that could induce us to change spiritual directors would

Once we have found a good spiritual director, we shouldn't go shopping around for opinions and spiritual advice from a variety of persons every time we have doubts.

include our inability to attain the trust and confidence necessary for
fruitful direction, the deterioration of the relationship from a healthy
spiritual one to a merely natural or even ambiguous one, or the realization over time that the director lacks the necessary knowledge,
prudence, or discretion to guide our spiritual and moral lives.

4. Preparation

A fourth and final quality of a good spiritual direction is *preparation*
on the part of the one seeking direction. Improvisation and spontaneity may work in other areas, but they can severely limit the fruit
of spiritual direction. To avoid forgetting important points of your
spiritual work, it may help to write out a brief outline of what you
intend to present to your spiritual director. The outlined points will
keep you on track and help you to make good use of the time you
have together.

Poor preparation can result in two negative outcomes: either uncomfortable silence and generalities when you can't remember what
has been going on in your spiritual life or, conversely, a lengthy,
wandering narrative that abounds in details irrelevant to spiritual
direction. Keeping on topic can be an act of charity toward your
director. Whenever possible, the spiritual director shouldn't have to
guess your meaning, wade through descriptive anecdotes to get to

your point, or draw it out of you with a long series of questions. Good preparation can avoid all these pitfalls.

Preparing your spiritual direction can also help you directly through self-examination. Accountability to another also means accountability to oneself. When looking over your spiritual work to prepare what you will say in spiritual direction, you will inevitably realize many things about your spiritual life that you would never have seen otherwise. Throughout both the preparation time and the actual session, the Holy Spirit is at work, enlightening, prodding, encouraging, and counseling.

An invaluable point of reference for your preparation is a spiritual program, drawn up together with your spiritual director. To this point we will now turn.

CHAPTER 15

Drafting a Plan of Action

The Usefulness of a Spiritual Program

If every year we rooted out one defect, we should soon be perfect men.

Thomas à Kempis, *The Imitation of Christ*

Few builders would dare begin construction on a house without a blueprint. Only a foolhardy builder would simply start pouring cement or nailing two-by-fours together without first devising a plan of action. Construction requires a certain logic, an order of tasks, and above all a clear idea of the desired finished product. The more detailed the floor plan, the more likely the project will proceed smoothly without glitches.

Granted, the spiritual life differs from house construction in many ways. The spiritual life centers on an interpersonal relationship between you and God, rather than a "job" that you set out to accomplish. As a relationship, the spiritual life requires flexibility and a give-and-take not found in impersonal projects. Moreover, as we saw in chapter 8, our role in our spiritual growth is secondary to that of the Holy Spirit, the Sanctifier, and many factors of the equation lie outside of our control. Nonetheless, as far as your cooperation with God's plan is concerned, a spiritual program can make the difference between effective spiritual work and spiritual drifting.

Good administration is characterized by good planning. The results of our enterprises depend not only on good execution, but perhaps even more so on foresight and preparation. Jesus asked, somewhat rhetorically, "For which one of you, when he wants to build a tower, does not first sit down and calculate the cost to see if he has enough to complete it?" and again, "What king, when he sets out to meet another king in battle, will not first sit down and consider whether he is strong enough with ten thousand men to encounter the one coming against him with twenty thousand?" (Luke 14:28, 31 NASB). Why apply a different standard to our spiritual work than we do to our professional work? Why rigorously chart out every detail of a business plan, then leave our spiritual lives up for grabs? Life's chief enterprise—holiness—certainly merits as much attention and planning as more mundane affairs.

Why rigorously chart out every detail of a business plan, then leave our spiritual lives up for grabs?

In a word, a spiritual program is a brief, structured, written plan of spiritual and moral work that outlines an ideal, goals, obstacles, and concrete means to achieve our objectives. Whereas such a plan cannot take into account every facet of our spiritual activity, it can set the bases and provide a basic structure for spiritual growth.

The Benefits of a Spiritual Program

Jesus never said that a spiritual program is necessary for salvation. It isn't even strictly necessary for growing in holiness. It can, however, provide benefits that make it highly recommendable. After all, adding machines aren't strictly necessary for accountants, but they certainly facilitate bookkeeping, and once you have used them, you wonder how you ever got anything done without them. Though many people wrote books prior to the computer age, I doubt very much that I would be writing this work without my trusty PC.

The main advantage of a program is the structure and focus it offers for spiritual work. By isolating a few key points of work, a good spiritual program keeps us from dispersion in a thousand directions. The Roman Legions came up with the military strategy of "divide and conquer," and that strategy works in the spiritual realm as well. We cannot possibly progress in every area at once, and attempting to do so would be both overwhelming and futile. Imagine trying to work on charity, humility, magnanimity, diligence, constancy, purity, gentleness, patience, and temperance all at the same time! Not only would you probably see meager results, you would also quickly get fed up with spiritual work altogether.

Imagine trying to work on charity, humility, magnanimity, diligence, constancy, purity, gentleness, patience, and temperance all at the same time!

A spiritual program keeps us focused on specific goals with concrete, practical means to reach them. Instead of wasting time wondering what points we should be working on from day to day, and what means we should employ to reach our goals, we are gently prodded in a single direction. This focus assures continuity—and results—in our spiritual work.

Of course the use of a program generates other collateral benefits as well. For one, it serves as a helpful guide for our examinations of conscience and a gauge of our spiritual progress. As a point of reference, it helps us evaluate our spiritual work. Moreover, having our program approved by our spiritual director gains the added merit of working under obedience, with the assurance that the points of our program represent God's will for us. Its use also helps forge self-discipline and tenacity, especially when we get tired of working on the same points or when our initial enthusiasm dies down.

The Structure of Your Spiritual Program

Before composing a spiritual program, you will need to do some deep self-examination: *What sort of person am I? What are my main qualities and talents? What is my predominant defect? If I were to change one thing about myself to become more like Christ, what would it be?* The need for self-examination cannot be over-emphasized. Many people develop programs without correctly identifying their root sins. They develop "programs of the moment" that reflect their current situations and not the ongoing difficulties that underlie their faults. Many vain people write programs to attack sensuality, while lazy persons may mistakenly focus on overcoming pride and proud persons set out to tackle temperance. Honest self-examination can help identify our most necessary point of work.

It takes much reflection and prayer to know yourself well. If you have the habit of frequent confession, reflect on the matters you often confess and try to dig to the root causes. Your spiritual director can be especially helpful in this examination process and in drawing up your program.

Although a spiritual program should be adapted to fit the particular needs of each person, certain fundamental elements should typically be present. I offer the following outline as a possible structure for your spiritual program. Feel free to follow it verbatim or to modify it to suit your needs.

IDEAL

Ancient Greek philosophers came up with a guiding principle that is as true as it is counterintuitive: start from the end. The clearer the goal, the easier it is to pinpoint effective means to reach it. If you know your destination, you can plot out the best route to get there. Since Jesus Christ is the model for Christian living, he is obviously the ideal for any spiritual program. Yet to make your ideal more specific, you may wish to identify a particular virtue practiced by Christ, and imitate him especially there.

For example, if you are a lazy person and habitually fail to do all that God is asking of you, you may wish to choose as an ideal Christ in his total, active commitment to fulfilling his mission. If pride seems to be your dominant defect, you may identify as your ideal Christ, meek and humble of heart. If you tend especially toward vanity and self-centeredness, you may aim for the ideal of Christ in his self-forgetfulness and love for his Father and all people.

If pride seems to be your dominant defect, you may identify as your ideal Christ, meek and humble of heart.

Obstacles

Know thine enemy. Here it pays to identify the root cause of many of your sins and failings, the predominant defect that keeps you from being more Christlike. Along with the root cause, list several of its typical manifestations in your life. The more clearly you see what needs to change, the more effectively you can work on it.

For example, maybe your predominant defect is rationalism, which manifests itself in a lack of faith and trust in God, in a blindness to the action of grace in your life, in an overreliance on your own strength, and in a pragmatism that tends to trample people in order to reach objectives. Or maybe your root defect is human respect and a fear of losing face, which prevents you from taking risks or standing by your beliefs, so you keep your Christianity to yourself instead of sharing your faith with others.

Though all of us have numerous defects and negative tendencies, choose the one that seems to be the deepest-rooted and most destructive. That way your spiritual work will stay focused.

In your conversations with your spiritual director, he or she can help you know yourself better and locate the area where you most need to work.

ALLIES

Just as we have enemies and obstacles, we also have many means at our disposal to become holy. It helps to remember here the precious Christian resources of prayer and vigilance, the strength of the sacraments, the role of self-denial, and the particular graces that God has given us to help us be faithful disciples of Jesus.

> *Just as we have enemies and obstacles, we also have many means at our disposal to become holy.*

OBJECTIVE

In a single sentence, endeavor to express what you hope to accomplish with your program, concentrating especially on the virtue you most need to grow more similar to Christ your ideal. For example, "I seek to grow in my charity toward others, putting their needs before my own and serving rather than looking to be served."

MEANS

Here make a list of a few very practical measures that you will employ to achieve your objective. Taking into account your specific circumstances (people you live and work with, schedule, job, responsibilities, temptations, etc.) and the manifestations of your predominant defect as you have determined, try to outline concrete resolutions that, if applied faithfully, will assure results. Do not neglect specifically spiritual and supernatural means, remembering your need for God's grace and the fact that "unless the LORD builds the house, they labor in vain who build it" (Ps. 127:1 NASB).

Ten Qualities of a Good Spiritual Program

Given the nature of a spiritual program and its role in our spiritual work, we can outline a series of qualities that a good program should have. Though this list may not be exhaustive, it gives a good idea of some of the key attributes that we should try to incorporate into our spiritual programs.

1. CONCRETE

An ambiguous program makes for ambiguous results. Seek to be as concrete as possible, both in the objectives you establish and the means you choose to attain them. Avoid vagaries; be specific and practical. This specificity will make it easier both to apply and to examine the program. The *means* especially should be so specific that you know immediately whether you applied them or not. Though it may seem like a limitation, concreteness makes for better results. For example, a poorly formulated means might be "I will be a more prayerful person," while a better formulation would be "I will offer my day to God each day when I wake up, go to church at least twice a week besides Sundays, and meditate on the gospel for ten minutes each day."

2. BRIEF

Since your spiritual program is a tool rather than a treatise, it should be lightweight and maneuverable, not cumbersome. Avoid wordiness and keep commentary to a minimum. Though it should be complete, a good program sticks to the basics. This facilitates quick review of the program every day and makes it easier to keep the points in your head. Remember that when fighting Goliath, David threw off Saul's unwieldy armor and went after the Philistine with a sling and five stones. A good rule of thumb limits a program to no more than two pages; if you can fit it in one, better still.

3. FOCUSED

Work on one point at a time and avoid the temptation to want to include everything. We all need to work on many virtues and overcome many vices, but devoting our energy to a single area increases our chances of success. That doesn't mean abandonment of other virtues, but a special emphasis on one virtue in your work and self-examination. Make sure that all the means you draw up point in the same direction, with a direct tie to your main objective.

4. PERSONAL

This is *your* program, not an abstract, one-size-fits-all program. Even your Ideal should be adapted to your real situation. What would Jesus do in *your place*, with *your temperament*, with *these specific people*, etc.? God made you to be a saint, which doesn't mean becoming somebody else, but becoming the *you* that you were meant to be.

> *God made you to be a saint, which doesn't mean becoming somebody else, but becoming the* you *that you were meant to be.*

5. POSITIVE

Direct your program at conquering virtue and imitating Christ, not just eliminating vice. Sin and vice are not the object of your program but the obstacles that you must overcome to reach your goal. Your program aims at building, not destroying, even though some tearing down may be necessary in order to build. But keep the focus positive.

6. DEEP

Aim at the core of your spiritual and moral life. If you need chiefly to grow in charity, don't settle for a program that helps you be more punctual to appointments or get out of bed quickly in the morning. Cosmetic changes won't make you the saint you are called to be.

Deep programs hurt because they attack the root of self-love, but anything less wouldn't be worth pursuing.

7. SUPERNATURAL

Spiritual work differs from mere self-help in two important ways. First, self-help relies solely on willpower and personal effort to accomplish its goals, while spiritual work teams up with God's grace, without which no lasting spiritual progress can be made. Second, spiritual work strives above all for holiness and union with God, rather than mere self-improvement. Your spiritual program should aim beyond worldly concerns to address your supernatural life of faith, hope, and charity.

> *Spiritual work teams up with God's grace, without which no lasting spiritual progress can be made.*

8. ORDERED TO CHARITY

If your program doesn't help you love better, it is not making you holier. Remember that the goal of the spiritual life is not personal perfection but love of God and neighbor. To avoid spiritual narcissism, keep love at the heart of your efforts, with the focus on others rather than on yourself. Even if your program aims at humility or poverty of spirit or some other virtue, it does so to help you love others better.

9. CHRIST-CENTERED

A Christian doesn't work on virtue for virtue's sake, but as a means of growing more like Christ. Christ is not a good model of an ideal that transcends him; he *is* the Ideal. We strive for virtue in order to resemble Christ; we do not strive for resemblance to Christ in order to attain virtue. Christ is not the means, but the end of our efforts, and your program should reflect this.

10. Realistic

Utopian plans, drafted in a moment of fervor, bear not fruit but frustration. Teresa of Àvila wrote, "The devil sometimes puts ambitious desires into our hearts, so that, instead of setting our hand to the work which lies nearest to us, and thus serving Our Lord in ways within our power, we may rest content with having desired the impossible" (*Interior Castle*). When drawing up your plan of work, remember who you are and the circumstances in which you live. Aim high, but not so high that you cannot reasonably fulfill the resolutions you put forward. In the spiritual life you will inevitably suffer setbacks, but some setbacks can be avoided through a healthy realism.

The crafting of a good program is only half the battle. To bear fruit, the program must be regularly consulted and faithfully followed. Remember, it is a work plan and not a theological or spiritual treatise; it is a means and not an end in itself. What a shame it would be to invest time carefully drafting an elaborate program only to file it away to gather dust in some drawer! As much as possible, try to have daily contact with your program and use it as a guide for your spiritual direction as well.

This being said, as good as your program may be, let it serve you, but do not serve it. Be faithful but flexible and ready to accommodate new circumstances and inspirations over time, under the guidance of your spiritual director. Modify your program if it doesn't yield good results. The program shouldn't be a straitjacket that restricts you but a channel that directs you and a booster that drives you forward. At the same time, a good program shouldn't require modification after every inspiring talk or sermon you hear!

Before I wrap up this book, I need to address one more topic. A Christian is called not only to change himself but to change the world around him. "Keeping the faith" doesn't mean we shouldn't share it with others. On the contrary, every Christian is called to participate in the Church's evangelizing mission, and a vibrant spiritual life propels us to evangelize.

CHAPTER 16

Practicing and Preaching

Letting Others in on the Secret

This is no time to be ashamed of the Gospel. It is the time to preach it from the rooftops.

Pope John Paul II, World Youth Day, Denver, 1993

P eople have an understandable fascination with "last words." We assume that a person will say something particularly profound and revealing before departing this world. In his brief farewell address before ascending into heaven, Jesus could have said many things to his followers. He could have reminded them once more to "love one another." He could have sent them on a needed retreat to think over their last three years with him and the paschal mystery they had so recently experienced. He could have reiterated his call to humility and service.

Instead, in his last recorded words, Jesus issued a direct and forceful command: "Go therefore and make disciples of all nations, baptizing them in the name of the Father and of the Son and of the Holy Spirit, teaching them to observe all that I have commanded you; and lo, I am with you always, to the close of the age" (Matt. 28:19–20 RSV). It's as if Jesus were saying: "Your training period is over. Now get to work." This short program has been handed

It's as if Jesus were saying: "Your training period is over. Now get to work."

down for centuries in the Church as Jesus' "missionary mandate," which sets forth the fundamental task of Christians in the world.

Note well that Christ's words take the form of a universal imperative. He issues a general command to *all* his followers, not a special charge for an elite group. There are not two categories of Christians, those called to keep the commandments and those called to actively evangelize. Active Christian apostles are not some sort of Christian Navy Seals or Army Rangers. The call to go out to the world and bear witness to Christ is not a specialized commission, but an essential task for every rank-and-file Christian.

Some Christians do receive special vocations, but *all* are called to be missionaries. A missionary is, after all, simply "one who is sent," and all Christians are "sent" out to the world to evangelize. The word "missionary" proceeds from the Latin verb *mittere*, meaning "to send." That is the same as saying that all Christians are called to be apostles, since the word *apostle*, too, derives from the Greek word *apo-stéllo*, meaning "to send out." Thus Christian evangelizing activity has typically been called the *apostolate*.

Jesus himself is the first apostle, "sent" by the Father. To be an apostle means to share in Jesus' own salvific mission and to be his

To be an apostle means to share in Jesus' own salvific mission and to be his presence in the world.

presence in the world. Jesus drew a close parallel between his own mission and that of his followers: "As the Father sent me, so I am sending you" (John 20:21). We are, as Paul says, "ambassadors" of Christ (2 Cor. 5:20). We go to the world not in our own names, but his. By virtue of baptism every Christian is an apostle—"called," but also "sent."

In the first chapter of this book we discarded the notion that the essence of Christianity is merely the avoidance of evil. That would be like saying that the essence of a soccer game is the avoidance of penalties, or that the essence of writing is the avoidance of grammatical errors. We play soccer to make goals, and we write to communicate ideas and move hearts. True, we do these things while observing the "rules," but the rules are simply boundaries within which we can work. The rules are not the object of the game. The Christian life is a call to fullness of life, and it entails sharing this life with others. Christians are not just passive beneficiaries of Christ's sacrifice; we also share in the mission of redemption.

From Disciples to Witnesses

Look what happened to the apostles after experiencing Christ's resurrection, and especially after receiving the Holy Spirit on Pentecost. They underwent a radical transformation. After the Resurrection they were no longer only *disciples* (the word means "learners" or "apprentices")—now they are his witnesses, his apostles, his missionaries. Before the Resurrection the disciples were locked away in a room like frightened children; after the resurrection they boldly proclaimed him before all with no fear for their lives.

Before the Resurrection the disciples were locked away in a room like frightened children; after the resurrection they boldly proclaimed him before all with no fear for their lives.

Peter, for example, was hardly recognizable as the same man. On the night of Jesus' arrest he fled the scene as Jesus was taken prisoner in the Garden of Gethsemane, and later that same night he vigorously denied he even knew Jesus! But just a few weeks later, on the morning of Pentecost, that same Peter was publicly preaching Jesus Christ to anyone who would listen. He no longer seemed to care about the personal danger. He was a new man, a true apostle.

What is it that caused this transformation? Two things, really. First, the disciples met the risen Christ. They realized that everything he had said was true, and that he really was the Lord. Like children awaking from a bad dream, they realized everything was all right. They saw that all that Jesus had suffered formed part of the divine plan of salvation, and he was still in charge. Time after time in their preaching, the apostles would refer to Christ's resurrection. On Pentecost, for instance, Peter said: "This Jesus God raised up, and of that we all are witnesses" (Acts 2:32 RSV). The apostles were his "witnesses" and they gave testimony to what they had seen and heard.

Saint John offers us a sterling example of this witness in his first letter.

> That which was from the beginning, which we have heard, which we have seen with our eyes, which we have looked upon and touched with our hands, concerning the word of life—the life was made manifest, and we saw it, and testify to it, and proclaim to you the eternal life which was with the Father and was made manifest to use—that which we have seen and heard we proclaim also to you, so that you may have fellowship with us; and our fellowship is with the Father and with his Son Jesus Christ.
>
> (1 John 1:1–3 RSV)

We, too, the apostles of today, are called to bear witness to what we have seen and heard, to give testimony of the love of God that we have experienced in Jesus Christ.

Second, the apostles received Christ's own Spirit—the Holy Spirit. The courage and enthusiasm they showed were no mere human feat. It was the Spirit of Jesus himself, which he confers upon his Church. After his resurrection Jesus told his disciples: "You will receive power when the Holy Spirit comes on you, and then you will be my witnesses not only in Jerusalem but throughout Judaea and Samaria, and indeed to the ends of the earth" (Acts 1:8). The Holy Spirit enabled

This Spirit is not only the saint-maker, he is also the apostle-maker.

and empowered the apostles to be effective witnesses. This Spirit is not only the saint-maker, he is also the apostle-maker.

This is true for today's Christians as well. We received that same Holy Spirit, a spirit of fortitude and vigor. He gives us the courage to evangelize and puts the right words into our mouths.

Contemplative and Conquering

So what does a book on the spiritual life have to do with apostolate? Our doubts may spring from an exaggerated rift between action and contemplation, as if the two stood in opposition to one another. In reality they complement each another and form the two axles around which the Christian life revolves. Christian prayer blossoms spontaneously into action, and apostolic action drives us to prayer.

When you have discovered something really wonderful, you cannot hold it inside for yourself alone. We humans have a need to *communicate*, to share our joys and sorrows, to make others participants in our experiences. Our knowledge of Christ and our love for him impel us to preach him. When we contemplate him in prayer, we are driven to share him with others. When the apostles were ordered not to speak about Christ, Peter and John answered with bold simplicity: "For we cannot but speak of what we have seen and heard" (Acts 4:20 RSV). Similarly, a Christian who has experienced the love of Christ cannot hold it within. We want others to find what we have found.

The good news we have to proclaim is not some breakthrough in medical science like a cure for cancer or AIDS, or a new method of energy production, or even a remedy for world hunger. It is even better. It is the Good News of salvation in Jesus Christ. God so loved the world that he sent his only Son, so that whoever believes in him might not perish but have everlasting life. This Good News is meant for everyone, but it will not preach itself. How can people believe if they never hear the message proclaimed? And how can they hear, if Christians do not bear witness to what they have seen and heard? Christians are commissioned to go out and to preach the faith that they have embraced.

The contemplation of this Good News in prayer propels us to share it with others in the apostolate, but the apostolate also forces us back to our knees in prayer. We need the purification, strength, and consolation that God offers in prayer. In prayer we fill our water jugs with the fresh water of the Spirit, and in the apostolate we carry that water to a world dying of thirst. The more we give of this water, the more we need contact with God in prayer to refill our jugs. Otherwise, we simply have nothing to offer.

In prayer we fill our water jugs with the fresh water of the Spirit, and in the apostolate we carry that water to a world dying of thirst.

The Christian life cannot be chronologically divided between prayer and apostolate. Rather that half and half, or some other ratio between the two, the Christian life is *fully* contemplative and *fully* active all the time. Our apostolate should be permeated by prayer and our prayer suffused with apostolic zeal. We are called to be apostles at prayer, and contemplatives in our activity. Remember Saint Benedict's motto: *Ora et labora,* "Pray and work." If we pray without working we deprive God of our talents as channels of his grace; if we work without praying our work cannot bear spiritual fruit, since without him we can do *nothing*. Prayer and the apostolate go hand in hand.

No Closet Christians

The images and analogies that Christ used when describing his followers all bear a common characteristic: we are called to change the world around us. In other words, a Christian isn't called simply to be good but to make the world around him better too. Christians are not wall hangings, but catalysts driven by the love of God. Jesus referred to his apostles as the "light of the world." Moreover, to avoid any possible confusion he spoke of that light being made visible to others so they may see. No one lights a lamp, he asserted, "to put it under a tub; they put it on the lampstand where it shines for everyone in the house" (Matt. 5:14–15). He further enjoined them to let their light shine before men, so that all who saw their good works would give glory to God.

> *Christians are not wall hangings, but catalysts driven by the love of God.*

As "light of the world," Christians are called to illuminate reality and to show things for what they really are vis-à-vis eternity. We are to offer the truth of faith, a treasure more precious than gold. There should be no such thing as a "closet Christian," a Nicodemus-like figure who privately believes yet publicly refuses to let his belief color his decisions or his dealings with other people.

Jesus also called his disciples "salt of the earth." We know full well that, outside of deer and livestock, no one eats salt for its own sake. Salt is not its own proper dish, to be eaten alongside potatoes, meat, and vegetables. People use salt to change the flavor of all these foods, adding zest to what could otherwise be bland fare.

Similarly, Christians do not exist for themselves. In fact, they have no reason for being apart from their influence on the world around them. Christ's disciples have received the challenge of changing the flavor of the world around them, imbuing their workplaces and social milieus with the values of the gospel. Christians do not set up a separatist camp parallel to the rest of human society but seek rather to permeate all of society with the gospel.

Salt has no nutritional value, so if it fails to do the one thing it is good for—provide flavor to the meal—it is truly good for nothing. Any ideal of Christian holiness that is limited to reaching personal, individual perfection is fundamentally misguided—like good salt locked away in a box or a lamp stuffed into a closet.

Any ideal of Christian holiness that is limited to reaching personal, individual perfection is fundamentally misguided.

Christ calls us to take a stand, to get off the fence. Earlier we reflected on the vice of mediocrity. In reality, there is no greater shame for a Christian than to "be like everybody else." Jesus stated that "if salt has lost its taste, how shall its saltiness be restored? It is no longer good for anything except to be thrown out and trodden under foot by men" (Matt. 5:13 RSV). A Christian who "tastes" like the world around him has lost the sense of his Christianity.

Jesus calls us to be active: "He who is not with me is against me, and he who does not gather with me scatters" (Luke 11:23 RSV). Jesus doesn't want us to stand idly by, basking in our faith. He calls us to "gather," to labor in his vineyard. As "gatherers," we are to be Christ's active coworkers for the salvation of souls. The one who does not gather scatters, and the one who does not labor gets in the way, like deadwood that keeps the living branches from growing and expanding.

Christ claimed that his disciples would be *recognizable* by their love. You have undoubtedly heard the challenge, though it bears repeating, that if today you were arrested and hauled into court for the crime of being a Christian, could the prosecution come up with enough evidence to convict you?

The world would rather assimilate Christianity than confront it head-on. Many would like to water down its message and condescendingly shelve it among many alternative "lifestyles" and paths of salvation. The world invites us to a false humility, whereby Christ would not be *the* Way, but *one* way among many, whereby he would not be *the* Truth, and certainly not the *whole* truth, but a respectable slice of truth to be added to the many other slices and splinters of truth to be found elsewhere. Yet this is not the Christian message. The gospel has a distinctive tone of radicalness and uniqueness which, if lost, would strip Christianity of its reason for being.

The gospel has a distinctive tone of radicalness and uniqueness which, if lost, would strip Christianity of its reason for being.

Enemies of the Apostle

There are all sorts of good reasons not to be an apostle, but none of them matters. The fact remains that this is what Jesus asks of us. The mission can make us uncomfortable because we feel hopelessly inadequate for it, because it curtails the pursuit of all sorts of other personal aims and objectives, and because it implies the risk of standing out and even of looking silly—one of the most painful forms of persecution. Just for the sake of being prepared and dealing with the excuses that are sure to present themselves, let's briefly look at a few of the enemies of the apostle.

1. LAZINESS

The first enemy that the apostle faces is his or her own laziness. It is simply easier not to concern oneself with the evangelizing mission of the Church. After all, haven't we got enough to do with work, friends, and family? Why add another area of responsibility? The idea of being an apostle almost surely threatens our comfort zones, and no one likes to be pushed beyond those.

Yet how much damage is caused by laziness and passivity in Christians! Again, "all that is necessary for the triumph of evil is that good men do nothing." How true this is for the Church. And for a solution, we mustn't wring our hands and look to others, but to ourselves. If everyone looks to someone else, nothing will get done. If everyone looks to himself and begins to live his Christian faith seriously, then the world will change.

We often shudder on contemplating the evil done by certain persons in history and wonder what the world would have been like without them. Yet we should also think of those who have done great good. How terrible it would have been had they refused their challenges and opted for more comfortable lives! What if the twelve apostles, after Pentecost, had simply retired to a peaceful existence instead of risking their lives preaching the gospel to the far corners of the world? What would the world be like without the witness of Augustine, Francis of Assisi, Thérèse of Lisieux, Martin Luther King, Billy Graham, or Pope John Paul II? Who knows how much better the world would be if all those called to the apostolate had generously embraced this vocation?

2. FEAR

Along with laziness, we may also experience fear. Normally this doesn't mean fear of physical harm (though sometimes this, too, may be asked of us), but above all, fear of ridicule. No one wants to be known as a Holy Joe or a Pious Patty. Again, the herd instinct makes us shun standing out. It was the apostle Paul who coined the phrase "fools for Christ" and it was as unpopular then as it is now. But each of us is called to make a choice and to risk being taken for a fool.

But each of us is called to make a choice and to risk being taken for a fool.

Jesus invites us to acknowledge him, not only in the silence of our hearts, but before others as well. His words could well give us pause: "Therefore everyone who confesses Me before men, I will also confess him before My Father who is in heaven. But whoever denies Me before men, I will also deny him before My Father who is in heaven" (Matt. 10:32–33 NASB). But if Jesus challenges us to overcome our fear, he also provides the remedy. He reminds us that he is with us always and gives us his Spirit without measure.

3. SUPERFICIALITY AND WORLDLINESS

Finally, sometimes we fail as apostles simply because we don't believe enough or love enough. If I am not convinced that discovering Jesus Christ is the greatest thing that ever happened to me, how will I be impelled to convey that faith to others? If I am caught up in the world with its worries and cares, and these become my priority, my vocation as an apostle may not even show up on my radar screen.

Only the one who is convinced will convince others. It is not a question of going through the motions, saying all the right things, and applying the right formulas. The enthusiasm of knowing Jesus Christ, of having been seduced by him, cannot be improvised or put on. The Samaritan woman at the well became an effective apostle to her fellow townspeople because of her contagious enthusiasm and joy after meeting Christ.

As apostles, we have nothing to offer but Jesus Christ. It isn't our qualities, our eloquence, our careful planning that will win others over to Christ and his gospel, but the action of grace working in an apostle that fills others with a desire to know Christ.

When our apostolic zeal begins to wane, we should probably first examine our own faith in Christ. Jesus taught that where our treasure is, there will our hearts be also. *Where is my treasure? What thoughts and concerns fill my heart? Where do Christ and his gospel really rank in my personal priorities?*

We should likewise examine our life of prayer. Contact with the living Christ stokes the fire of the apostolate. The closer we are to him, the more we have to give. When we approach his heart that burns with love for humanity, we cannot help but be caught up in that same love.

The Many Faces of the Apostolate

Accepting Christ's challenge to the apostolate doesn't mean quitting our jobs and undertaking a drastic change in lifestyle. We don't need to move to Nicaragua or preach Christ to the Inuit in the Arctic. The apostolate doesn't require years of study, or a special license to practice (though adequate preparation is extremely helpful). By the very fact of our baptism we are equipped as apostles. I know an elderly woman with little formal education whose kindness and authentic love of the Lord are a constant light to those around her. In her own gentle way, she surely touches more souls than many learned scholars who don't share her humility and faith.

It isn't our qualities, our eloquence, our careful planning that will win others over to Christ and his gospel, but the action of grace working in an apostle that fills others with a desire to know Christ.

The ways of evangelizing and bearing witness to Christ are manifold. Few are called to pull out a soapbox and preach Jesus Christ on a Manhattan street corner. Often, in fact, the in-your-face approach to evangelizing is counterproductive and serves only to drive people away.

This wasn't Jesus' approach. Pull out your Bible, open to the fourth chapter of John's Gospel, and feast your eyes on the consummate Evangelizer. Jesus met a Samaritan woman at a well, and though he knew that she wasn't living an exemplary life (she currently lived with a man with whom she was not married, after having had five prior husbands), Jesus reached her heart suavely, starting an innocent conversation by asking the woman for a drink. The results were splendid.

> *Jesus reached her heart suavely, starting an innocent conversation by asking the woman for a drink. The results were splendid.*

Jesus announced the Good News in a different way to each person, tailoring his approach to their needs. Paul imitated Christ's example, making himself "all things to all men" in the hope that some, at least, would come to believe (1 Cor. 9:22).

The mission begins not in far-off lands, but at home, at the office, with those nearest to you, and those the Lord places in your path. How else will Christ reach the people in your workplace, in your home, in your factory, at your school, if not through you?

Bearing witness to Christ can be as simple as treating people the way Christ would, loving them the way Christ would. It is Christ himself who wants to work through us, to be present in the world wherever we are, to continue to go about doing good in and through us. He asks us to lend him our hearts with which to love, our mouths through which to speak, our hands with which to serve, to the point where we can say with Paul: "It is no longer I who live, but Christ who lives in me" (Gal. 2:20 RSV).

Sometimes we mistakenly think that getting active in the Church means taking on liturgical roles or formally working for the Church in an institutional function. We reduce the life of the Church to the Sunday sermon and the internal life of the community. But as we have seen, the mission of the Church is fundamentally missionary and proactive. Rank-and-file Christians are uniquely equipped to change the world around them. The laity, unlike the clergy, seek the kingdom of God fundamentally by engaging in temporal affairs and by ordering them according to the plan of God.

Sometimes bearing witness to Jesus will entail actively announcing the Good News of salvation. Other times it will mean preaching the justice and love that characterized his life. Sometimes it will mean listening to others' problems with an open ear and praying earnestly for them. In the end, nothing is more attractive or convincing than genuine Christian charity, that love for others that earnestly seeks only their true good.

Not only is charity the distinguishing mark of the true Christian, it is also the most effective apostolic tool he possesses. We can do nothing for souls unless motivated and spurred on by authentic love. Christian love is marked by gentleness and respect. The Church has nothing to *impose* on others and wishes simply to *propose*.

Likewise, other people to whom we witness are not notches to be added to our belt but fellow pilgrims trekking toward the common homeland. When people experience true and unconditional love, they experience God. Many eloquent words will not move hearts the way selfless love will.

> When people experience true and unconditional love, they experience God.

A Christian is not merely called to *do apostolate*—the way he or she might commit to a few hours a week as a volunteer—but to *be an apostle*. Christian baptism consecrates us as apostles of Jesus Christ, which constitutes a new way of *being*, not a contractual commitment to a certain amount of time. Apostolate is simply what an apostle *does*. It is a twenty-four-hours-a-day, seven-days-a-week identification with Christ the Apostle. In his prayer, his work, his recreation, his travels, his sufferings—a true Christian carries with him the identity of "one who is sent." In his words, in his gestures, in his reactions, in his way of treating others, a Christian bears witness to his Lord.

This might be a good moment to ask ourselves: *Whom do I know who could use God's love? How can I love that person as Christ would? How can I make Christ's love present where it is especially needed?* In this way, our good intentions can bear fruit in practical action.

Loaves and Fishes

Of all the Scripture passages, few capture the apostolic dimension of the Christian life better than the miraculous multiplication of the loaves and fishes to feed five thousand people (Mark 6:34–44). You remember the scene. Jesus tried to escape for a little R & R with his disciples to a faraway place, but the crowds found out about it and beat him there. When Jesus saw the crowd, he was moved with compassion because they were like sheep without a shepherd, so he set about teaching them. But then night fell, and the impatient apostles, who had envisioned things differently, practically ordered Jesus to send the crowds away to find food for themselves. Jesus' response stopped them up short: "Give them something to eat yourselves."

Puzzled, the apostles quickly took stock of their resources and assured Jesus that there was no way they could do what he asked. The amount of food needed would have cost two hundred days' wages, while all they had were five loaves of bread and two fish. Not dissuaded, Jesus had them assemble the people in groups of fifty on the grass. Jesus then took the loaves and fishes, blessed them, broke the bread, and gave it to the disciples to distribute to the people. We all know how the story ended. The loaves and fishes not only managed to make the rounds; the disciples even collected twelve hampers of leftovers after the five thousand had eaten their fill.

This scene typifies the way Jesus works with us. Instead of sending the crowds away or simply producing the necessary food to feed the multitude, Jesus looks around for human helpers. He first makes us aware of how inadequate our resources and talents are for the task at hand, but then he commands us to do it anyway. He takes

He takes the little we have and multiplies it, so that it not only suffices but also exceeds the needs we are to satisfy.

the little we have and multiplies it, so that it not only suffices but also exceeds the needs we are to satisfy.

If you feel weak and overcome by the thought that the task exceeds your ability, join the club. This was the general response of every prophet and missionary before you. Just as surely as Jesus meant it when he said that "without me you can do nothing," so Paul hit the nail on the head in saying that "I can do all things in him who strengthens me."

Christ calls us to be saints and apostles, an impossible task for mere humans, but a thrilling adventure when united with his grace. In this exciting, all-important endeavor, his last words give us constant strength: "In the world you will have troubles. But take courage. I have conquered the world!" (John 16:33).

Notes

CHAPTER 4

1. Vatican Council II, Pastoral Constitution on the Church in the Modern World, *Gaudium et spes*, 16.

CHAPTER 5

1. Pope Benedict XVI, encyclical letter *Deus Caritas Est*, December 25, 2005, 36.

CHAPTER 9

1. Pope John Paul II, apostolic letter *Rosarium Virginis Mariae,* October 16, 2002, 1. There he also wrote: "The Rosary, though clearly Marian in character, is at heart a Christocentric prayer. In the sobriety of its elements, it has all the *depth of the Gospel message in its entirety,* of which it can be said to be a compendium."

2. "To Our Lady" reprinted with the permission of Macmillan Publishing Co., Inc. from *The Child on His Knees* by Mary Dixon Thayer. Copyright 1926 by Macmillan Publishing Co., Inc., renewed 1954 by Mary D. T. Fremont-Smith.

CHAPTER 11

1. Mother Teresa of Calcutta, *The Love of Christ* (San Francisco: Harper & Row, 1982), 82.

CHAPTER 14

1. Mother Teresa, *The Love of Christ*, 68.